At Grandmother's Table

At Grandmother's Table

Women Write about Food,
Life, and the Enduring Bond
between Grandmothers and
Granddaughters

Edited by Ellen Perry Berkeley
Drawings by Simi Berman

Fairview Press • Minneapolis

Cataloging-in-Publication Data

At Grandmother's table : women write about food, life, and the enduring bond between grandmothers and granddaughters / edited by Ellen Perry Berkeley ; drawings by Simi Berman

p. cm.

Includes index.

ISBN 1-57749-107-6 (paperback : alk. paper)

1. Cookery. 2. Grandmothers—Miscellanea. I. Berkeley, Ellen Perry.

TX715.A855 2000

641.5–dc21

First hardcover printing: September 2000
First paperback printing: September 2001
Printed in Canada
05 04 03 02 01   7 6 5 4 3 2 1

Cover design by Laurie Ingram Duren™
Drawings © 2000 Simi Berman.

Text Credits

The poem "Coming Home" © 1996 by CB Follett was first published in *Sistersong: Women across Cultures,* The Grandmother Issue, Fall 1996. Portions of "The Goose That Laid the Golden Egg" by Hannelore Hahn are adapted from her memoir *On the Way to Feed the Swans* © 1982, published by Tenth House Enterprises, Inc., New York, N.Y., 1982. The poem "Plain String," © 1996 by D.H. Melhem, was first published in *Graffiti Rag* in 1996. The description of her grandmother's kitchen is adapted from an untitled prose poem, © 1995 by D.H. Melhem, appearing in *Rest in Love* (2nd edition) by D.H. Melhem, published in 1995 by Confrontation Press (English Department, C. W. Post of Long Island University, Brookville, N.Y.). The poem "Asking My Grandmother," © 1995 by Takayo Noda, was first published in *The Quiet Stream Is Running Through* to accompany the exhibition "Dimensional Collages" by Takayo Noda at Tiffany Windows, New York, N.Y., November 16–29, 1995. Brief portions of "It All Comes Out in the Wash" by Keri Pickett are adapted from *Love in the 90s: B.B. & Jo. The Story of a Lifelong Love,* © 1995 by Keri Pickett, published by Warner Books, Inc., A Time Warner Company, New York, N.Y., 1995. The essay "Abbondanza" (formerly titled "Italian Chutzpah") © 2000 by Sharon Lloyd Spence.

Photo credits

Portrait of Claire Louise Herder Steers by Sol Young Studios of New York, New York

Portrait of Katharina Theodora Weidenbach by Heinn Leimkühler of Essen, Germany

Photograph of Bella Ordansky Schneiderman with her husband by White Studio of Brooklyn, New York

Photograph of Josie Lou Lydia Walker Blakey with her granddaughter by Keri Pickett Photography of Minneapolis, Minnesota / Swanstock

Portrait of Pauline Wilson Burg by H. Zamsky of Philadelphia, Pennsylvania

Acknowledgments

To my husband Roy, who helped in so many ways, all along the way.

To my cousin Joan, who smacked her lips, long ago, over our grandmother's borscht.

To my friend Simi Berman, who made our working together never seem like work, and who always liked the colors I wore.

To my mother, who gave me time with my grandmother and delighted in our closeness.

To the good people at Fairview Press – Lane Stiles, Stephanie Billecke, and Steve Deger – whose professionalism was exceeded only by their enthusiasm, and who let me know early and often that they considered quality our primary goal.

To the excellent recipe testers – Jane Billecke, Scott Billecke, Gary Brown, Amy Curtis, Michelle Dilley, Helen Donnay, Louise Duncan, Laurie Ingram Duren, Leslie Gibson, Amy Harris, Margaret Harris, Perrie Heitler, Carolyn McCormick, Joel Meyer, Julie Ann Meyer, Jean Murray, Marianne Nora, Natalie Nowytski, Barbara Nye, Naomi Nygaard, Barbara June Patterson, Scott Robertson, Cathy Schwingler, Judy Stifter, and Brook and Amber Van Dyke – who turned complicated and imprecise directions into recipes we can all enjoy.

To everyone who wished me well on this project, even those whose work was ultimately not included in the book.

To the contributors, who are the book.

To the grandmothers, who are with us always – at *our* tables.

ontents

the 1870s

the 1880s

the 1900s

Recipes

Soups

Salads

Breads

Side Dishes

Main Dishes

Desserts

Preface

Today's grandmothers are as likely to be playing tennis as baking pies. Some do both, rinsing away the gray and, in their spare time, holding down a full-time job. A stereotype? Possibly. But no less a stereotype than the notion that the grandmothers of an earlier time were ample-bosomed, white-haired, and homebound.

At Grandmother's Table gives us a far richer view of the women we have called Grandma, or Gram, or Grossmutter, or Nonna. Here we see the substance of their brave and often difficult lives. We see the enormous contribution of these women – to their families and to their communities. We see the importance of their relationships with us, their granddaughters, in the lessons they taught us, the values they gave us, the strengths they lent us, and (not least) the foods they served us. It does not demean these women to say that we sometimes evoke them most readily by preparing the dishes they prepared. Indeed, by cooking what they cooked we are in contact again with their lessons and their values, their warmth, their courage, their comfort, their love.

This is a book about connections. We aren't the first generation of women to feel pain and sadness, to love deeply, to struggle fiercely, to know a contented peace or quiet pride or exultant joy. In connecting across the boundaries of time, we can see the concerns of our grandmothers as not unlike our own. And in connecting across the dividing lines of our own time, we can see our deepest selves reflected in women of very different backgrounds, beliefs, advantages, and pursuits. Whatever else we may label ourselves, we are all granddaughters.

The book honors a varied group of grandmothers. Some were born to families who had lived here for generations, some were the children of immigrants, some were immigrants themselves, and some never set foot on this land. They represent different circumstances, different heritages. And because they also represent different eras, they appear in the book according to their date of birth. This makes for an interesting history: we see the grandmothers marching into modern times, and we see the granddaughters making their own journeys. In these pages, a young woman rages at her grandmother for growing old; a woman who loses her husband comes to understand the trauma of her grandmother's young widowhood; a woman in her middle age finds the compassion to forgive her grandmother's long-ago stinginess.

The granddaughters in this book are as diverse as the grandmothers. Their single bond – other than being granddaughters – is their connection to this project. Some are my long-time friends and colleagues: a mentor, a protégée, people met along the way. Some were suggested to me. And some saw my notices in the newsletters of organizations to which I belong: the American Society of Journalists and Authors, the International Women's Writing Guild, and the League of Vermont Writers. All essays were written for this volume – written with great diligence, considerable joy, and not a little difficulty.

"I feel as though I've given birth to my grandmother," said one contributor. Said another, "Exploring the relationship with my grandmother is like gardening in an old riverbed, forever coming across another rock." Indeed, some would-be contributors found their family history too painful to put on paper. In other cases, I had to respect the privacy of several contributors whose truths were not for telling: one woman would not reveal in print that her grandmother had raised an illegitimate grandchild as her own child; another woman would not reveal the number of wives her father had had. Apart from such details – and do we really need to know them? – these stories are as true, as faithful to the people involved, as writer and editor could make them. We can never know the full history. What is known, and what is added through personal recollection, is solid enough.

A word about the illustrations. Youthful photographs of our grandmothers are especially poignant, since we don't often think of these women as young. Group photographs are similarly haunting when we see a striking resemblance across the generations. But photos tell only part of the story. I therefore asked artist Simi Berman for line drawings to complement a few of the word-pictures. Her drawings celebrate the special relationship between granddaughters and grandmothers, a relationship where each person finds something precious and comforting in the attention and companionship of the other. Close your eyes and remember such moments with your own grandmother: what you did together, where you walked, what you looked at, what you laughed at.

And, of course, what you ate together. Turn to your own handed-down recipes, those worn cards with their long-ago handwriting, their faded type. Whether you were close to your grandmother or not, whether you even knew her, she had a profound influence on your life and your palate. Relive – or create anew – the special memories that her recipes evoke.

In fact, this book owes its existence to my own experience with a treasured recipe. Some years ago, when my cousin Joan and I were each going through difficult times, we spent a day together: a rare treat. We shared our troubles and then, on a whim, made our grandmother's borscht. Our own trials were somehow lessened by all of this – by our closeness, surely, but also by the knowledge that our grandmother suffered her own disappointments, savored her own triumphs. Grandma Fish's borscht is more than a beet soup. It was part of her life, and part of our lives with her. Special foods are like that.

Like our grandmother's borscht, the recipes in this book have been handed down for generations. I thought of grading the recipes according to their acceptability by modern nutritionists: the scale would have extended from unbelievably wholesome to outrageously sinful. But that seemed too judgmental. I thought of grading them according to their ease of preparation, but that also seemed too judgmental. People love to cook for the intensity of it, or the relaxation of it, or the precision of it, or the artistry of it – each of us has her own reasons.

In cooking from these recipes, use your creativity. Substitute ingredients freely. If you like your enchiladas spicy, by all means add hot sauce or chili peppers. If you don't like turnips in your chicken soup, leave them out. Make flexibility your only rule. Make these recipes your own.

And maybe – just maybe – you'll be prompted to put onto paper some words about your own grandmother. Can't you just hear the encouragement and praise from that special person! She happily ceases to be a stereotype when she takes her place on the page – the unique and special woman who is grandmother to a unique and special granddaughter.

ELLEN PERRY BERKELEY

$\mathcal{R}$eading, Writing, and Love-Apples

Jennie Breece Robison
1844–1930

BY JANE JACOBS

The generations are long in my family. My grandmother was born well before the start of the Civil War and lived to see the start of the Great Depression, but she and I overlapped for fourteen years at the end of her life; I knew her well.

Back in 1856, when she was only twelve years old, she went to the superintendent of schools in her small Pennsylvania town and asked to be appointed teacher at a pretty little schoolhouse she had admired. Twelve years old! He replied, "Why, that's the toughest school in our district. They'd eat you alive." But he treated her like an adult, telling her to come back after she had graduated and he'd see that she got a school. Four years later, when she had finished her education, she got a one-room school of her own and a salary of $20 a month. Since she lived at home – they grew up slowly, in some ways – she was able to spend her first month's salary on maps and framed pictures of Roman ruins. Those were for the classroom. Her second month's salary was for herself: a looking glass.

Grandmother taught until she was twenty-nine, then married a country lawyer and had five sons and four daughters, one of whom was my mother. Until she died, Grandmother was a beloved teacher, as well as the champion speller – winner of many dictionaries – in that part of the state.

Although she was almost immobilized from rheumatism during much of the time I knew her, I hardly realized this at the time because she never complained and was so obviously enjoying herself. The two of us were typically engrossed in our books, she in her rocking chair and I on the floor at her feet, a bowl of hard candies on a table within reach of us both. Now and again we would read good parts of our books to each other. Or she would tell me a story, usually about her sister Hannah who had taught on Indian reservations and in Alaskan villages, or about washday when she was a child and they made their own soap from wood ashes and fat, or how, on winter days, they could skate twenty miles on the canal. She had lived all her life in the Bloomsburg area of Pennsylvania where she was born, one of twelve children of Daniel Breece and Mary Ann Case. Several generations earlier, her forebears had come from Scotland and England to settle in New Jersey and in central Pennsylvania.

"While the family watched in consternation, he sliced one and ate it with sugar and cream. When he was observed to be alive and well the next morning, the news spread quickly."

When she was an old lady, she was constantly visited by former students who, to me, looked as old as she was. Apart from conversing with these and other visitors, she spent most of her time reading. She once mentioned that she had recently read a great new writer named Ernest Hemingway, so I resolved to read him too. (I think she'd have enjoyed my own books, which began appearing more than thirty years later. I wish we could have discussed them together, eating candies as we went along.)

Whenever old pupils showed up, she proffered the candy and then talked politics with them – town, state, and national politics. I got the distinct impression that her visitors respected her opinions. But my interest in these matters being minimal at the time, I usually went back to my book or wandered into the yard to watch her youngest daughter grafting fruit trees or killing a chicken for dinner. We never learn all we can from our grandmothers, but some of her unflagging interest in public affairs did sink in.

Grandmother's Fried Tomatoes with Gravy

Grandmother's mother, I am told, remembered well when people in Bloomsburg didn't eat tomatoes, which were believed to be deadly poisonous. They were called "love-apples" and were grown only as ornaments; children were strictly forbidden to touch them.

One evening, a cousin of my great-grandmother's arrived from New Jersey on horseback and, upon seeing a bowl of love-apples adorning the parlor, declared them to be edible! While the family watched in consternation, he sliced one and ate it with sugar and cream. When he was observed to be alive and well the next morning, the news spread quickly and the town took to inventing and trading tomato recipes.

Grandmother's fried tomatoes with gravy were one of these Bloomsburg concoctions. They were her best dish, even better than her creamed onions, her applesauce, her roast chicken.

In our family, fried tomatoes are a main meal, not merely a side dish. We never make this recipe with out-of-season tomatoes, which just aren't as delicious as local sun-ripened fruit. It is also satisfying to realize that harvest time has come again and one needn't stint on the Best Tomatoes in the World! Perhaps because this dish is seasonal, the recipe has been surprisingly long-lived, like many a special holiday treat. I still make it, as do my two sons and my daughter, and my granddaughter has been dredging the slices with flour since she was a tot; she will undoubtedly be cooking it too, during the heights of tomato seasons to come.

6 bacon strips, or
    6 tablespoons vegetable oil
6 fully ripened tomatoes
½ teaspoon salt
1 cup flour
1½ to 2 cups milk

Fry the bacon, then remove it from the pan and set it aside. (If you're using vegetable oil, omit the bacon and heat the oil now.)

Slice the tomatoes thick and dredge each slice in salted flour. Fry each slice in the fat or oil until the flour is nicely browned. The slices will break up somewhat, and small bits of tomato and flour will collect in the pan.

Place the fried slices in a serving bowl, draining the fat and juice from the bowl back into the pan. When all the tomatoes are fried and in the serving bowl, add flour to the hot pan, stirring constantly to blend the flour with the fat, juice, and residual bits of tomatoes. Then, still stirring, gradually add milk to make a thick (but not stiff) gravy.

Pour the gravy over the tomatoes in the serving bowl. If you're using bacon, pile the crisp bacon on top. This recipe serves 2 people.

emima's Secret Life

Jemima Wallace Thomson
1855–1934

BY NANCY MEANS WRIGHT

We might have passed in the dark. I was barely conceived when my grand-mother moved on. And yet she has been an enormous influence in my life and a recurring stimulus to my writing. I have invented and reinvented her in poems, stories, novels. How often I've reached down into that deep well to pull up a bucketful of Jemima!

She was a fifth child, born in Leven, Fifeshire, Scotland. The older four bore the name Beveridge; Jemima had no surname. I discovered this years later when I looked up her birth in the Scoonie Kirk register. There, in spidery handwriting, was the single word: "Illegitimate."

Imagine the notoriety for the mother, aged thirty-three, in that tiny parish. A husband vanished, and next door a young man named Wallace. Did she openly declare him the father? Was he already married? Had he another sweetheart? My great-grandmother Jessie, that close-mouthed John Knox Presbyterian, never told. But when her oldest daughter died in New York City, leaving a brood of seven children, and the widowed husband Alex sent for red-haired Jemima to help out, Jessie shipped the girl off under the surname Wallace.

She was seventeen, and alone. I imagined her journey for a short story pub-lished in *Seventeen*. She'd never met this man and now she was to live with him — maybe marry him, her mother whispered as they took leave at the ship. Marry! But marry they did, and in quick succession Jemima bore my mother and seven others, of whom two died. Did she love Alexander? She never said. But how much time was left for affection with thirteen children to care for? To survive, Jemima organized the crew into work details. One was in charge of making over dresses and coats, one headed the wash crew, my mother redecorated the old hats.

"Even when she grew older and overweight, her eyes dim with cataracts, Jemima would squint through tiny round glasses into the beef or kidney stew and sip happily from a dripping spoon."

But Jemima was the chief cook; no child was going to get *that* job! My brother recalls her as a ready source of fudge and sweets. A cousin remembers the warm hugs, the platefuls of chocolate icebox cake. Even when she grew older and overweight (all that candy!), her eyes dim with cataracts, Jemima would squint through tiny round glasses into the beef or kidney stew and sip happily from a dripping spoon. Of course, with her poor vision she was apt to put turtle food in the turkey stuffing — as one day she did!

Perhaps the poor vision was responsible for her agoraphobia: she was painfully shy and, except for the obligatory church attendance, kept to the house. The shyness and poor vision and the John Knox guilt seem to have bypassed my mother and landed squarely on me — along with a questing temperament. For my grandmother wrote a poem once, and my older sister, who loved to plunder Jemima's bureau drawers, recalls one line: "I wander in my dreams."

Where did you wander, Grandmother? What limits of time and space did you want to break through? No one can tell me. I can only keep on inventing. Perhaps, in my imaginary travels, I'll stumble on the truth.

Jemima's Oatcakes

Oatcakes were a daily part of Jemima's diet, and a way of filling the bellies of thirteen hungry children. If Jemima used a bannock-stick or spurtle to make the oatcakes, she didn't pass it on. But according to an older cousin, she did have a grocer who carried Scottish oatmeal (also called steel-cut oats). My mother and her siblings definitely preferred oatcakes to the unembellished, thick oat porridge they forced down each morning. They could lather the oatcakes with jam, marmalade, butter, and sometimes fried herring!

2 cups Scottish oatmeal, uncooked (or American oatmeal run through the blender)

¾ to 1¼ cups flour

½ teaspoon salt

1 tablespoon melted fat or vegetable oil

1 cup water

Preheat your oven to 350 degrees.

Mix 1½ cups of the oatmeal with ¾ cup of the flour, then add the salt. Make a well in the center; pour in the melted fat and water, and form the mixture into a dough. If the dough is too wet, add more flour.

On a board covered with the remaining ½ cup oatmeal, knead the dough and roll it out to a thickness of ¼ to ⅛ inch.

Cut the dough into 4 quarters (Jemima called them "farls") and bake the quarters on an ungreased cookie sheet for 35 minutes. The cakes should be dry on the outside and somewhat moist in the middle. Serves 6 to 8 people.

Jemima's Steak and Kidney Pie

Presbyterian Jemima was a teetotaler — except when it came to cooking. Some recipes, including her steak and kidney pie, contained a cup of beer! I can imagine my grandmother sending an older boy out to buy it, insisting that he remind the grocer it was for cooking only. How much tasting, one wonders, did she do with this recipe? Jemima's secret life!

The Filling

4 lamb kidneys
3 pounds round steak
½ cup flour
2 tablespoons butter
2 large onions, chopped
2½ cups boiling water
2 teaspoons salt
½ teaspoon pepper
2 tablespoons Worcestershire
    sauce
1 cup beer

The Pastry
(for two 1-crust pies)

2 cups flour
1 teaspoon salt
6 tablespoons butter
⅓ cup cold lard or shortening
Ice water as needed
2 egg yolks

To prepare the filling: soak the kidneys in cold salted water for 30 minutes. Remove the skin, trim off the fat and the veins, and cut the kidneys into ½-inch cubes. Set these cubes aside.

Remove the steak fat and set it aside. Then, cut the steak into 1-inch cubes.

Roll the kidney and steak cubes in the flour.

Melt the steak fat in a skillet, add the butter, and fry the onions until browned. Add the steak and kidneys and brown the cubes on all sides. Remove the meat to a large pot.

To the fat and onion mixture, add boiling water, salt, pepper, Worcestershire sauce, and beer. Dribble this mixture over the meat. Cover the meat and simmer for 2 hours until tender.

Spoon all the meat and half the gravy into two 10-inch pie pans. Reserve the rest of the gravy for later.

To make the pastry: sift the flour into a bowl and add the salt. Cut in the butter and cold lard, then sprinkle 5 or 6 tablespoons of ice water over the top. Mix with a fork until the dough sticks together.

Form the dough into a ball. Divide the ball in half and press each piece into a flat, round disk. Chill these disks for at least 1 hour, then roll them out on a floured board.

Preheat your oven to 350 degrees.

Fit the crusts over the meat in the pans, cutting several slits for the escaping steam. Brush the pastry with the egg yolks. Bake for 45 minutes, or until the crust is browned. Reheat the remaining gravy and spoon it on top before serving. This recipe serves 8 to 10 people.

A Forbidding Formality

Selina James McDonnell
1859–1952

BY HILDA McDONNELL FARRELL

Picture Queen Victoria, in black bombazine dress and black pearl-buttoned boots, seated on a horsehair chair in Buckingham Palace, and you have my childhood image of my grandmother, herself of distant royal blood. Dutiful young Congregationalist, she had converted to Catholicism to marry the handsome Irishman to whom she bore thirteen children. I could never reconcile that romantic image with the austere personage I met on my Sunday afternoon visits with my father to her home.

My grandmother presided over an imposing house in Dorchester, Massachusetts, where also lived numerous maiden aunts and bachelor uncles, as well as my beloved cousin Eileen. We two young friends spent these visits roaming secret stairways and passageways and the tiny rooms under the eaves, while downstairs in the drawing room (how familiar, years later, was *The Forsyte Saga*) our elders pondered the imminent doom of Western civilization. Their gloomy discourse continued during tea, at which Grandma poured.

But my grandmother was far more than the ceremonial woman with whom I had only a formal acquaintance. Too many years later, I learned how she had once interpreted *Libera nos Domine,* a phrase from the Mass, as "Liver on a stormy day." My grandmother? I was aghast.

Not only was I unaware of her irreverent sense of humor, I didn't know that she had buried her first two babies, victims of a diphtheria epidemic that swept the English countryside, while her husband, an expert in repairing church organs, was in remote Russia accommodating the czar.

Hoping for better opportunities for their children, my grandparents immigrated to Canada in the early 1900s. In Toronto they met virulent religious hostility and extended hard times. Francis, adored husband and father, died soon after they arrived, and my grandmother struggled to hold the family together. The children worked from an early age in factories and shops; the males formed a band that played at socials. Not until they came to Boston did the clan begin to thrive.

Sadly, I do not recall ever having a real conversation with my grandmother. Only now, learning more about her, do I see our similarities. We both were oldest daughters. We both were widowed at forty-eight, left to raise large families that each included six sons. We both enjoyed the pleasures of cooking and entertaining and raising our children. Today, when I visit Eileen, who, with her dog, still lives in the big old house, I realize that Grandma and I were both collectors of colored glassware, an interest we never knew we shared.

I am told that my grandmother's interests were vast and deep. She never went beyond third grade but was often thought to be a university graduate. I hear with disbelief stories about her wonderful disposition and how she sang constantly at her housework. How could I have known only coolness from this woman who might have been my friend? Had she been irritated by some curiosity or obstinacy or aloofness in me that she rejected in herself? I did not mourn her when she died. Now, I wish the time had arrived when we might, perhaps, have learned to love each other.

Grandma's Rock Cakes

At teatime in my grandmother's mahogany-paneled dining room, the long damask-covered table was graced by two cozied pots: one for strong tea, the other for boiling water. Next to them were delicate cups and saucers, gleaming silver flatware, and spoons nestled in a cut-glass bowl. The repast included homemade bread (a delicacy when spread with bacon drippings), jam, sliced meat and cheese, fruit, and perhaps a trifle or the blancmange I hated so. And rock cakes.

Rock cakes were one of my grandmother's specialties: sweet biscuits, similar to scones, that she had known from childhood. I am told that every family in her English town made its own variation of these little cakes; the only constant (for whatever arcane reason) was the mandatory use of the silver fork.

4 cups flour

1 cup sugar

4 teaspoons baking powder

½ teaspoon nutmeg

¼ teaspoon salt

½ pound (2 sticks) butter, or
   1 cup beef drippings or
   vegetable shortening

1 cup dried currants

1 cup milk

1 egg, beaten

Preheat your oven to 375 degrees.

Stir together the flour, sugar, baking powder, nutmeg, and salt. Rub in the butter using your fingers, then stir in the currants.

In a separate bowl, combine the milk with the beaten egg. Mix the liquid ingredients into the dry ingredients with a silver fork. The batter should be stiff and somewhat lumpy. Do not overmix.

Drop the batter one spoonful at a time onto an ungreased baking sheet. Bake for 16 to 18 minutes, or until the cakes are lightly browned. Watch the cakes during the last 5 minutes of baking to make sure they do not overbake.

This recipe makes 6 dozen delicious "rocks."

he Lost Stories

Leonia Ragan Berry
1860–1955

BY JANE BERRY MARCELLUS

Ask any of the Berrys of Dickson County, Tennessee, about family history, and you'll get an earful about the men.

There's Michael Berry, the family patriarch, who rode horseback out of the North Carolina woods early in the 1800s to spread the word of Methodism to Tennessee settlers. He preached sixty consecutive years, mostly around Dickson County because once his thirteen children came, he could hardly remain itinerant.

The generations of men who followed established a tradition of questionable behavior, despite an upbringing punctuated by readings from a big black Bible and baptisms in the local creek. My cousin is alleged to have returned from World War II with enough German diamonds to fill half an upturned fedora. Another relative had six wives, maybe eight, if you take for fact the rumors of an overheard conversation in which he admitted he could not remember.

But stories about Berry women are harder to extract. Until recently, all I knew about my father's mother was that her name was Leonia and that as an old woman she had wavy white hair, round wire-rim glasses, a thin mouth, and my father's wide, straight nose. In one photo, she wore a dark dress with a lace collar and a cameo pinned close to her throat. Her expression was, well, grandmotherly: kind but dignified, somewhere on the border between bemused and wise. It was a look that said she knew things she saw no reason to tell.

I never met her. She died, at ninety-five, the year before I was born. Only in my thirties did I begin to wonder who she was.

From my half-sister Betty, thirty-three years my senior, I learned that on most Sundays Leonia made something called "stack-apple pie," and that late in life she wore a kind of loose cotton underwear she may have designed herself.

Surely someone remembered more. I flew to Tennessee and talked to cousins. My Berry first cousins are all forty or so years older than I am, a family peculiarity that routinely sets people to doing math in their heads. From the cousins I discerned a certain formality toward her. In a region where cousins are "cud'ns" and "aunt" rhymes with "saint," they referred to her as "Grandmother," pronouncing the "n" and "d" distinctly.

Otherwise, I learned very little. What did she like to do or read or talk about? What did she think about women's suffrage, which was ratified in Tennessee the year she was sixty? Did she remember the Civil War, which ended the year she was five? Did she like cats, begonias, ham? And why did the conversation always revert to the men?

I visited the house where she lived as a girl. It sits by a creek on a dirt road, near a town so tiny it is not on most maps. Behind the house is a small graveyard where her father and two mothers, both named Sallie Jane, are buried side by side. Sallie Jane Robertson Ragan gave birth to my grandmother and died three years later; Sallie Jane Gilmore Ragan raised her. Because the family had no money for headstones, they poured concrete over the graves and wrote the names and dates with a stick. After a century of rain and sun, the handwriting is eroding.

Who was Leonia? I'll never know. And that means I'll never know if we share the same dry humor, the same jagged anger. I'll never know if, like me, she preferred vanilla over chocolate and refused to wear uncomfortable shoes. I'll never know what it was like for her to deal with all those errant men. Without the details, I am left with a stereotype.

Storyteller Luisah Teish writes in her book *Jambalaya* about the West African tradition of providing a feast for one's dead ancestors in order to evoke them. I would like to make my Grandmother Berry's stack-apple pie to evoke her; if anyone finds the recipe, I will. But even that will tell me little. I'd rather have more stories. Stories may warp reality, but they mark the place where a life was lived.

"I'll never know if we share the same dry humor, the same jagged anger. I'll never know if, like me, she preferred vanilla over chocolate and refused to wear uncomfortable shoes."

Grandmother Berry's Apple Float

Grandmother Berry's stack-apple pie is described as "more of a cake, really." An old man whom Betty knew in Nashville remembers that my grandmother used to cut him a piece every Sunday when he was a boy and leave it on the fence post near her house. Why he could not come to the house is a mystery. But so are many things.

The recipe for stack-apple pie is lost. But my cousin Nell remembers our grandmother making "apple float," and so I include it here as the nearest way I can evoke my grandmother, Leonia Ragan Berry.

10 tart apples
1 to 1½ cups water
½ to ¾ cup sugar
½ teaspoon cinnamon
3 pasteurized egg whites

This is how Nell remembers it:

Peel, core, and chop up your apples. Place them in a large saucepan, add the water, then add your sugar and cinnamon. Cook the apples until they are soft. When finished, drain off the water and mash the apples into applesauce.

Place the applesauce in the refrigerator to cool, about 2 hours.

In a separate bowl, beat the egg whites until they form soft peaks, then gently fold them into the applesauce. Chill before serving. (There was no icebox, Nell said, so our grandmother chilled the float in the nearby spring.) Serves 10 to 12 people.

he Zen Master

BY TERESA R. AMUSO

Teresa Caruso Amuso
1863–1954

It is a hot summer day and I am teaching an Elderhostel session on Eastern philosophy. They are an active group, wanting concrete answers: "What, *exactly*, is Zen?" I receive only silent stares when I reply, "If you can name it, the masters say, it isn't Zen."

I try to explain. "Zen is being in flow with the universe. If you're making a flower arrangement, you don't just plunk a pile of flowers in a vase. If you place a stalk of blue delphinium, the round pink rose will demand to sit at its feet. You see?" Some faces still look blank. I tell them about archery, being one with the target; about the martial arts, responding motion for motion with an opponent; about Frank Lloyd Wright insisting that his students study Zen. I show pictures of Zen gardens, their stones raked in unending patterns.

I then disclose to these people, living in the autumn or winter of their lives, one of the marvelous powers of a Zen Master. "A Zen Master controls his own death. When ready, the master announces the exact time of his passing, goes into meditation, and wondrously passes into the next dimension."

Back home, I am caught in the hallway by a portrait of my paternal grandmother – formidable, inscrutable. I take a glass of ice tea and relax on the deck, looking over the bay. My mind drifts. . . .

I am a child of nine watching my grandmother. In exact patterns, she rakes the pebbles on the paths woven through her garden, the handle of the rake ludicrously waving over her diminutive frame. She is seventy-six. I feel a strange sensation. Not exactly fear. I realize suddenly that I have always been in awe of her.

In the spring, summer, and autumn she would work in her garden. After cutting the choicest blooms in season – the purple irises, the Japanese peonies, the lush roses, the golden chrysanthemums – she would make her pilgrimage, walking the two miles to the cemetery where she would place her flowers on her husband's grave. She had begun walking with her Giuseppe in the Italian countryside as part of the ritual of a betrothed couple, accompanied, of course, by a family member who would allow him to pick and present a flower to her. Now her walks continued alone, in a different place and time, but still with Giuseppe in her heart.

Grandmother lived near us in Pittsfield, Massachusetts; our houses were connected by a little street called Cove. Every Sunday after church my two brothers and I would cut across the backyards of Cove Street to make our "formal visit" to Grandmother. We always fussed about going, but the truth was I wanted to go, finding myself drawn to this stern woman even during the week. I knew somehow that it was important – as though there was something I was supposed to learn from her, something timeless that she had brought with her, perhaps from the old country.

We would be in our Sunday best. Grandmother dressed impeccably; she would never have tolerated scruffy children. We would sit quietly at the kitchen table, answering questions about school and about catechism with the nuns.

At an appointed time, Grandmother would go into the dining room, unlock her oak china cabinet, and take down an apothecary jar. In the jar were *competti,* wonderful hard candies (Easter-egg-colored) with an almond in the center. She would count out an exact number for each of us, our reward for the visit.

Years passed in much the same way. One day, when I was twenty-four, I saw that my parents were perturbed: Grandmother had announced that she was going to die on the following Sunday. It was nonsense, said the doctor – she was in excellent health – but we had better humor her. On Sunday she summoned the family for one last visit. The priest and the doctor were there, too. Grandmother said her good-byes as we all formally kissed her cheek. She held each infant great-grandchild for a long moment with the closest thing to a smile I'd ever seen on her face.

At one point, feeling cold, she asked my father for her gray sweater. He ran down to the kitchen and took from a peg the first sweater he saw. As he placed it around her shoulders she looked at her *green* sweater and threw it harshly to the floor. I had to leave the room, mumbling about the bathroom, to avoid laughing in this solemn moment. Solemn moment, indeed! I thought. She'll live another ten years. But just as I reentered the room, she looked deep into my eyes as though she had waited for my return. I gasped as she quietly closed her eyes and died.

. . . Coming out of my reverie, I look over the bay and suddenly realize that though Zen is ineffable, in some deep part of myself I've always understood. I've learned it over the years from my Italian grandmother – the Zen Master!

Grandmother's Biscotti

Like most Zen Masters, Grandmother was a vegetarian. Her diet was austere and frugal. I have a fond memory of Grandmother pouring coffee from her dented dripolator, which rested on the old black cooking stove, then taking out her tin of homemade biscotti and sitting with me as we quietly and contentedly dipped our biscotti into oversized coffee mugs. Like Proust dipping his madeleines into his tea, every time I dip a biscotto into coffee, the taste brings me back to my grandmother's, where I learned so much from my own Zen Master.

3 to 4 cups flour
1 teaspoon baking powder
½ teaspoon baking soda
Dash of salt
½ teaspoon grated orange peel
½ teaspoon grated lemon peel
4 tablespoons (½ stick) butter
1¼ cups sugar
3 eggs, beaten
½ cup milk
1½ teaspoons anise extract
1 teaspoon vanilla extract
1 cup chopped walnuts

Preheat your oven to 375 degrees.

Mix 3 cups flour with the baking powder, baking soda, salt, and grated peels.

In a large bowl, cream the butter and the sugar, then mix in the beaten eggs. Alternately add the dry ingredients, the milk, and the extracts. Then add the chopped walnuts. You may need to add a little more flour until the dough is the consistency of piecrust dough.

Divide the dough into three pieces. Roll out each piece to roughly 4 x 6 inches. Place all three pieces onto a greased, 11 x 16-inch cookie sheet. Stretch the ends of each piece to touch the top and bottom of the cookie sheet. Pat the dough down flat to a thickness of about ½ inch.

Bake until lightly browned, about 15 to 20 minutes. Take the cookie sheet out of the oven and cut each piece into 1-inch slices.

If you like soft biscotti, allow them to cool before serving. If you prefer crispy biscotti, turn the pieces over and brown them in the oven for another few minutes. You may wish to brown the sides of the biscotti, also. Makes 2 dozen biscotti.

Never Shall I Forget Her Calm Eyes

Helene Stockhausen-Korsten
1864–1945

BY ADRIANA MILLENAAR BROWN

Grossmutter never panicked. I never heard her raise her voice, not at my little brother, nor at Milenkow, our Yugoslav prisoner-of-war gardener, who by the grace of the Teutonic gods was allowed to dig up precious potatoes for us in that bitter fall of 1944 in Berlin. Nor did Grossmutter shriek like my aunties whenever the sirens went off. They would yell into the black night: "*Schnell,* the children, blankets, quick." I shivered. Sleepy tears would roll down my cheeks. But as soon as I felt the firm hand of Grossmutter and heard her gentle *"Mein Herz,"* my heart stopped throbbing. Grossmutter's imperturbability had touched me like the fairy's wand that I so badly wanted to see sparkle through our cherry grove, where the brook wandered away from the nasty barbed-wire section for Milenkow and his fellow prisoners.

Even when sleeping or daydreaming, whenever my nerve ends picked up the humming of fighter planes, I ran to Grossmutter. I threw my arms around her poised head, thrusting my trembling body against her still limbs.

"*Mein Herzchen,* it's okay." Grossmutter soothed me momentarily. But then, inevitably, my demons popped up: "Grossmutter, what if they bomb us? What if our roof catches fire? What if Papa is hit? Milenkow in his bunk? Our potatoes, my cherry tree?"

My heart would stand still. Always it stood still when I heard the drone of the fighter planes, the wail of the siren. I was confused in the middle of the night, the middle of a daydream, the middle of my first school year, the middle of a potato meal. It was then that my heart locked. A bomb always struck part of me, no matter how hard Grossmutter rubbed my back. She rubbed it until the morning, until the light shone through a hole in the blind or until my brave little brother yelled through the cellar: "Papa says it's the Allies again. Hurrah." Every day our Dutch Papa bicycled across Berlin to his office at the Swedish Embassy. He was the only Dutchman who was asked – indeed, begged – by his government to stay behind in the capital of his country's conqueror to help the neutral Swedes in their job of protecting Dutch interests.

That winter we fled to a distant land, a neutral land: Sweden. I never saw Grossmutter again. She died on a long trek from Weimar to Cologne the following winter. My mother told me that she starved to death. But I shall believe she died because she never again felt her little granddaughter's agitated body against hers, would never again prove to the frightened child that nerves can be willed into submission in spite of imminent bombs.

Never shall I forget her calm eyes where I read the sorrows she had swallowed, the losses she had acquiesced in. Pride was not her trademark. Revenge never settled in her being. Greater glory for her country, for her fallen sons, never entered her mind. An accommodating woman, she was grateful that her husband plied up and down the Rhine, trading. She was thankful that her sunshine – my mother – had married an Ally, and though he was the enemy he remained an ally. Grossmutter felt blessed by her God, who had given her the equanimity and harmony she shared with her musician father, her composer mother, and all before her who had lived in Colonia Agrippina since Roman times.

Lenchen's Potato Cakes

Our meals, in that last year before we escaped, were scant. But we always had some old potatoes, a few carrots, a parsnip or rutabaga, and duck eggs. I remember the smell of the goose fat that Grossmutter used when frying the best potato cakes I have ever tasted. Where did the nutmeg come from? Had it been smuggled from Holland and given to my father?

2 small potatoes, grated
 (about 2 cups)
3 carrots, grated (about 2 cups)
1 parsnip, grated (about 1 cup)
1 rutabaga or turnip, grated
 (about 1 cup)
1 onion, grated
3 eggs, beaten
2 tablespoons flour
1 teaspoon nutmeg
1½ teaspoons salt
Freshly ground black pepper
Melted fat or vegetable oil
 for frying

Grate the potatoes, carrots, parsnip, rutabaga, and onion (or run them through a food processor). Place the grated vegetables on a tea towel and wring the towel to extract the moisture. Put the gratings into a bowl. Stir in the beaten eggs.

Combine and sift the flour, nutmeg, salt, and pepper. Add the flour mixture to the vegetables. Shape into patties ¼ inch thick and 3 inches in diameter.

Heat 2 tablespoons of fat in a skillet and sauté the cakes. Be careful not to crowd too many in the pan or they won't brown properly. Brown each side until crisp, adding melted fat as necessary. Serve hot from the pan, decorated with a red cherry on top. Makes 2 dozen potato cakes.

Another Way to Touch

Mary Burroughs Hard
1865–1963

BY MARY HARD BORT

Whenever I take the big, old, heavy, dark-brown mixing bowl from the cupboard, I think of Grandma. That tiny, frail lady cradled that big bowl between her body and her curved left arm, stirring doughs and beating batters with the strength of someone twice her size. The very sinews stood out on her thin arms as she mixed cakes and cookies, custards and pancakes, biscuits and desserts, for her farm family. She never owned an electric mixer, a food processor, or an electric (or gas) stove. She tested oven temperature with her hand, she measured with chipped and no-handled teacups, bent and tarnished spoons, and she hummed as she cooked and baked and tested and stirred. The results were delectable – and impossible to duplicate, even using her own recipes. My sister and I have concluded that we can't rival the rich cream and milk from the farm's Jersey cows, the eggs fresh from the chickens – or Grandma's touch.

Grandma had been left a widow before she was fifty years old, when her daughter and three sons were young adults. An Englishwoman by heritage, she rarely showed emotion of any kind. She seldom laughed and almost never touched, kissed, hugged, or demonstrated any tenderness or love. Her extended family, which included her siblings, their children, and various cousins, knew her as a benevolent matriarch, a kind and thoughtful friend and supporter. Only one of her children, my father, married or left the farm. Except for that, her domination seems to have been complete – and even he returned when she asked for his help during the dark days of the Depression.

Grandma's personal standards were high and immutable, and everyone in her family was expected to follow the practices she considered basic to civil living. All meals were served in the dining room, never in the kitchen, on a table set with cloth napkins, full china and silver service, and water glasses. When the men came in from the barn they removed their shoes, which had been carefully brushed on the porch, and their shirts. Before going to the table they washed faces, necks, arms, and hands at the kitchen sink, then put on clean shirts and house shoes. Many years after Grandma died, when Uncle Jesse was living alone in her house, he still set the table meticulously for each solitary meal.

"She tested oven temperature with her hand, she measured with chipped and no-handled teacups, bent and tarnished spoons, and she hummed as she cooked and baked and tested and stirred. "

I don't remember that Grandma ever hugged or kissed me, but I certainly knew that she loved me. We were good friends. I regret only that I didn't ask her about Grandpa, or her youth, or her years of teaching in the little red school-house on River Road in Manchester, Vermont. Today I am heavily involved in researching and preserving the history of this community, to which I have returned. If she had told me more, would I have been less involved? I wonder.

Grandma died just before her ninety-eighth birthday. She had been ill and in pain for several years after a broken hip, and she was quite deaf. She could no longer see to read, and her mind often wandered to places we could not go. In spite of these deficits, she loved to see her great-grandchildren and she seemed to hear every word they said to her. I watched in horror one day as my two-year-old son whirled her 'round and 'round in her wheelchair, then hopped on the footrest for a ride. She laughed with delight.

How lucky I was to have had her as part of my life. I learned from her the satisfactions of preparing food – of nurturing in that way. She touched, kneaded, crumbled, and tested with her work-worn hands. She folded gently, she shaped and stirred and tasted with authority, and when she was done she presented her gift of love to family and friends.

Of course she touched us – in her own way.

Grandma's Thousand Island Pickles

In the fall, the air filled with the aroma of spices and vinegar (made from our own apples) as the pickling season got underway. Thousand Island pickles, also called ripe cucumber pickles, were my favorites. I've only recently learned that my sister called them sweet pickles and loved them too. They were always served in a particular cut-glass dish that I now own, and I can taste those pickles each time I use it.

4 quarts large, ripe cucumbers, pared and sliced into 1-inch squares (ripe cucumbers are yellow, not green)
4 small onions, diced
1 tablespoon salt
2 cups sugar
1 quart cider vinegar
2 teaspoons turmeric
4 teaspoons mustard seeds

Fill a large canning kettle with water and bring it to a boil. (Canning kettles contain racks that keep the jars from touching the bottom and each other. If you don't have a canning kettle, use towels to pad the bottom of a large kettle, or place a rack at the bottom.)

Clean several Mason jars and lids. Place both jars and lids into the boiling water, then reduce the heat. The jars and lids should be fully immersed in the water, and the jars should not touch one another.

Meanwhile, put the cucumbers and onions into a large kettle, then add the salt, sugar, and vinegar. Place the turmeric and mustard seeds in a cheesecloth bag, then put the bag into the cucumber mixture. Heat this to a boil.

When the pickles are tender (but not mushy), use tongs to remove the Mason jars and lids from the canning kettle. Drain the jars and, while the jars are still hot, place the pickles and their brine inside. Leave a ½-inch space at the top. Twist on the lids, then place the jars back into the hot water. Allow the water to cover the jars by at least 2 inches.

Bring the water to a full rolling boil, then cover the kettle and lower the heat. Keep the water boiling steadily for 10 to 20 minutes.

Turn off the heat, use tongs to remove the jars, then set the jars on a rack to cool for 24 hours. When the jars have cooled, test the seals by inverting the jars and checking for leaks. The jars must be airtight. Makes 4 quarts.

Grandma's Doughnuts

Doughnuts were a staple for our hard-working farmers, eaten as an early morning pick-me-up before milking, as a sort of dessert with breakfast, or as a snack at bedtime. When still warm and sugary, doughnuts gave two young sisters incomparable pleasure, even though we were always told that hot doughnuts weren't good for us.

1 egg

1 cup sugar

8 teaspoons melted fat or
  vegetable oil

1 teaspoon cinnamon, or
  ½ teaspoon nutmeg

2 cups milk

1 teaspoon baking soda

2 teaspoons cream of tartar

Dash of salt

4 cups flour, or enough to
  make a soft dough

Lard or vegetable oil for
  deep-frying

1 cup sugar

1 tablespoon cinnamon

Cream the egg and sugar, then add the melted fat, cinnamon, milk, baking soda, cream of tartar, and salt. Stir this well. Gradually mix in the flour until the dough is soft and no longer sticky.

Heat 3 or 4 inches of lard in a deep kettle. Meanwhile, on a floured board, roll out the dough to ½- or ¾-inch thickness. Cut out rounds of dough with a doughnut cutter. (If you don't have a doughnut cutter, use a juice jar or cookie cutter for the rounds, then use a bottle cap to cut out the centers.) The dough will be very soft.

When the lard is 350 degrees, carefully drop in 2 or 3 pieces at a time. If the lard begins to smoke, reduce the temperature.

Fry the doughnuts, turning them once, until they are a rich, golden brown. Place them on brown paper to drain and cool.

While the doughnuts are still warm, place the sugar and cinnamon in a paper bag, put the doughnuts inside, and shake the bag gently. Makes 2 dozen doughnuts.

eeing

Amy Ellen Clarke Woodward
1869–1956

BY SALLY S. FINN

Nana looked at me by moving her gentle fingers over my face, for as Mother said, "Your grandmother has been blind from the year you were born." At first I thought these words implied some responsibility on my part, but they simply identified the year – 1929 – when Amy Ellen Woodward, mother of seven, lost her sight.

For the rest of her life, she could not see the sons and daughters she had raised. When they were young, their father worked six days a week at the lumberyard near the railroad tracks, then relaxed afterward with a pipe and a pint in his Morris chair in the dining room, but none of my aunts can recall Nana sitting at ease. Amid all the other women's duties of the time, she sewed magnificently; photographs of five daughters bear witness, as do the infant garments from my own layette. Did she miss using such skills? No one ever heard her complain. Nana's accepting outlook on a shadowed world showed me how to look for what is bright and good in every day, every circumstance.

Until the age of seven, I lived in a flat, two streets over from my grandparents' house in Bayonne, New Jersey, equally at home in both places. I remember only a few walks with Grandpop, and a dinner where he presided, and then a gathering in the parlor for his wake. He left his wife only the house, which Amy Woodward was determined to keep. Two daughters continued to live at home, and she accepted their contributions for the household, not for herself.

Nana coped with a darkened world by learning to use her other faculties brilliantly. Her movements were sure, aided only by the splayed fingers of her left hand gently sweeping the space before her. She devised new ways to cook. Amy Woodward knew her neighbors by their footsteps, and a whiff of perfume on the breeze identified which flowers bloomed along the walk.

Because she lived patiently with her handicap and managed each day so well, I was aware in my childhood only of her bosomy, comforting presence. Steep steps led to the "stoop" where Nana and I rocked in a chair and where there wasn't "room enough to swing a cat." She laughed when she realized that I envisioned an unhappy airborne kitty, then she was careful of my feelings as she explained the cruel cat-o'-nine-tails used for flogging sailors long ago. Then and always, she divined my thoughts from some nuance of voice.

"I treasure her wavering signature on congratulatory notes and cards marking every milestone of my growing up."

Her voice was grand, whether she was singing Gilbert and Sullivan or joining *The Gospel Singer* on the radio. But hearing words rather than seeing them sometimes made for confusion. During World War II, Nana spoke vehemently about "those awful Moxies" – the word "Nazi" was strange to her ears and translated into the name of that early carbonated drink she had never approved of.

But she was quick to grasp new ideas. Throughout the years, she was my advocate for adventures that my parents hesitated to allow. She supported two weeks of Girl Scout camp and insisted that I ride a mountain tramway (no doubt eager for my subsequent account). I treasure her wavering signature on congratulatory notes and cards marking every milestone of my growing up. She was there to kiss me and the parchment of my college degree, a family first.

Moments with Nana spelled contentment. We washed the dishes – and the dog. She knew poems by heart and we recited together. We talked about everything. She told me to follow my heart although the religion of my intended was not her own.

I knew only peace and love in her company. She remains with me now – my sightless Nana – looking over my shoulder and pointing out the best things in life.

Nana's English Fruitcake

Amy Ellen Clarke emigrated from England with two brothers in 1878. Orphaned, the children were escorted on a sailing ship by their maternal grandmother, who did not remain in America. The older brothers apparently went "out West"; Amy was left with cousins in New Jersey. In time she found work and a "place" in another home and never saw her grandmother or brothers again. Over the years she clung to customs from her early childhood: roast beef at Christmas and a cake recipe she had carried across the ocean. No family gathering was complete without this rich, dark fruitcake.

While teaching me how to make it, Nana told me about this eighteenth-century recipe. As most cooks know, the sugar content and moistness of fruitcake assure that it can be prepared well ahead of time, and that it "keeps" even after being cut. For these reasons, this recipe often appeared at weddings as "the groom's cake." English historical accounts indicate that early travel by coach between manors and villages took days. Relatives coming to a wedding expected to remain a week or more and to be provisioned for the return journey. The angelic white bride's cake was consumed at the festivities, but portions of the groom's cake were carried away in a single rider's "wallet" or in the hamper atop a coach. On the journey home, each young female would slip a slice under her pillow, believing that her dreams in a wayside inn would reveal her future husband. Generations later, when my son married, the departing guests were offered dainty slices of this firm cake, tied up in ribbons and clear wrap to let the jewels of fruit show.

Over the years, different branches of our family tree have developed variations of Amy Woodward's recipe. Individual preferences determine the choice of fruit. Chopped fruit mixes are handy, but if you have time to make your own blend, look for less-processed fruit sold in bulk. Also, stick margarine may be substituted for salt pork. (Even forty years ago I didn't buy salt pork, much less have a butcher who would "chop the pork fine.")

You can make this dense, chewy cake weeks before your special occasion. Just wrap it well and store it in a tin, perhaps one from England!

1 pound large muscat raisins,
    seeded
1 pound dried currants or
    small seedless raisins
1 pound mixed candied fruit,
    chopped (or a mixture of
    ½ pound sliced citron,
    ¼ pound sliced orange
    peel, and ¼ pound sliced
    lemon peel)
1 cup chopped walnuts
Dried dates and figs, candied
    cherries and pineapple, and
    other fruits as desired
½ pound salt pork, chopped fine
    (or ½ pound [2 sticks]
    margarine plus a dash of salt)
1 cup dark molasses
1½ cups sugar
1 cup warm water
6 cups flour, or enough to bind
    the fruit
½ tablespoon baking soda
2 teaspoons cinnamon
2 teaspoons nutmeg
1 teaspoon allspice
1 teaspoon ground cloves
½ cup brandy (optional)

Preheat your oven to 325 degrees.

Assemble the fruit and nuts. Chop, as necessary, into ¼-inch cubes.

Melt the salt pork and put it into a very large bowl. Add the molasses, sugar, and warm water. Let the mixture cool.

In a separate bowl, mix the flour, baking soda, cinnamon, nutmeg, allspice, and cloves. Alternately add the flour mixture and the fruit/nut mixture – one cupful at a time – to the molasses mixture. The batter will be quite heavy and will take some strength to stir. (You may add the brandy now, or drizzle it over the cake after it has baked and cooled.)

Grease and line your cake pans (see note below) with parchment paper before pouring in the batter. Bake the cakes according to the following directions:

One 9-inch ring pan	*2 hours*
A pair of 5 x 9-inch standard loaf pans	*1½ hours*
Half a dozen 3 x 5-inch miniature loaf pans	*40 minutes*

To avoid overbrowning, check the cakes 20 minutes before they are supposed to be done (8 minutes for the miniature cakes). Use a long toothpick – it should come out relatively clean.

To remove a cake from a pan, allow it to cool 15 minutes, or until it starts to shrink away from the sides of the pan. Use a narrow spatula or flat-bladed knife to loosen the edges of the cake. Turn the cake onto a wire rack and allow it to cool completely. Once the cake has cooled, remove the parchment paper.

Note: A straight-sided ring pan is ideal for a large cake; do not use an angel food cake pan. If you use several small pans, place them higher in your oven.

outhern Comfort

BY RUTH FERBER

I had three grandmothers. On my mother's side, I had a grandma whom I knew well. When she was a newborn baby, she and her fifteen-year-old mother were dragged out of the house on a mattress by Union soldiers who then set their house on fire. That was the way things happened in those terrible years.

I had a Grandma Emily on my father's side – Emily Elizabeth – whom I never knew. But I had another Grandma Emily on my father's side – Emily Jane – and I didn't know she wasn't our blood grandma until much later. A widow, Emily Jane moved into my grandpa's house several years after his wife died, to help his youngest daughter take care of him. Did he marry her? No. He didn't have to, he explained to his daughter. We all called her Grandma because she was the only paternal grandmother we knew and because we adored her.

She returned our love in full measure. When we ten grandchildren descended upon Grandma and Grandpa for summer vacation, we were welcomed with oodles of hugs and kisses. The parents left quietly. Excitedly we staked out our special places. Our beds were just quilts on the floor, but each of us was allowed to choose our own spot – in the parlor, in the kitchen, in the dining room, on the porches – a heady bit of freedom for such carefully brought-up youngsters.

She spread her love equally among us, but since I was the oldest, she made me responsible for the youngest ones. To me, this meant that she needed and trusted me, and I always felt that a special bond existed between the two of us. The other grandchildren would be outside playing hopscotch or I Spy, while I would be inside doing chores. Grandma called me her "precious helper," and I admit to the not-very-admirable trait of feeling proud to be teacher's pet.

I didn't spend all my time bathing and diapering the babies. Grandpa had a country dry-goods store, and I loved hearing the old-timers swap stories around the potbellied stove. I wasn't so charmed with their dipping and chewing tobacco – they left the smaller door of the stove open so they could spit and squirt up a storm, making a spewing sound on the coals that sent chills up my spine.

Grandma also had a vocation. My "real" grandmother, Emily Elizabeth, had been the town dentist, getting her instruction and tools from her uncle, a Memphis dentist. When Grandpa turned over his dead wife's tools to Emily Jane and taught her all he had observed, she pulled teeth for practically everyone in their small Mississippi town. (During the Depression few people had the means to travel to the nearest dentist in Memphis.) With anesthesia unavailable, she kept a jug of corn whiskey handy, especially for the men who complained of "a heap of pain." Of course, most of the men made this complaint. They kept asking for another swig or two, and Emily, being a merciful lady, never refused. Giggles abounding, the younger grandchildren would escort the drunk man safely home as he wobbled all over the road. I would follow behind to supervise.

We used to argue about who should inherit Emily's tools; we all wanted to be dentists like Emily. Instead, we became nurses, secretaries, schoolteachers, a newspaper reporter, and a textile-industry executive who invented a new textile machine. Not a dentist in the bunch, but I'm sure Grandma Emily was proud of us all.

She was an impressive woman, not least because she raised her own tender pullets in the backyard, and she would casually wring a chicken's neck and leave it to flounder around on the ground before it came to its eternal rest. We always behaved at Emily's house. Who would defy a woman who held death in her fingers?

There was one night when Emily's authority reigned. Grandpa had hidden a colored man in his cellar, a man falsely accused of raping a white woman. Emily gathered us around her and swore us to secrecy. "The law" was after him, she said, and if a bunch of rowdies reached him first, an innocent man would be lynched. She knew she could trust us, she said. But suddenly she was gripped by terror thinking what might happen to the man in the basement – and to us all – and her tone changed. "If any one of you opens your mouth, I'll wring your neck." That sealed our lips! Meanwhile, the rapist was caught and all ended well at Grandma's house. It always did.

Grandma Emily's Indian Chicken Curry

Grandma Emily's specialty for festive occasions was Indian chicken curry. She grew her own spices with seeds from a mail-order house. This recipe came from a drummer (a traveling salesman) who was courting one of her daughters. The recipe is very hot. (So was he, according to the daughter.) This may seem a complicated recipe, but it isn't. I have the cooked chicken ready the day before (sometimes I buy a cooked rotisserie chicken from the supermarket) and can whip it up in no time. I do not vary the spice amounts; as far as I'm concerned, they're perfect.

¼ cup vegetable oil

3 medium onions, sliced

4 to 6 ounces mushrooms, halved (about ¾ cup)

1 tablespoon curry powder

1 tablespoon ground coriander

1 teaspoon turmeric

1 teaspoon ground cumin

2 teaspoons poultry seasoning

6 bay leaves

¼ teaspoon cayenne pepper

1 teaspoon fresh ginger, diced

2 garlic cloves, chopped

⅓ cup raisins

⅓ cup unsalted peanuts

2 (14½-ounce) cans chicken broth or beef consommé

1 large boneless chicken breast, cut to bite-sized pieces (or 2 cups cooked chicken pieces)

¼ cup cornstarch

½ cup cold water

Flaked coconut (optional)

Heat the oil in a large kettle and lightly brown the onions and mushrooms. Drain off the excess oil, then add the curry powder, coriander, turmeric, cumin, poultry seasoning, bay leaves, and pepper. Stir to mix, then add the ginger, garlic, raisins, peanuts, and consommé. Cover and cook gently for 20 minutes, stirring frequently.

Meanwhile, sauté the chicken pieces until they become opaque, then set them aside. (Skip this step if you are using precooked chicken.)

In a bowl, combine the cornstarch and water, stirring until it is smooth. Add this to the liquid simmering on the stove, then add the chicken. Stirring constantly, cook the sauce until it thickens, about 5 minutes. You may need to add water as the curry cooks (especially after the cornstarch has been added) to reach the desired consistency.

Remove the bay leaves, sprinkle coconut flakes on top of the curry, and serve it with mango chutney and rice. Makes 4 to 6 servings.

From Horse Power to Nuclear Power

Mary Isabel Rudd Swayze
1870–1957

BY CB FOLLETT

Coming Home

When less than a year,
I came with my widowed mother
to live at my grandmother's,
the house she and her husband built on a street
so bowed with elms it was called Forest,
the house where my mother grew.

Two widows, one weathered, one raw.
My mother coming home lost and adrift.
My grandmother settled
into each seam of her house.

Into this house and her welcome, we came,
wounded daughter/mother.
And my grandmother willing.

If I disturbed her, she never said.
If she wished the return of old peace,
she didn't show it. Sometimes
when I raced through the house
chased by my yappy terrier, I would hear her
groan from the next room.

We lived over twenty years while her hair
turned from dark to gray to a white so pure
it was blinding. She put up with sleepovers,
long telephone calls, white rats that escaped
and climbed her bedroom curtain.

I tried on whaleboned corsets
with their unbelievable waists,
stone martens that snapped at each other
with stiff, hinged mouths, her wedding dress
kept in the tissue of her past.

We played gin rummy, later canasta,
and when she was old
I'd meld the wrong cards so *she* could win.

While I was at college, she failed into a nursing home,
Mother unable to give enough care. I'd go
see her but she was no longer there. Her mind
imploded, her beautiful hair
pinched into a pink bow.

My grandmother lived from gaslights to atomic bombs. She lived through two world wars and the Great Depression, from the aftermath of the Civil War to Elvis Presley. She was brought up on Riverside Drive in New York City, raised in comfortable circumstances with servants and beautiful clothes, and considered a great beauty with her fourteen-inch waist and "bedroom" eyes.

Funny how circumstances can change. Her parents bitterly divorced, and both remarried. Along came a little brother and my grandmother felt pushed out of childhood. Worse yet, her mother permitted no contact with her father, in fact so poisoned the child against her father that even as an adult my grandmother refused all contact. She married a promising young man from a wealthy family in Sussex County, New Jersey, but his fortunes did not prosper and my grandmother had to take on more and more of the housework. Only one woman remained to do the cooking and cleaning, but during World War II she went off to work in a factory downtown and never returned. By that time, my grandfather was long dead, all the children had married and left home, and one of them, my mother, had returned with a three-month-old baby just before the war.

By then, my grandmother routinely walked to the railroad tracks to gather chunks of coal that had fallen while the coal cars were being loaded; she constantly cleaned coal soot off the sills and furniture, and she learned to cook because she had to.

"She was raised in comfortable circumstances with servants and beautiful clothes, and considered a great beauty with her fourteen-inch waist and 'bedroom' eyes."

Grammy's Ladyfingers

My grandmother turned out to be an excellent cook.

Her ladyfingers were one of the treats I remember best, their name connoting delicate behavior of which I could never be accused. Even in those days, most people bought ladyfingers from the bakery, but my grandmother made her own and didn't use the special pans, either. It was my job to separate the whites from the yolks. She would form the fingers on a paper, pinching them with her plump hands, her diamond winking among the ladyfingers as she worked down the rows. I would get to lick the bowl, but she was a stingy bowl scraper and used most of the leavings to make one last piece.

Ladyfingers were for special occasions: guests, sometimes holidays. I was allowed to have one only when the evening was over, and only if there were leftovers. I would sit halfway up the front stairs of her New England Victorian. From there I could see into the dining room, resenting each helping. Because I rarely see ladyfingers served these days, the memory of them is sweet, something special between my grandmother and me.

3 egg whites
⅛ teaspoon salt
⅓ cup powdered sugar
2 egg yolks
½ teaspoon vanilla extract
⅓ cup cake flour, sifted

Preheat your oven to 350 degrees.

Combine the egg whites and salt in a metal bowl. Beat until the egg whites are stiff as the waves in an ocean storm. Then, while still beating, gradually add the powdered sugar.

In a separate bowl, beat the egg yolks until they're thick and the color of summer lemons. Gently fold these into the egg whites. Add the vanilla, then gently fold in the sifted flour, keeping the egg whites as full of air as possible.

On cookie sheets, form the dough into 4 x 1-inch fingers. (Although my grandmother did this by hand, beginners may have more luck using a pastry bag.) Bake for 12 minutes or until golden on top. Makes 16 ladyfingers.

Note: Grammy sometimes sprinkled powdered sugar on top (like a drizzle) before baking or (like a snowstorm) after baking. She often cut the cooled ladyfingers in half and made sandwich cookies with tart jelly or fresh fruit in the middle. Occasionally, she put cinnamon in the batter, filling the kitchen with expectations of Santa and gifts.

Margaret Mitchell and Black-Eyed Peas

Katie Pearl Spinks Chester
1872–1956

BY ELIZABETH LINDER DaGUE

Six years after Robert E. Lee surrendered at Appomattox, my maternal grandmother was born on the family farm near Camp Hill in southeastern Alabama.

Her father had been drafted during the last two years of the war. A graduate of Georgia Military Academy, he built bridges and tunnels with the Confederate Corps of Engineers in Virginia. In his Civil War diary, Rollie Randolph Spinks named men who fainted during the Confederate tunneling around Petersburg. But he never complained, even when bartering for food or walking home at war's end.

Rollie's stoicism was strong in his daughter Katie Pearl, my Gran. In those hardscrabble years when the Civil War was remembered as if it were yesterday, Southern life held few luxuries. After her marriage to Oscar Chester – farmer, cattle trader, and pharmacist who originated and sold his own Kidney Elixir – my Gran needed money of her own. There was precious little cash for cows, none for clothes. Her solution was to raise chickens and sell eggs.

With some of her "hen" money she bought books. Reading came after the midday dinner, a bath, and a clean dress. The fragrance of rose talcum wafts back to me today, along with the image of my Gran in her high-backed rocker on the sleeping porch in summer, book in one hand, pleated paper fan in the other, lost in the printed page. The smell of wood smoke in autumn brings back indoor afternoons, a pale light through the window of the back bedroom, the smell of burning coal, the glow of a fire in the grate, and my Gran reading by the window.

Though they had little money, my Gran's family treasured books and respected her buying them now and then. After all, "hen" money bought them.

My Gran had an eclectic taste in books. I remember two books discussed one summer over fried okra and black-eyed peas: Pearl Buck's *The Good Earth* and

Ernie Pyle's account of ordinary soldiers in World War II. My Gran read everything from *I Married Adventure* (who could forget that title?) to *The Yearling* and *The Robe;* and because these books were in her house, where my mother and I lived when I was young, I read them, too. Later, when my father finished advanced training in his medical specialty, our family was reunited and we moved to Birmingham. I borrowed my Gran's copy of *Gone with the Wind* and read it by flashlight under the bedcovers. My mother had forbidden me to read it. Too young, that's what I was.

"The fragrance of rose talcum wafts back to me today, along with the image of my Gran in her high-backed rocker on the sleeping porch in summer, book in one hand, pleated paper fan in the other, lost in the printed page."

Today I'm a buyer of books that I wish my Gran could have read, for during her entire life she devoured the printed word much as her family devoured her food.

I remember my garrulous Gran when she had auburn hair and freckles and dished up butter beans and talk on summer Sundays; but I also remember my solitary Gran in late afternoon, with her books. Like Henry Thoreau, she traveled far in one place.

Gran's Blackberry Spice Cake with Burnt Caramel Icing

The garden behind the house where my Gran lived all her life required plowing by a hired man and a mule. After that, dressed in her garden hat and long-sleeved cotton coat, my Gran seeded, weeded, and harvested. My Edenic memories include spicy, dense blackberry cake she made from berries brought from the farm, and scuppernong wine she made from grapes off the arbor behind the house. Gran didn't live in Eden, though, because she shelled, and peeled, and shucked, and then cooked and canned on a wood stove for almost all the days of her life – she retired the wood stove only after World War II had ended.

The Cake

1½ cups flour

¼ teaspoon salt

1 teaspoon baking soda

1 teaspoon nutmeg

1 teaspoon cinnamon

1 teaspoon allspice

¼ pound plus 4 tablespoons
   (1½ sticks) butter

1 cup sugar

3 eggs

3 tablespoons buttermilk

1 teaspoon vanilla extract

1½ cups fresh blackberries

The Icing

1 (5-ounce) can evaporated
   milk, plus enough water to
   make 1 cup of liquid

¼ pound (1 stick) butter

3 cups sugar

Preheat your oven to 350 degrees, then grease and flour a pair of 9-inch cake pans.

In a medium-sized bowl, sift the flour with the salt, baking soda, nutmeg, cinnamon, and allspice; set this aside.

Cream the butter and sugar. Separate the eggs, setting the egg whites aside, and add one yolk at a time. After each yolk, add ⅓ of the flour mixture, beating well after each addition. Stir in the buttermilk.

In a separate bowl, beat the egg whites until they form high, dry peaks. Mix in the vanilla and blackberries, then fold this into the batter.

Pour the batter into your cake pans and bake for 25 to 30 minutes. Use a toothpick to check for doneness. Allow the cake to cool several hours before icing it.

For the icing: mix the milk, butter, and 2½ cups of the sugar in a heavy saucepan. Bring to a boil, then reduce to a simmer. Stir frequently.

Meanwhile, melt and brown the remaining sugar in a heavy skillet over medium heat. Do not allow the sugar to burn. Add the browned sugar to the milk mixture and cook until the mixture reaches 234 to 238 degrees on a candy thermometer, or until a small amount of the mixture forms a soft ball when dropped into ice water. The ball should be firm enough to roll between your fingers.

Remove the icing from the heat and beat it until creamy. The icing will be very thick. Spread the icing on the top, on the sides, and between the layers of the cake. (As the icing cools, it will be difficult to spread.)

Lost Loves

BY ELLEN PERRY BERKELEY

Helen Liberman Fish
1873–1939

I was sunny and sweet, as a little girl, and plump. My father fondly called me "Butterball." Grandma Fish was also sunny and sweet and plump. She and I had the same shape to our face, the same small nose and mouth. I was named after her. And we matched in one other way: Uniquely for us both, we each received from the other a love unblemished by criticism or preoccupation. And then she died. At that time, for me, death came mostly to evil creatures in fairy tales. Her death was the first of anyone I had known and loved.

She died quickly, over a weekend, of staphylococcal pneumonia. I had written a poem for her, and my mother brought it to her in the hospital: "A little frog / Sat on a log / Trying to dry in the sun / Ho ho, he thought, what fun / Ho ho, he thought, what fun." But Grandma died without hearing my poem; my mother didn't think to pretend otherwise. We grieved privately in our family. I remember only that Mommy came to my room, later that day, and said, "You haven't been crying, have you?" I could find no honest answer to this question. "No," I lied.

I cannot recall, now, a single thing that Grandma and I said to each other. We went deeper than words. How deep I understood only fifty-odd years later, when my grief slammed into me one afternoon. I couldn't find a precious trinket of Grandma's that had been mine for years: a tiny box barely an inch in diameter, woven from strips of something golden. I searched wildly. "It's gone, it's gone," I wailed. What could have become of it? Would I never see it again? Ah, but there it was, on the floor, the little box that held nothing but history and memory and love. As I clasped it to me with a sob, I had some understanding of the panic I must have felt at the death of Helen Liberman Fish so long ago.

I had been Grandma's eager pupil in all the homemaking arts disdained by my modern mother. Grandma let me sprinkle the chopped nuts on her butter cookies before they baked (the trick was to get the nuts on the cookies, not on the baking sheet), and I remember being good at it and earning her praise. She showed me how to sew – little stitches, all the same size – and we were both proud of my efforts. She made gorgeous clothes for my Betsey, the huge doll that Daddy found at a fire sale. Betsey had a flannel nightgown to match my own, and a green velvet coat with fur collar that matched nothing I owned. Grandma made no clothes for my Shirley Temple, sensing that all you did with her was change her outfits, while with Betsey you laughed, you did things, you had a friend. I wrote often to Grandma, sending my poems and news and love. And then she died. I was not yet eight.

"By 1891, Jews were being deported from Moscow, denied admission to government service, and admitted to educational institutions according to strict quotas. It was time to leave. But the time was wrong for Grandma."

Only later did I learn about her, as much as anyone knew. She had been a beautiful young woman, fair-haired and blue-eyed, one of eight children in a family permitted to live in Moscow. (This was unusual for Jews; her father was a merchant, perhaps an important one.) Also, extraordinary for a Jewish child, she had been admitted to a Russian school – but because she was Jewish, she was forced to stand all day at her lessons. Nevertheless, there she learned Russian and English and began her lifelong love of poetry.

The family immigrated to America somewhere around 1890. Restrictions against Jews had increased under the rule of Alexander III (1881–1894): Jews were now forbidden to settle outside the towns and villages, even within the Pale of Settlement where Jews had been confined since the first decade of the century. By 1891, Jews were being deported from Moscow, denied admission to government service, and admitted to educational institutions according to strict quotas.

It was time to leave. But the time was wrong for Grandma. She left behind a sweetheart, a young violinist who had – as she once confided to my mother – beautiful hands, a beautiful heart, a beautiful soul.

Hyman Fish, who became my Grandpa, was not beautiful. He was tactless and critical, although generous, principled, and intellectually rigorous: loving justice more than people, my aunt suggested. He arrived from Lithuania with three rubles to his name – which was then Yudelevitch – and, starting as a peddler, went on to make overalls, own a lining store, deal in wholesale woolens, and lose money in real estate.

Grandma had four children within five years and later a fifth; the fourth was my mother, who forever felt unwanted. In the early days, Grandma spent long hours helping in the lining store, and throughout the years she endured Grandpa's ridicule of almost everything spiritual that moved her.

Her own birthday was never celebrated. "Was she too busy, or were we?" my mother wondered. And then, as my mother told it, Grandma became an anxious, thin, and sad little woman. But her love for me was never anxious, never sad, and in my memory she will always be plump and sweet. I will always know that I was cherished by her. I hope she knew that she was cherished by me. I hope, too, that she had been cherished by her own lost love, the violinist with the beautiful soul. I don't like to think of Grandma being sad.

Grandma Fish's Borscht

Pop Fish dictated his autobiography, primarily to my mother, as he lay dying in 1945, and in it he mentions his wife only minimally: "Meanwhile I had gotten married and set up four rooms with new furniture bought in Hartford." He had a notions store in Hartford, before Grandma got homesick for her sisters and they returned to New York City. While in Hartford, so the story goes, Pop once raged at Grandma for buying a twenty-cent remnant from his competitor. The chief rival of H. Fish was G. Fox, later the preeminent department store of Hartford.

Grandma thought she was a rotten cook at the start, but Grandpa liked everything she made. His own mother, back in Vilkamir, had been a strong and simple woman who ran a flour mill with her husband, dispensed justice within the shtetl, and lived healthily on the simplest foods — radishes, bread, borscht.

Borscht was a staple for Grandma Fish, too. Here is her recipe, dutifully copied — and often prepared — by my mother. I have only my grandmother's simplest recipes from my mother, who never found the culinary arts as challenging as the other arts and became a sculptor and potter instead. This recipe is gloriously easy. Note the precise language — not "gradually," not even "very gradually," but "very, very gradually." It seems important to pass this along very, very precisely.

The Soup

1 (15-ounce) can of beets,
    drained and grated
1 (15-ounce) can cold water
Juice of ½ lemon
Salt
1 egg

The Extras

Sour cream
2 to 3 small potatoes,
    boiled and chopped
    into bite-sized pieces

"To one can of beets, add one can of cold water, the juice of ½ lemon, and a pinch of salt. Bring this to a boil; simmer for 5 minutes.

"Beat the egg well. Very, very gradually, drip the hot beet mixture into the beaten egg. Cool the soup and then refrigerate it. Keep it in the refrigerator until you need it.

"If you are not dieting, put a tablespoon of sour cream into each soup bowl. Boiled potatoes, too.

"This recipe will give 6 people a good taste, or 3 people a substantial meal."

Grandma Fish's Caramel Custard

Grandma's sweetness was legendary. I remember her indulgent smile at my every interruption, her proud smile at every accomplishment. Even when Grandpa's rough sense of humor rankled her, she still smiled sweetly: a placid smile.

Grandma's sweets were also legendary. Here is another simple recipe that I have from my mother, Esther Fish Perry, who had it from her mother, who probably had it from her mother.

The timing is a bit casual (can you see the shrug in "5, maybe 10, minutes"?), but I promise you that this recipe works beautifully and will make any granddaughter ever so slightly more plump and sweet and sunny.

The Custard

5 eggs
4 cups whole milk
½ cup sugar
½ teaspoon salt
1 teaspoon vanilla extract

The Caramel Sauce

1 cup sugar
1 cup boiling water

For the custard: "Heat the oven to 325 degrees. In a bowl, beat the eggs slightly and set them aside. Scald the milk on the stove and set this aside, too.

"Put the sugar in an iron spider. [I have it on good authority that a pot of any material can be substituted for an 'iron spider.'] Turn the stove to medium and stir the sugar constantly until it melts down to a light brown syrup. Lift the pan from the fire occasionally, to prevent burning.

"Add 1 cup of the scalded milk very gradually, being careful that the milk does not bubble up and over. Stir until the sugar is completely dissolved, then add the rest of the milk.

"Allow the sugar-and-milk to cool, then add it to the beaten eggs – very, very gradually so the eggs don't curdle. Add the salt and vanilla, then strain all of this into a buttered mold or baking dish, or individual custard cups. Bake in the oven in a pan of boiling water until the custard is firm in the center – 20, maybe 30, minutes. Try it with a knife. If the knife comes out clean, the custard is done. Chill the custard and serve it with caramel sauce."

For the caramel sauce: "Melt the sugar down to a smooth, light brown syrup. Then, very gradually, add the boiling water. Let simmer 5, maybe 10, minutes. Spoon it over the custard. This syrup will keep, if you have any left [but this granddaughter thought it best never to have any left]." Makes 6 to 8 servings.

Fellow Conspirators

BY MARY ANN HORENSTEIN

My grandmother and I were always close. The tie that bound us, although we didn't often discuss it, was our common enemy – my mother.

We were angry at my mother for very different reasons. My grandparents had been wealthy until the Crash of 1929. But unlike some of his friends, my grandfather did not pick himself up and start over. At the age of fifty, feeling like a loser, he gave up his business and never worked again. My mother and father supported my grandparents for more than forty years. Was my mother angry? You bet! But my grandmother was angrier still; she hated being dependent on her daughter.

My own anger wasn't so specific. Lots of teenage rebellion. I was disappointed to be an only child and couldn't think of anyone to blame but my mother. Also, I thought my mother a bit silly, someone with whom I couldn't have a serious conversation.

But my grandmother was always available, always thoughtful, always ready to talk. When I was about ten, I made the short train trip by myself to stay with my grandparents in New York City. We made valentines together, Gran and I – cutting, pasting, decorating, writing verses. (My mother hadn't understood why I found it unacceptable simply to *buy* valentines.) This trip began a new phase of my life. Whenever my parents had plans that didn't include me, or whenever I needed to be away from them, I took off for Gran's. We went to the movies, to dinner, for a walk along Riverside Drive. Each time I visited, I was in heaven.

When I married, at twenty-one, Gran took me to the butcher for a lesson in buying inexpensive cuts of meat. Then we went home together and cooked. Cooking together – and discussing life while we cooked – was an important part of our relationship. She would occasionally mention that my mother was too busy to make soups and stews, and we'd smile at each other. We knew we were different from my mother. We loved her, and we knew she was a good and loving person, but she just didn't fit into our narrow society.

When my children were young, my mother would come to visit with her maid, who would cook dinner and sometimes clean the house. Meanwhile, Mom would take the children for an adventure and I would have some much-needed time alone.

But Gran would come to babysit. Especially after my grandfather died, she would arrive every month or two for a few days. Sometimes she'd stay home with the children while I was out. She'd read to them, play with them, talk to them. When I returned, it was always to a peaceful home. The children were happy; even the dog was calm. Gran exuded confidence, competence, comfort with herself, and acceptance of others.

She continued to visit into her mid-nineties. My children were in school and I was working, but in the late afternoon and evening we'd cook, she, my daughter, and I. (Not my sons – the sexual stereotypes were firmly in place with Gran – but the boys wouldn't be far away, eavesdropping and enjoying the aromas.) We'd have all the goodies for dinner. And we'd talk. She'd tell us tales of her childhood, her family, her courting days. One of six children, she was the grandchild of Hungarian émigrés. At eighteen, she married her childhood sweetheart and bore my mother and a son. In her suburb of Chicago, she was one of the few women who worked – she and her sister owned a clothing store when they were young mothers. Perhaps she was more available to me than she had been to her own daughter.

Did my grandmother have a loving relationship with my mother when Mom was a girl? I hope so. But in my growing-up years, and until the day she died just before her hundredth birthday, Gran was the important adult and female role model for me. I've never stopped missing her.

Gran's Mushroom and Barley Soup

Gran didn't wait until she died to distribute her few treasured possessions; she wanted the joy of giving them to people she loved. So one day, when she knew she wouldn't cook much more, she gave me two black cast-iron frying pans and a soup pot. I think of her each time I use them.

This is her recipe, written down by me after watching her cook. I make it often.

7 to 8 pounds beef marrow bones
1½ pounds stewing beef
1 cup barley
1 (28-ounce) can stewed tomatoes
2 bay leaves
1 teaspoon salt
1 teaspoon pepper
1 teaspoon thyme
4 medium yellow onions
3 ribs celery, with leaves
3 to 4 carrots
½ pound string beans
1 garlic clove
1 to 2 pounds mushrooms

Put the bones, meat, barley, and tomatoes in a soup pot and cover with water. Heat to boiling. Add the bay leaves, salt, pepper, and thyme. Then, cover the pot and cook slowly for approximately 3½ hours. Skim off the fat.

Cut the onions, celery, carrots, string beans, and garlic into small pieces; add them to the pot and cook for 15 minutes. Then slice the mushrooms and add them to the pot. Cook for another 20 minutes or until all the vegetables are soft.

Remove the bones and save them for the dog. (If you have no dog, save them for the neighbor's dog; you'll have a friend forever.) Save the marrow from the bones. While it is still warm, spread it on slices of rye bread for a tasty treat.

Remove the meat from the stew, cut it into small pieces, and return it to the pot.

Refrigerate the stew. Skim off the fat before reheating. Makes 15 to 20 servings.

The Survivors

Ida Sachs Travis
1875–1960

BY LILLA M. WALTCH

In the early 1900s, after scraping together her earnings from a small stocking factory that she ran in her village in Lithuania, my grandmother sent her new husband to the Land of Opportunity – and then waited for him to send for her. He never did. A year or so after his departure she managed to get together enough money to come along after him anyway.

Once in Boston she devoted herself to caring for an unappreciative husband, whose small grocery store was barely solvent, and raising the two daughters born here. The elder daughter was my mother.

By the time I came on the scene, Grandma was in her late fifties and afflicted with diabetes. With her gray hair in a bun and her feet in slippers that had holes cut out for her corns, she seemed like an old woman to me. She spoke Yiddish most of the time, and her poor English and failing vision kept her isolated from a world in which she was out of place.

I always worried that she would die, and I couldn't bear to lose her; I loved and needed her. We all lived together – my grandparents and my parents with their two children (and another soon to come) – crammed into the third floor of a three-decker in Dorchester. These were Depression years. My grandfather's store was failing. My father was struggling to make a living as an engineer. In that atmosphere of anxiety and dissatisfaction my grandmother's love was like a soft pillow under my head.

She always listened to whatever I wanted to tell her, always chuckled with pleasure and said, "You're so smart, *ketzele* (kitten), you could do anything."

My mother was often angry with me, calling me "bad girl" and retreating to her bedroom and slamming the door as if she couldn't stand to be near me a moment longer. I would knock on the door and beg, "Please make up with me.

Please." Without her approval, I felt diminished. Worthless. Bad. But she would never answer and, finally, I would give up and go to my own room and lie crying on my bed.

Then Grandma would come in and put her arms around me. I could smell the clean cotton of her housedress along with a sour odor of vinegar and dust. Her skin was like loose silk, the wrinkles on her cheeks like pleats in the soft fabric. The skin under her arms hung down like a curtain. "Come, *ketzele*," she would say, "don't listen to her. You're a good girl. Let's bake cookies. Just the two of us." She would take my hand and lead me into the kitchen, and together we would get out the big crockery bowls, the flour and butter and poppy seeds. She hummed as she worked, and I could feel my spirits lifting as we beat the eggs and stirred the fragrant mixture.

It wasn't until many years later that I began to realize what I meant to her. I was her beloved grandchild, of course, but I was also her chance to grasp at life. She could live through me — through my triumphs, my sorrows, my joys. She could guide me, praise me, encourage me. And for each of us, being an outcast was no longer our defining characteristic.

In her eighties, when her health was failing, she brought the children's book I had written to the nursing home where my mother had reluctantly sent her. Grandma hadn't read my book, not because it was so recently published, or because her eyesight was so bad, but because she had never learned to read English. Yet she knew the story and characters well, and she showed the book proudly to everyone she met there.

Growing up, I often wondered why a woman of her intelligence and resourcefulness had been unable to adjust more successfully to life in America. Now I better understand how difficult it must have been for her, moving to a strange country, making a life with a man who was indifferent to her, and raising children in an alien culture. She gave me the love and support I needed so desperately. I gave her another chance at life.

Grandma's *Mon* (Poppy Seed) Cookies

Baking was Grandma's way of making her world better, of making her family happier. When I was feeling down in the dumps, she would invite me to help create food that would cheer others. In doing so, we cheered ourselves. Sometimes my mother would complain that we were messing up her kitchen. Grandma would say, "I've got to do something. I'm not dead yet. Come, ketzele, let's bake." Grandma's mon (poppy seed) cookies were appreciated by the whole family. To this day I make them to please my family and myself.

¼ pound (1 stick) unsalted
    butter
½ cup sugar
2 eggs
1 teaspoon lemon juice
2½ cups flour
¼ teaspoon salt
1½ teaspoons baking
    powder
½ cup poppy seeds

Preheat your oven to 350 degrees.

Cream the butter and sugar. Add the eggs and beat well. Stir in the lemon juice.

In a separate bowl, sift the flour. Mix in the salt and baking powder, then add the poppy seeds. Stir the dry ingredients into the butter. If the mixture becomes crumbly, use your hands to mix the dough.

Roll out the dough on a floured board. Cut out the cookies with a large, round cookie cutter or the top of a glass. (Grandma used a juice glass.)

Bake for 15 to 20 minutes. Makes 2 dozen cookies.

A "Proper" Tea

Lillian Spence Wood
1875–1964

BY DIANNE S. LODGE-PETERS

My Nana died at eighty-nine, having never lost her Yorkshire accent although she lived in this country from the age of six. Yorkshire's my native tongue, too; I learned it from her. I'd come home from school and, happy or sad, I'd talk to her over cups of " 'ot Oolong tea" and *kern* teacakes. From her I learned that "there's naught amiss what supping tea won't cure."

My Nana, Lillian Spence, married Levi Wood, a metalsmith, at the turn of the twentieth century and lived out her years in the Merrimack River Valley of Massachusetts. I grew up on the same Oakland Avenue as my mother and aunts did, graduating from the same Methuen High School. But I went on to college and then to graduate school, mostly because of Nana Wood.

She never went beyond the third grade. She couldn't even tell time in the ordinary way: "Clock's going up for five," she'd say. She couldn't spell or punctuate. She wrote words by their sound. "Vacation" was *v-a-k-a-s-h-u-n*. Her letters to me in college began with a capital letter and ended eight pages later with a period. In between was all the family and neighborhood news. Her phonetic spelling – "insolent" for "insulin," for instance (she was a late-life diabetic) – enabled me to read Chaucer immediately and in the original, smack off the page. I was astounded. What a gem of a grandmother I had! Of course, I had already heard about Arthur and Gawain, St. George and the Dragon. Nana had told me the old stories over our afternoon tea.

It was Nana who showed me I could bake yeast bread, despite the revelation from my high school biology teacher that bacteria were Living Things. To me this meant they had a "mind" of their own. I was uneasy about tampering with them.

"It doesn't matter if they're alive, luv. You're smarter than they are."

Family stories were important to my family not just for telling later generations how life was lived before they were born, or for telling the children who they were and how and where they belonged. Family stories were important because they showed us our family's *traditions* – the handing down of our lives and patterns of living. Family stories told us how we survived as a family. In mine, we showed affection not so much by hugging and kissing, but by listening to the sounds of words and the real meanings beneath them. We showed our love by laughing at ourselves: That bacteria were alive and sentient was the family joke on me, and I love to tell it on myself.

My Nana taught me who I was in the language of my ethnic heritage. She made sure I knew all the old stories and songs. (Later, when I was studying for my doctorate in anthropology, I learned that these were classic medieval folktales.) She gave me the confidence and the patience to make yeast bread, to win a college scholarship, and to stick with the dissertation until it was finished.

Nana taught me about trust: The dough *will* rise if you let it. She also taught me about trusting myself. God love her, I've never lost this. To me, she's the smartest person I have ever known.

Nana's *Kern* (Currant) Teacakes

My son Benjamin (who is named for Nana's twin brother) often comes by with his boys after school, for tea and talk, just as I went to Nana's when I was little. I see Nana in Ben, in the way he shows his sons how to "sup" tea from the same cups and saucers that she used with me. Four generations in our family have learned that the recipe for confidence means a "proper Oolong tea" in bone-china cups, a plate of kern *teacakes, and a tableful of "luv."*

Kerns are currants. Teacakes are eight-inch rounds of yeast bread sliced crossways into "fingers" (not wedges); they are meant to be dossled, *or dunked, in hot tea.*

½ cup dried currants

¼ teaspoon lemon juice

¼ cup canola or safflower oil

¼ cup sugar

¼ teaspoon salt

4 or 5 anise seeds, ground (you don't want to use so much that it's tastable – just the littlest of hints)

1 cup fat-free milk, scalded and cooled to lukewarm

1 tablespoon (1 envelope) active dry yeast, softened in ¼ cup warm (not hot) water

1 egg, slightly beaten

4 cups flour

Plump the currants by covering them with boiling water. Add the lemon juice and set it aside.

In a large bowl, stir together the oil, sugar, salt, ground anise, and lukewarm milk. Add the yeast water, then add the egg. Stir well. Next, stir in 2 cups of the flour, one cup at a time, beating well after each cup.

Drain the currants and fold them into the dough. Add ⅓ cup of the flour and mix well. The dough will be wet.

Oil the top of the wet dough. Cover the bowl with a dampened cloth and let the dough rise until doubled (about 1 hour) in a warm, draft-free place.

Stir down the dough. Then, stir in ½ to 1 cup of the remaining flour, or enough to make the dough kneadable. On a floured board, knead the dough until it is smooth and elastic (about 5 minutes). Divide the dough into four equal pieces. Shape each piece into a mound about 4 or 5 inches in diameter; place the mounds on a greased cookie sheet and press them flat. Let these rise uncovered until doubled. Do not allow the mounds to touch each other.

Meanwhile, preheat your oven to 375 degrees.

Bake the teacakes until browned, about 30 minutes, and slice them before serving. Makes 24 to 32 "fingers."

$\mathscr{S}$he Walked in Silence

Florence Virginia Wood Willis
1876–1942

BY FLORENCE LADD

$\mathbf{M}$ama Willis stood proud, erect, and tall in a long cotton skirt covered with an apron, her arms folded over a simple blouse. Her walnut-brown face was adorned only with steel-rimmed eyeglasses, thin gold-loop earrings, and the black grosgrain ribbon that tied her fine gray hair in a knot atop her head. With cordial greetings, but without kisses or embraces, she welcomed us to the wood-shingled house on Jones Street in the North Carolina tidewater town of New Bern, where my parents, my sister, and I visited for a week or two every summer. The house, built by my grandfather, a carpenter, was a symbol of prestige and family pride. My mother had been born in that house. Her nostalgia grew palpable as the annual homecoming approached.

The drive from our house in Washington, D.C., to my mother's hometown took us along the highways and country roads of then-segregated Virginia and North Carolina. Aware of the risk of a fierce racial encounter if anything went awry – engine trouble, perhaps, or a flat tire – Mom and Dad were on edge while on the road. As we approached the house where Mama Willis awaited us on the narrow front porch, my parents were jubilant at having made the journey without incident.

Aloof and reserved, no excess in her gestures, Mama Willis led the way to the bedrooms upstairs. We followed with our baggage. I somehow knew she was happy to see us, but I wanted to *feel* her delight. I wanted to throw myself onto her apron and be lifted in her arms. Named Florence for her, I wanted a namesake's welcome. I wanted her embrace.

Since I had been named for Mama Willis, I wondered about ways in which I was expected to emulate her. During our visits, I looked up to her – literally (she was just under six feet tall) and figuratively – with keen interest. She was diligent

and alert, but often silent. When she spoke, she had something essential to say. People paid attention. Whatever she said seemed important, wise, and useful. It was simple speech, plain talk — an explanation, a direction, or an expression of gratitude.

It was her silence that I embraced, and her silence that embraced me. I admired her air of self-containment and calm. And it was her kind of intelligence to which I aspired. Hers was a strategic mind — she knew how to use language pointedly and effectively. I now realize that she had a relatively modest vocabulary. With only eight years of schooling and little time to cultivate language, she practiced concise speech and protracted silence.

Silence was our medium of communication. In silence at her side, I held the pail of clothespins as she hung the laundry out to dry in the early morning sun. Then she turned to the garden and gathered bouquets of daisies and dahlias: one for her African Methodist Episcopal Church, one for an ailing neighbor, and one for the dining table. Amid the bountiful vegetables, she stooped to pinch off string beans and pluck tomatoes from their vines; I watched her silently dig up new potatoes and strip ears of July corn from stalks. She fed the flock of fluttering fowl before selecting two or three for dinner. I saw her deftly wring their necks, behead them, and then pluck them in steaming water and prepare them for frying. I was awed by her strength and courage.

Mama Willis kept house and cooked for a family of five: herself, Pa Willis, and Aunt Nettie's three children. (Nettie, who had Bohemian tendencies, was pursuing a second marriage in Brooklyn.) During our visits, Mama Willis cooked for nine. When she was not at work in her own house, she earned a few dollars — and earnest prayers, no doubt — as housekeeper and cook for New Bern's Catholic priests.

At home, she cooked on a cast-iron, wood-burning stove, even in the unrelenting heat of the Carolina summer. After dinner, my garrulous mother joined Mama Willis in the kitchen. Mom, fearful of silence, filled the warm kitchen air with her idle, incessant monologues. Together they washed dishes in a tub of water heating on the stove, water drawn from the pump in front of the house. The chores of the day finally over, Mama Willis settled in a rocking chair in the corner of the dining room. Mom joined the others — Pa Willis, Dad, and my cousins Charles, Gus, and Louise — at the table. While they discussed the events of the day as reported in the *Sun Journal* and debated prospects for the future, Mama Willis quietly rocked. My ears were tuned in to the talk, but my eyes were fixed on her. Pa Willis held forth on a variety of topics, his opinions delivered in a deep, authoritative voice. Mama Willis kept silent. Years later, I wondered about her silence.

Florence Virginia Wood had been born eleven years after Emancipation to parents who had been slaves. Henry Willis (who had moved to New Bern from Portsmouth, an island off North Carolina's coast) was the son of a Cherokee mother and a mulatto father who had not been a slave. Pa Willis had an attitude of entitlement. Did his lineage imbue him with the confidence to express his views in a forceful voice that silenced hers? Or had years of domestic chores, in the service of others and in her own domain, rendered her quiet (as well as visibly weary)? Had she been silenced, over the years, by the labor required to purchase the land and building materials for a house, acquire furniture, buy a piano, provide piano and organ lessons for my mother, then send her to Winston-Salem Teachers College? After years of rearing her own children, Mama Willis had three grandchildren thrust upon her. Had her voice been stilled by duty and responsibility?

When Mama Willis suffered a fatal heart attack on a Sunday in May, I was a month away from my tenth birthday. I was neither old enough nor bold enough to frame the questions I now want to ask about her life in New Bern, a small, segregated town where she had lived her entire life. (I am told that she never visited Florence, South Carolina, for which she was named. Her father, when freed from slavery, traveled in the region and fancied place names. Virginia, her middle name, signified his attraction to another state, another place she never visited.) Was it that she had little to say about the small world that surrounded her life? Decades after her death, I continue to wonder what I might have learned if I could have penetrated her silence.

Despite the hardships and limitations of her life, hers was a silence of contentment and good cheer, strength and dignity, calm and self-sufficiency. And mindful silence was one of her gifts to me, a capacity for quiet contemplation that has sustained me in difficult times.

Although I have lost the memory of Mama Willis's voice, I can still hear her silence, and I treasure it.

Mama Willis's Pecan Pie

The memory of my grandmother's silence is as delicious and fulfilling as the memory of her pecan pie.

We were typically pulled to the table by the aroma of chicken frying, corn steaming, and biscuits baking. After Pa Willis said grace, Mama Willis added, "May we remain alive in the hearts of others and mindful of their presence," which I learned years later was her refrain, her prayer. After the blessing, she surveyed the circulation of steaming dishes to be sure that everyone was well served. And while we ate — I had a notorious capacity for her fried chicken — she was back and forth to the kitchen to replenish platters with more of everything. Finally, she brought out her luscious pecan pie, a treat made with last season's harvest from a neighbor's pecan trees. The room hummed with the sounds of anticipated pleasure.

The Filling

3 eggs, lightly beaten
½ cup brown sugar
1 cup corn syrup
4 tablespoons (½ stick) butter, melted
1 cup chopped pecans
1 teaspoon vanilla extract
¼ teaspoon salt

The Crust

Unbaked 9-inch piecrust

The Topping

½ cup heavy cream, whipped
¼ cup pecan halves

Preheat your oven to 350 degrees.

To the beaten eggs, add the brown sugar and corn syrup. Whisk this until it is smooth. Blend in the melted butter and the pecans, then add the vanilla and the salt.

Spoon the filling into a piecrust that has been baked for 5 minutes. (I buy a crust already prepared. Mama Willis, of course, mixed the ingredients herself for a fine, flaky crust.)

Bake the pie for 35 minutes. Cool it to room temperature.

When you're ready to serve this wonderful pie, make it even more wonderful by spreading whipped cream over the surface and decorating the top with pecan halves.

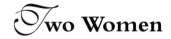

Two Women

Theresa (Tamam) G. Flutti Deyratani
1876–1967

Plain String

Thanksgiving evening. I have just wiped
a few plates left to drain; I wipe them
clean of spots, they sparkle. And I remember
you, Grandmother, carefully drying
the spoons we had quick-dried
after holiday dinner,
how you studied each spoon for dampness
that might blemish it,
how you sought to impose
on the plain order of your life
perfection, an Aristotelian sense
of ideal form and purpose.

And these causes, your humble act instructed
in other tasks: basting stitches were to be
small and even, before a final sewing,
so that even the things unseen
might leave their aura of excellence.
I remember the string full of knots;
a peculiar chore to untie them.
A work of patience. I learned it.
And then the reward:

AT GRANDMOTHER'S TABLE • 71

cat's cradle — forms
for their own sake.
The white string, the depth of line,
the quick twist into
simplicity, both of us holding it.
That I could share with you something fine,
designing the air into epiphanies!

String, an instrument,
four hands to conduct and orchestrate
with filaments and webs and geometries
together, together not only our hands to their
single tasks, but joined now in dialogue.
You speak, then I speak.
Our language of plain string.

Like my mother, my grandmother was beautiful, but there most resemblances ended. Born in Beirut, Lebanon, my grandmother was brought up in a Prussian orphanage; my mother was born in Mersin, Turkey, to doting parents. Grandma gave birth to fourteen children, nine of whom survived; my mother, Georgette Melhem, bore me as her only child. Grandma lived to be ninety-one; my mother died of cancer at sixty-three.

As disciplined and disciplining as my mother was permissive, Grandma needed to be highly organized to care for her large brood. It was hard for me to think of her in a romantic situation, with her Victorian and reclusive ways, her focus entirely on her family, her dress always for mourning. She wore only long black dresses and skirts, and jet beads. (Much later, on her sole holiday tour, a trip to Cuba with her youngest daughter, she permitted herself the indulgence of one navy dress printed with tiny white flowers.) Yet sometimes I caught a glimpse of her girlishly long gray-and-white hair, which she fastidiously coiled into a bun above the nape of her neck and anchored with jagged hairpins and two small silver combs. Her early years suggested romance of a restrained yet intensely aesthetic quality. A schoolteacher fluent in Arabic, English, French, Greek, and German, she was charmed by the fine voice and handsome demeanor of a music teacher from Damascus, whose singing she could hear whenever she passed his classroom. After a brief courtship they married and moved to Mersin, where they immediately started a family and where my grandfather became a successful importer of dry goods.

In 1920, when in his late forties, my grandfather boarded a train on a business trip and stopped overnight at a hotel en route. Police found his watch and his wallet on a night table, but he had vanished, never to be heard from again. Thought to be a victim of a political assassination, he was declared legally dead after a year's intensive search. When his ailing mother was told of the loss of her only son, she collapsed on the spot and died. One of my aunts never reconciled herself to his demise. She consoled herself by imagining that her father had stepped out of his old life into a new life, anonymous and less stressful.

While resolutely trying to absorb this tragic event, the grieving widow came to a crucial decision. Two years later, Grandma immigrated with her children to the United States, where her eldest son was studying at Union College in

Schenectady. My father, whose family had been friends with my mother's family in Mersin, had already begun falling in love with the gentle teenager who was my mother. He had left for America before her. They were reunited in Brooklyn.

Grandma loved the United States and adored Franklin Roosevelt. She was an ardent radio listener (before TV), kept up with the news, and referred to the abundant Roosevelt haters as *shaitan* (devils). A single mother, she nonetheless saw all her offspring educated: each had, at minimum, a high school diploma, and one uncle graduated magna cum laude from City College. She was very proud of me, her first grandchild, and when she learned of a good report card or a prize I had won she would exclaim, *"Brava aleikeh, ya shatra!"* (Brava, you smart one) and would try to bestow on me a fifty-cent piece – a reward I fled in embarrassment. Later I realized that her gesture was also intended to thank my mother for her faithful daily arrival (me in tow) to assist with the household chores.

I remember Grandma's kitchen in Brooklyn, around the corner from Bedford Avenue where we lived. The fiery steam heat rose both at dawn and at dinnertime from the coal-stoked furnace in the basement. During the day, the kitchen was warmed by the cooking and washing. I can see my mother and my grandmother sitting at the white enamel kitchen table, kneading dough, shelling peas, measuring pine nuts into the chopped lamb and onions, soaking the crushed wheat for *kibbeh,* filling dozens of meat pies, stuffing chicken and squash and green peppers and eggplant, rolling stuffed grape leaves and stuffed cabbage like cigars, making dumplings for yogurt soup among cans of sesame oil and boiled butter, peeling scores of potatoes for baked lamb necks and shanks and roast chicken, boiling rice, browning rice and onions, adding rice and tomatoes to large pots of marrow-bone vegetable soup, all the while sitting and chatting over familiar tasks that were done must be done would be done every day without respite. I sat between them on a stool in the corner where I watched and listened, tasting dough and stuffing, my rewards for being content to observe and accept, with my silence, their love.

Waiting for them to acknowledge me, I absorbed the strange names of relatives and friends I would never meet, Beit this and Beit that, houses remote as the house of Atreus, incidents and characters recalled and savored as I anticipated the mention of meaningful names dropping from the flow of Arabic between them: aunts and uncles who lived in the house, my mother's sisters and brothers.

And I bore witness to a daily translation of two women's lives into pots and pans, the circumscription of kitchen walls, with heat rising amid the smells and rhythm of effort, into patterns and patience, interchangeable days carried by movements worn to such precision that hands and objects seemed to extend each other. In my child's density of pleasure, I did not wonder how many times their bodies might have yearned beyond clothesline and tar roof. When I contemplated their lives many years later, I saw the dough sticking to their fingers, the clock hands restraining.

Grandma's Lentil-Spinach-Macaroni Soup (*Adas B'Hamod*)

In our own kitchen, I watched my mother prepare the dish below; she had learned it from her mother. My grandmother's version of this traditional Lebanese fare included macaroni, which stretched the recipe into a hearty vegetarian meal. My mother's contained more spinach – a substitute, I was recently assured by a Lebanese chef, for the scarcer Swiss chard.

Lentils made frequent appearances throughout Grandma's cuisine. And my mother, whose poetic nature disclosed the beauty around us, planted lentils in our window box for the simple pleasure of watching them sprout and grow.

The title of this dish is spelled phonetically. I could not confer with any family member. Alas, none survives. But I do possess an invaluable recipe book, compiled for me by my daughter Dana, organizing the culinary odds and ends I have amassed over the years. Included are a series of my mother's own carefully handwritten notes. The name of this dish literally translates as "lentils with sour flavor."

1 onion, minced or sliced and
    lightly browned in butter
4 to 6 cups water
½ teaspoon salt
1 cup dried lentils
1 cup small elbow macaroni
½ pound shredded fresh spinach
Juice of ½ large lemon

Place the browned onion in 4 cups of water, add the salt, and bring the water to a boil. Then add the lentils. Reduce the heat and simmer for 45 minutes, or until the lentils are tender. Add water as necessary.

Stir the macaroni into the lentils. After a few minutes, when the macaroni is nearly cooked, add the spinach and lemon juice. Cook briefly and serve. The soup will be thick. *Sahtan!* (To your health!) Serves 4.

A Shared Sensuality

Julia Manning Jones Marriner
1877–1964

BY FRANCES FERGUSON BUTTENHEIM

My grandmother was a sensual woman. Her husband always said gloomily that they "grew up in the ashes of the Civil War," but MuJu was blessed with a pervasive, contagious pleasure in the good things of life. When I picture her, it is late afternoon in the sultry heat of a North Carolina summer. She is in her chemise, just up from her nap. This was a daily ritual, observed with cool cloths and fans behind shutters drawn against the heat. After the nap came a leisurely bath and clouds of Blue Grass dusting powder. Then my grandmother would slowly make her way downstairs, cross the yard, and pick a gardenia to tuck down in the neckline of her dress: "in my bosom," she always said. In season, bowls of gardenias sat on every table in her house.

As a child, I knew that my grandmother loved fragrant things. On hot afternoons we sometimes strolled to a nearby house smothered in honeysuckle and just inhaled. City child that I was, dazed by such delicious abundance, I knew that MuJu understood and shared my pleasure, that she never considered these outings a waste of time. Early on I learned from her that pleasure is its own reward and that you should never pass it by. "If you have a choice between work and a party," she said to me once, "always go to the party. The work will wait for you, but the party may not."

I inherited many things from MuJu. Some are tangible, like her silver tea service, but more are intangible – attitudes, enthusiasms, and susceptibilities. I inherited her green thumb and her pleasure in growing fragrant things: pink roses, gardenias, and a sweet autumn clematis that enveloped her back porch as summer lengthened into fall. I inherited her love of games, her skill at cards, her enjoyment in handling cool, smooth mahjong tiles. One of the few times I

remember her really angry was when I cheated at Crazy Eights, stacking the deck when she stepped out of the room. I never cheated again.

I inherited her love of books and language on long, hot afternoons when she read my favorite books to me over and over again. We did *The Secret Garden* until we both knew all the key passages by heart. Years later, she passed on to me her fascination with Russia and the Romanovs. I, in turn, passed that on to my own daughter, now married to a Russian and living in Moscow. I like to imagine MuJu and Dmitri happily conversing, oblivious of the language barrier. She would have loved him. "So good looking," I can hear her saying. "*So* attractive."

MuJu and her three sisters divided the domestic arts among themselves. Aunt Mamie was musical and taught piano; Aunt Sally, the family seamstress, had a puckered mouth full of pins; Aunt Leila operated a still in her bedroom. But my grandmother's province was food. I still use her pink cotton apron. MuJu was an instinctive cook, never measuring, never using second-rate ingredients. She enjoyed eating, taking as much pleasure in a vanilla ice-cream cone as in a lobster dinner or my father's vodka martinis. And she was an adventurous eater, happy to try bird's nest soup or anchovy pizza when visiting us in Manhattan. Food was another pleasure to be savored, as she savored gardenias, or a good book, or her granddaughter.

MuJu's Yellow Cat
(Popover with Bourbon Hard Sauce)

My grandmother never said that certain foods were "good for you," just that they were "mighty good." She wouldn't have known about cholesterol, though I doubt that it would have worried her; two of her favorite dishes were salty country ham with a thick layer of fat on top, and figs swimming in heavy cream. She wouldn't have given up either one. Her specialty was "yellow cat," a dessert unique to our family. Yellow cat is a large popover, hot from the oven, liberally doused with a hard sauce of butter, sugar, and bourbon. Her cook made the popover but my grandmother made the sauce, patiently creaming the butter, beating in the sugar, pouring in the bourbon, grating a little fresh nutmeg on top. Consumption was always followed by a long nap.

The Hard Sauce

4 tablespoons (½ stick)
    unsalted butter
1¼ cups granulated sugar
½ cup bourbon
Freshly grated nutmeg

The Popover

1 cup sifted flour
1 cup milk, at room
    temperature
¼ teaspoon salt
1 tablespoon butter, melted
    and at room temperature
2 eggs, at room temperature
Additional butter for oiling
    the pan or muffin tins

To make the hard sauce: cream the butter and gradually beat in ¾ cup of the sugar. Add the bourbon alternately with the remaining ½ cup sugar. Grate the nutmeg on top.

Let the hard sauce sit at room temperature until you're ready to serve it. The sauce should be granular and almost liquid.

To make the popover: preheat your oven to 450 degrees.

Combine the flour, milk, salt, and butter. Add the eggs, one at a time, beating thoroughly after each addition. Continue beating the batter until it is smooth and the consistency of heavy cream.

Heat a heavy skillet, cake pan, or muffin tin in the oven until it is almost smoking. Quickly butter the hot pan and pour in the batter. (There are two schools of thought on this. Some cooks prefer pouring the batter into a cold pan that has been buttered and floured. Both methods have produced triumphs and failures.)

Bake for 15 minutes, then lower the temperature to 350 degrees. Don't open the oven. Continue baking for another 20 to 25 minutes until the cat is puffed and brown.

Cut the cat into wedges (if it was made in a large pan). Split the wedges open and douse the soft, doughy centers with hard sauce. Serves 6 people.

Reader be warned: this bourbon hard sauce is strong!

The Goose That Laid the Golden Egg

Julia Libstatter Hahn
1878–1948

BY HANNELORE HAHN

Oma Julia's married name was Hahn. She got it, of course, upon marrying my grandfather, Jakob. Their marriage had been arranged by relatives, since Oma Julia had been orphaned in early life. Oma Julchen (little Julia) dutifully performed her wifely tasks, but I perceived that life lay heavily upon her ample chest. She often sighed and was moved to tears for no apparent reason. Even as a child I knew that something deep and nameless was lodged in her.

The name Hahn means rooster in German, and Opa Jakob was indeed the undisputed head of household, the rooster of the House of Hahn. He ruled harshly, often resorting to corporal punishment on his three sons, one of whom would grow up to be my father with his own harsh ways.

In contrast to Opa Jakob's harshness was Oma Julia, a mother hen personified. Plump and soft, she tended to everything that was fructifying and edible. Their house faced a cobblestone street in Bad Hersfeld, a small Hessian town where I, a city child, bore witness to flocks of soft-backed sheep being herded home after grazing at the edge of town. Whenever the sheep returned, dinner would soon be ready.

Equally predictable and ritualistic were the habits of Opa Jakob. He would walk across the cobblestone street to the synagogue for morning prayers, then return for freshly baked Kaiser rolls and coffee in the dark oak dining room upstairs. Afterward, when he went down to the street to raise the roller shades of his bank and check-cashing establishment, the white tablecloth would be strewn with crusty crumbs and dotted with beige coffee stains.

Oma Julia had her own rituals. Each day she would take a pot of manure from the chicken yard and walk to the edge of town, where she kept a small garden of hardy vegetables and radiant flowers. There, in the quiet of stretching roots and opening seeds, she would think about what could be done to have a more interesting life. She sought escape from what she considered her hemmed-in existence. She hoped that when her children grew up and married, she could visit them in exciting cities like Berlin, Frankfurt, and Dresden. Thus, while plucking the feathers of a goose one day, Oma Julchen's eyes fell upon an ad in the newspaper spread under the goose's rump. The ad sought a "young Jewish male with legal training" for a large family business; also mentioned was the possibility of matrimony. Oma Julchen knew at once that her middle son, Arthur, was the right candidate.

The esteemed family Brach, who owned two malt houses (one in Czechoslovakia, the other in Germany), had placed the ad. They were Austrians living in Czechoslovakia. After Arthur, my father, had given a good impression of himself in writing, Leonhard and Louise Brach announced their wish to travel to Bad Hersfeld with their daughter Helene in order to visit Jakob and Julia Hahn.

No one in the Brach family observed the Sabbath, but Leonhard Brach considered that his arrival on a Saturday, though convenient for himself, would be unforgivable to the Orthodox Jakob Hahn. The Brachs, therefore, got off the train one stop before Bad Hersfeld, respectfully stayed overnight in a small hotel, and continued their journey on Sunday morning. They were met at the station by Isfried, my father's older brother, who carried a bouquet of long-stemmed red roses for Louise Brach. Then, moving on foot through town, the retinue (which included luggage-carrying porters) was met in front of the town hall by Rudi, my father's younger brother, who also carried flowers as a sign of welcome. My father, who had directed his brothers to position themselves at strategic points with flowers, awaited the family at the front door of his parents' house with a bouquet for Helene.

Upstairs, all was excitement and nervous energy. Julia, who had to apply last-minute touches to meat, fish, and fowl, had hired a white-gloved waiter from a nearby restaurant to lend elegance to the occasion. As they ate, everyone knew that only one thing remained to be settled: the dowry. In Yiddish it is called "talking *takhles.*" In America one speaks of "talking turkey." Surely every country and every language has a saying for that moment when it is time to strike a deal.

The two principals, Leonhard B. and Jakob H., one clean-shaven, the other with a Kaiser Wilhelm moustache protruding from each side of his face, knew what had to be done. Dark-suited, their gold watch chains across their vested chests, the patriarchs arose after the meal to take a walk. They returned relaxed and amiable. Things had gone well. They took their seats at the dinner table. Jakob H. rose to speak.

"Arthur and Helene are good children," he said. They had found each other and he saw no reason to stand in their way. Arthur would make a good husband and a worthy son-in-law to Helene's esteemed father, whose business he would enter and for whom he would do his best to make things prosper. "All is in good order and I have no objection to any of this," he continued, "except for one thing."

All eyes were upon him.

"What about Kosher?" he asked. "Without the assurance that my son's household will uphold the Jewish dietary laws, I cannot give my consent."

Silence.

Suddenly the determined and resourceful Julia had the answer. "I will send Liesl to Dresden to live with Arthur and Helene." (Liesl had come into the Hahn household as a young farm girl, and although she was not Jewish, she had been trained by Julia in all details of keeping a Kosher kitchen.)

Thereupon, Jakob H. dropped a glass to the floor, stepped on it, and said *"Mazel tov."* And the white-gloved waiter reappeared to serve Julia's addictive chocolate mousse. . . .

Thus was Julia able to visit us in the beautiful city of Dresden. But only fifteen years later, in 1937, my parents and I fled to Czechoslovakia and impatiently waited for our immigration visas to the United States. My father arranged for his parents, too, to cross the border and join us in Prague; from there they went to London to live with Berti, their daughter. All this uprootedness proved too much for Opa Jakob, who died soon afterward. But Oma Julia picked up once again, coming to live with us in New Jersey after the war.

We saw each other for the last time at the beautiful old Penn Station. I was eager to catch the train that would take me to my new life at college. She was tearful, clinging to me. Perhaps she knew that we would not see each other again.

But I see her often when I look in the mirror. I have her square face, her short stature, her ample bosom. I am like her in other respects, also. I have her resourcefulness, her determination, and her readiness to call in white-gloved waiter service.

Oma Julchen's Chocolate Mousse

In my recipe files is a yellowed index card on which I long ago typed my grandmother's pièce de résistance, *her chocolate mousse. Yes, she was short and plump, often sighing deeply. But despite her heaviness, both emotional and physical, she was the one who could make food addictive. Maybe the two go together.*

4 (1-ounce) squares bitter or
    semi-sweet chocolate
¾ cup sugar
¼ cup water
5 pasteurized eggs
1 tablespoon Cognac

Melt the chocolate in the top of a double boiler. Add the sugar and water; stir until dissolved.

Separate the egg yolks from the whites and set the whites aside. Beating vigorously, add the yolks, one by one, to the melted chocolate. Remove the mixture from the heat and add the Cognac.

Beat the egg whites until they form soft peaks, then fold them gently into the chocolate mixture. Pour the mousse into individual molds or a dessert bowl, then place the mousse in the refrigerator for at least 12 hours. The longer it stands, the better. It will keep for several days. This recipe makes about 4 cups.

The Warp and Woof of Our Lives

Carrie Melora Scales Stuart
1879–1966

BY GAIL MOSES RICE

She sits upright in her bed, this Grammy of mine. "Just a few dizzy spells, dear," she says, but she is eighty-five and I see her frailty. I am frightened.

I sit on her bed and we discuss family news. She has been reading *Reader's Digest* and shares her thoughts about an article on education. I am married now with a small son and a teaching career. We do not see each other as often as we would like.

As I rise to leave she grasps my hand. "I hate this being in bed and a burden to everyone. I have taken care of people all my life, and now they are looking after me. It's not as if I really want to do anything strenuous, but it would be nice to know that I could." I laugh, bend to kiss her, and leave.

Her words stay with me. Indeed, all her life she has taken care of us. First her elderly grandparents, when she was a young woman. Then her husband Monty, handsome, intelligent, erratic. Then five children (one of them my mother) and endless hired help. And through it all she cared for her blind elderly mother and a younger sister paralyzed by polio since infancy.

Somewhere along the years the slim, brown-eyed, russet-haired Carrie Melora Stuart became the plump, white-haired, merry-eyed Grammy Stuart who was one of the most important ingredients in the recipe of my life.

She was one of those rare souls, loved and respected by just about everyone. The warp and woof of our lives, sensible, sensitive, a veritable 911, she was called upon whenever something went wrong. We all felt better when Grammy was around. She always appeared on the scene with quiet assurance and loving concern.

As a child I often went to her. Her small dairy farm was a hundred miles away in Pepperell, Massachusetts: a very long trip for a motion-sick child. Grammy was always at the door with a big hug and kiss for her pale-faced visitor.

"Somewhere along the years the slim, brown-eyed, russet-haired Carrie Melora Stuart became the plump, white-haired, merry-eyed Grammy Stuart who was one of the most important ingredients in the recipe of my life."

I was not the only granddaughter, but I was perhaps closest to her in temperament and interests. We roared with laughter as I tried to learn the old tongue-twisting rhymes she was so good at. (I never did learn them all.) She found in me a ready listener for all her family stories — about our Scots-English ancestors, about her childhood, about her love for horses. Her skill at driving a horse and two-wheeled cart had been the envy of her peers and was now the proud delight of her granddaughter.

I was a shy child, introspective and easily worried. Her calm common sense and her loving attention, even when she was busiest, made me feel secure. She never treated me like a child, but like a person with whom she could share her thoughts. For many years I happily dismissed summer camp and other treats to spend vacation time with her. Such a fortunate child to have had her companionship and guidance.

On rainy days I loved to sit in her kitchen while she baked. I was always allowed to help, and my lifelong love of cooking (and most assuredly my cooking ability) I attribute to her. She was a dab hand at anything culinary.

Her pink-and-blue-figured apron hangs on a hook in my pantry. It is my kitchen charm.

Grammy Stuart's Holiday Pudding

Grammy had an old black book containing recipes written by her grandmother and mother. The measurements were hilarious: a half gill of this, a tumbler of that. I loved to read them aloud so that she could explain. The black book is long gone, but I have several of her recipes and I treasure them.

She has been gone from us for more than thirty years, and I still serve her plum pudding with foaming sauce at holiday time. She was a traditionalist, and I know she approves.

The Pudding

1 cup finely chopped beef
    suet, or ½ pound (2 sticks)
    butter, melted
2 cups fine, dried bread
    crumbs
1 cup molasses
1 cup chopped raisins
1 cup chopped dried currants
1 teaspoon salt
1 teaspoon ground cloves
1 teaspoon cinnamon
1 teaspoon allspice
1 teaspoon baking soda
1 cup milk
3 cups flour

The Sauce

½ pound (2 sticks) butter
2 cups light brown sugar
2 tablespoons flour
¾ teaspoon nutmeg
2 cups boiling water

For the pudding: mix together all the ingredients. Press the mixture into a well-greased pudding mold (see note below) and seal tightly.

Place a small rack or a folded dish towel inside a large pot. Set the pudding mold on top of the rack or towel. Pour water into the pot, enough to reach halfway up the sides of the pudding mold. Bring the water to a slow boil, cover the pot, and allow the pudding to steam for 4 hours. Check the pot every 30 minutes to make sure the water hasn't boiled away, and add more water as necessary.

Unmold the pudding and serve it with foaming sauce. Makes 10 to 12 servings.

To make the sauce: cream together the butter, brown sugar, flour, and nutmeg until the mixture is very light in color. The more it is creamed, the better it will taste.

Heat this mixture in the top of a double boiler. Add the boiling water and stir only enough to dissolve the ingredients; do not spoil the foam. Pour the sauce over individual servings of pudding.

Note: Ideally, you will want to use a steamed pudding mold, available in gourmet cooking stores. However, you can construct your own steamer out of a Bundt pan (or a medium-sized saucepan with the handle removed) and some aluminum foil. Simply grease the pan, press the pudding dough inside, and seal the top with aluminum foil.

The Big Heart of Little Grandma

Juliette Sansom Ravel
1880–1966

BY HUGUETTE VITU PECK

When my maternal grandmother was only seven, she became the substitute mother for her sister and baby brother; their mother had just died in childbirth. Their father, in despair at the loss of his wife, directed all his love to his children, taking them everywhere with him, even to the opera. They were raised in considerable luxury. Were they spoiled brats? Not at all. In fact, they became some of the nicest people in the world. For all her years, my grandmother was an additional mother to every generation in her family.

We called her Little Grandma because she was small – under five feet. She was very pretty, had the cutest nose, and had a great presence. She also had an iron will, which she exercised mostly on herself. And she could beat anyone at poker. She was alone a lot, but I never heard her say she was bored; she always had a game of solitaire or a book in progress. She loved all card games and happily taught them to us.

In the early thirties, at fifty-two, she had a double mastectomy. This was before radiotherapy and chemotherapy, and the surgeon had to cut a lot. When she came home and could not raise her arms, I often helped her dress. I happened to see her scar, nearly half an inch wide; it went from the inside of her left elbow, across her chest, to the inside of her right elbow. Undaunted, she lived to be eighty-six! (I think of this often, especially since a dozen years ago I was diagnosed with breast cancer myself.)

Then came World War II. Our family stayed in our country house on the Loire River, near Orleans, but I was sent to a convent boarding school in the north of France. As the war progressed and things got worse, the school decided to send me and two other girls back to our families in Paris. But the German troops had advanced through northern France. We three, and the nun traveling with us, found ourselves trapped. From May to September 1940, I virtually disappeared in the fighting near Dunkirk; my family did not know whether I was dead or alive, and I did not know whether they were dead or alive. After many moves and mishaps I was finally reunited with my family in the middle of October. I felt really safe, though, only when Little Grandma and I held each other. I learned later that she had spent practically the whole time watching the road, waiting for me to appear.

"Her beloved husband, Louis, had always worn a gold locket on his watch chain. After his death in 1930, Little Grandma finally looked inside the locket, slightly afraid of what she might find . . ."

In January of 1941, we moved to Grenoble in the Alps, and Little Grandma now spent her time running around in town or in the mountains to find food for the family. She ate as little as she could, to leave more for the young ones.

After the war we returned to Paris. Little Grandma lived with me, helping me with my children. When I moved to the United States with my American husband, she stayed behind with my mother and brothers. Having lost or given away everything she had to whoever needed it, she took it for granted that the family would take care of her. We did so with great pleasure, as she was always a joy to have around, always helping.

One year she braved the ocean and her fear of *mal de mer* to spend the summer with me in Connecticut. She was an instant hit with my husband's family. None of them could speak French and she could not speak English, but they understood each other wonderfully. She also beat them at croquet.

Her beloved husband, Louis, had always worn a gold locket on his watch chain. After his death in 1930, Little Grandma finally looked inside the locket, slightly afraid of what she might find. But she found a picture of *herself,* taken at a wedding where she was a bridesmaid and he was an usher. He hadn't even known her name when the picture was taken, but right then and there, Louis had fallen for Juliette. She was that kind of person. People loved her instantly, and for all of her life.

Little Grandma's Leek Soup

When she got married in 1900, Little Grandma didn't know how to boil water! Her father had given her a fairly large dowry, but a good part of it consisted of Russian bonds sold by the czarist government to raise money for the development of Russia. The bonds became worthless after the Bolshevik Revolution in 1917, and that is when Little Grandma learned to cook.

She loved rich foods. But in her thirties she developed eczema, and her doctor said that the only cure was a very strict diet. For nearly a year she ate only salads, boiled vegetables, and fresh fruits. It worked. Having become very conscious of what food can do to people, she often prepared a leek soup that contained hardly any fat.

2 large leeks
6 large potatoes
2 large onions
8 to 10 cups vegetable stock or degreased chicken stock
1 cup low-fat milk, warmed
Salt and pepper
¼ cup parsley

Clean the leeks carefully and cut them into chunks. (Use only the white and light-green parts; discard the dark green.) Peel and quarter the potatoes and onions. Put everything in a pot and add just enough stock to cover the vegetables.

Bring the stock to a simmer. After about 20 minutes, turn off the heat and let the soup cool a bit. Pass it through a vegetable mill, or use a food processor or blender to purée the soup in small batches.

Add the milk, salt, and pepper to the puréed soup, and reheat.

When the soup is hot, sprinkle parsley in the soup bowls, pour the soup, and serve. Makes enough for 8 people.

Note: To make the soup "rich," use half-and-half instead of low-fat milk, and put a pat of butter in each bowl.

Little Grandma's Scalloped Potatoes (*Gratin Dauphinois*)

This is another of Little Grandma's triumphs. She made it more or less rich, according to circumstances.

3 garlic cloves, crushed
1 quart milk
Nutmeg
3½ pounds potatoes
Salt and pepper
½ pound Swiss cheese, grated
2 eggs, beaten
Butter

Preheat your oven to 350 degrees.

Rub two cloves of garlic inside a large, ovenproof baking dish.

Put the leftover garlic, plus one more clove, into a saucepan. Add a quart of boiling milk, followed by a touch of nutmeg. Let this steep.

Meanwhile, peel and slice the potatoes fairly thin. Cover the bottom of the baking dish with potato slices. Salt and pepper them lightly and dust them with grated cheese. Add another layer of potatoes, salt, pepper, and cheese. Fill the dish with as many layers as possible.

Once the milk has cooled, remove and discard the garlic, then mix in the beaten eggs. Pour this over the potatoes. Dust the potatoes with the rest of the grated cheese and pat butter here and there according to taste.

Bake the gratin for 1½ hours. Cover the dish with foil for the last 40 minutes. Serves 8 people.

Note: To make this recipe less rich, use low-fat milk and low-fat cheese. Skip the butter. Instead of two whole eggs, you can use egg whites (with a dash of mustard) or egg substitute (sold in supermarkets). If you do not want to use any egg at all, make a white sauce with the milk.

rand Voyager

BY MAUREEN TERESA McCARTHY

Gertrude Quinlan McCarthy
1880–1980

The grandmother of my childhood had smooth cheeks and a mane of long silver hair, worn up in a French twist and secured by combs she had bought in Paris. The trip to Paris was apparently one of many, Grandma having acquired a taste for travel as a young girl. At seventeen, she had ventured up the Amazon on a raft with her father, carrying her own pearl-handled derringer. They had gone in search of oil fields inherited from her grandfather, who had fled the troubles in Ireland by way of Venezuela before settling in central New York. I don't know whether that search was successful, but life was comfortable for Gertrude Quinlan. Her father was a hard-working businessman who believed that people wanted comfort and beauty in their lives. Even during the Depression his greenhouses prospered.

She married an ambitious young man who was, of course, also Irish Catholic. Invited to join the family business, he eventually took over the greenhouses and added a florist shop. Gertrude worked there too. It was unusual for a woman to work in the early 1900s, especially when she had a good husband and nine children, but Gertrude was known for being strong-willed. Her will prevailed over her daughters, who thought that at seventy she was too old to prune her own trees, and that at eighty-four she was too old for still another trip to Europe. Grandma reminded them that she had ridden rafts, horses, ocean liners, carriages, and automobiles, and that she had decided she was going to fly in a jumbo jet. Her sons knew better than to argue with her, and off she went, in her navy-blue wool suit, white blouse with lace collar and cuffs, and matching navy pumps. No laced-up oxfords for her.

At ninety-five, her only trip was to the hospital, for a mastectomy, but she was as indomitable as ever. The day after surgery, the student nurse bounced into Grandma's room with a cheery greeting: "Hi Gert! How are we feeling this morning?" Grandma had already twisted her hair back with the French combs, and she sat as tall as her five feet would allow. "My name is Mrs. McCarthy and I am feeling fine. I have no idea how you are. Please get me my clothes; I am going home."

"Grandma reminded them that she had ridden rafts, horses, ocean liners, carriages, and automobiles, and that she had decided she was going to fly in a jumbo jet. Her sons knew better than to argue with her."

She went home, and she lived long enough to hold my son, her twenty-ninth great-grandchild, on her lap. When she died, at nearly one hundred, she left a touch of her spirit and her wanderlust to three generations. Her children were every bit as independent as she was, and her grandchildren have ventured beyond Paris to Istanbul and even to the edge of space in an F-16.

I don't know now whether all of my memories are true; my aunts have different versions. (Did the combs come from Paris? I know the rugs did.) But I do know that what I remember is true enough.

When I left for Europe in jeans, she wished for me a navy-blue suit, but she sent me off with her blessing.

Grandma's Applesauce Molasses Drops

My father adored his tiny, determined mother and had lunch or tea with her often. As his oldest daughter I was frequently invited, and it was then that I heard the stories about her travels, as we were served tea and cookies on her favorite thin china. Grandma believed in basic meals and simple desserts, but cookies were a staple. Applesauce molasses drops, rich and dark, were baked regularly. This recipe reminds me always of her.

2 cups all-purpose flour
   (or substitute 1 cup with fine
   whole-wheat pastry flour)
1 teaspoon baking soda
1 teaspoon cinnamon
½ teaspoon powdered ginger
¼ teaspoon nutmeg
¼ teaspoon allspice
Salt
¼ pound (1 stick) butter,
   softened
½ cup dark brown sugar
1 large egg
½ cup light molasses
¾ cup unsweetened applesauce
1 cup finely chopped walnuts

Preheat your oven to 350 degrees.

Sift together the flour, baking soda, cinnamon, ginger, nutmeg, allspice, and salt. Set this aside.

In a separate bowl, cream the butter and sugar, add the egg and molasses, then add the applesauce. (The batter will look curdled, but don't worry.) Stir this mixture into the dry ingredients, then add the nuts.

Drop by teaspoonfuls onto a greased cookie sheet. Bake for about 10 minutes, until the centers are firm to the touch. Serve on very nice china, with tea in matching cups. Makes 4 dozen cookies.

Gertrude Strickler Thomas
1881–1959

A Quilted Insight

BY MARILYN GUSTIN

"Do you want those old quilts Gran'ma made?" Mother asks. Doubtfully, I haul them out and toss them around me. Colors everywhere. Fifteen quilts, maybe. I sit among them, startled. Had I ever seen her at work on these?

No such memory arises. I recall quite different scenes:

I always slept with Gran'ma when we visited, but it wasn't cozy. As often as not, the night would erupt with her horrible howling nightmares. I'd be rigid with her fear. Gran'pa would waken her – but no thought was given to my terror. I always wanted to sleep in the living room.

By day, she hoarded: string, foil, coins. To can peaches, she peeled them with a lye bath, which I was forbidden to come near. Then she made soap with the leftover lye – to save money, she said. Oh, they had plenty of money. But Gran'ma never let go of anything. She gave me a quarter each birthday until I became a teenager. Then it was a dime.

Once she came up behind me to put her hands on my head. She struck me so hard that her bones hurt my scalp.

When my blind Gran'pa would call her from across the house, her answer was always the same. "Well?" she would demand, as if his very voice were an offense. Sometimes neighbors came to call. They were usually greeted by her harsh "Well, why didn't you come sooner? He sits here all day with nothing to do, you know."

Gran'ma was thin and wrinkled and everything about her seemed sharp. I recall a baby photo of me on her lap – held hard, I'm sure – my face contorted in yelling protest. The image shows perfectly how I felt about her.

Today, sitting among her quilts, I try to piece together a fuller picture. . . .

We were sitting on the front stoop together, watching a certain flower. It opened so quickly we could see the petals move. Had my wonder been shared by this tense little woman beside me?

Gran'ma owned an organ. She had bought it many years before – "with my own money," she always boasted. She played only hymns, by the hour. Never could afford lessons to play better things, she claimed. How hungry was her soul?

Now, these quilts. Here's one with yellow-orange poppies and flitting butterflies, each of them unique. Done in crayon, faded, but cheery still. The hues must have been intense when she colored them. I suddenly recall cheap muslin curtains with blue and pink morning glories climbing their edges. In crayon, not paint. Why? Money, she would have said, but now I wonder what else, what feelings, kept her from using good materials.

Today, surrounded by her stitches and colors, my memories don't feel the same. Gran'ma was indeed grim; she repeatedly hurt people she loved. What within her liked flowers and made music and created lovely things with bright colors?

Suddenly I want to gather her tiny frame in my arms and cry with her. Perhaps my tears would have softened the heart that must have ached under its thorny crust. Tonight, her bright butterfly quilt will lie on my bed. I will be warmed by it. I will salute her courage.

Gran'ma's Persimmon Pudding

In Gran'ma's southern California backyard, a persimmon tree grew. True to her waste-nothing style, she put persimmons in everything she cooked after the first November frost when the luscious fruit ripened.

Here's her recipe for a loaf that is moist, dark, and delicious. The recipe is precisely as she dictated it to my mother — a marvel of economy with words.

If you don't live in persimmon country, be sure to let the persimmons thoroughly ripen in a windowsill. Persimmons pucker the mouth like alum when they are not fully ripe.

The Pudding

1 egg
1 cup milk
2 to 3 persimmons
2 cups flour
1 cup sugar
2 teaspoons baking soda
1 teaspoon salt
1 cup chopped nuts
1 cup raisins
1 teaspoon vanilla extract

For the pudding:

[Preheat your oven to 350 degrees.]

Beat 1 egg, 1 cup milk, 1 cup mashed persimmon
[2 to 3 persimmons, depending on size]

Mix in 2 cups flour, 1 cup sugar, 2 teaspoons baking soda,
1 teaspoon salt

Add 1 cup chopped nuts, 1 cup raisins, 1 teaspoon vanilla

Bake in greased loaf pan for about 1 hour.
Serve with sauce.

For the sauce:

The Sauce

½ cup sugar
1 cup boiling water
1 tablespoon cornstarch
2 tablespoons butter
1 teaspoon vanilla extract
Salt

Mix ½ cup sugar, 1 cup boiling water,
1 tablespoon cornstarch, 2 tablespoons butter,
1 teaspoon vanilla, a pinch of salt

Boil until clear.

A Treasure for Picking

Claire Louise Herder Steers
1881–1969

BY CLAIRE L. STEIGER

Knowledge

I have learned the old ways
Of cutting and bringing in wood for the fire
To warm myself
Then carrying out the cold ashes

Of washing dishes by hand, the gentle rhythm
Recalling time by my grandmother's side
She washed, I dried, looking out
Over the Lake toward the White Mountains

When she died, I learned I had no hold on the world
Or on what I loved

I have learned all this and more
Will I ever know enough to go on living without you?

I was her first grandchild, daughter of her first daughter and oldest child, and I was given her name – Claire Louise. I felt like her favorite; I wanted to be like her and succeeded: we both had reddish hair, were intimidated by my mother, played the piano, and had gall bladder disease. I delighted in approaching her pro-creative ability when my fourth daughter was born. She had five children, four of them daughters.

She lived seven miles from us when I was a child and would drop in to read to me when I was sick. I would visit her, too, and it was always a treat to be the only child in her large Colonial house, with more rooms than I could find. There she taught me to eat oatmeal from the edge of the bowl – where it was cooler – to spare a tongue burning. But she also gave me fierce ear washings, and she threatened enemas if I didn't "perform" every day. She was afraid of tunnels and, unknown to my mother, would huddle down next to me in the back seat when crossing the Hudson River to visit cousins. We called her "Seese," following the lead of some cousins for whom she sang, "*Sees*aw, Marjory Daw."

She spoke proudly of her mother's ingenuity: after her father deserted them, her mother turned the home into a boarding house to support the family. But Seese never spoke of her roots in Ireland, home of her mother's mother, a Baptist from Dublin. Indeed, "Catholic" was whispered as if it were a dirty word. In a sense it was, to the Anglo-Irish who emigrated with the Catholics and didn't want to be tarred with the same brush of discrimination. What would she think of my brother and me: of our each marrying one of "them" and of my making Ireland my second home?

Once, to accompany a nervous friend, Seese took the Cornell scholarship exam. The friend didn't win a place, but my grandmother did, graduating in 1902. She was soon courted by Newton Ivan Steers, a handsome but roguish man who valued her beauty, intelligence, and education – all assets for an ambitious man. He worked for the DuPont Company and was credited with devising the underwa-ter dynamite cap that made possible the excavation for the Panama Canal. He retired as president of the New York branch of the film division, but died not long after, at sixty-eight, leaving my grandmother a widow at sixty-three. He was gen-erous, leaving bequests to each of his children and grandchildren.

"Seese never spoke of her roots in Ireland, home of her mother's mother, a Baptist from Dublin. Indeed, 'Catholic' was whispered as if it were a dirty word."

My grandmother remained thrifty, taking buses and subways in her mink coat rather than the taxis that her horrified children would have preferred for her. She was an expert but tactful bridge player. She loved games and taught me mahjong with ivory tiles she had purchased in China. (She and her husband had traveled to the Holy Land, the Pyramids, the Far East.) She knew Latin and German. She knew, and could see, all the constellations, and delighted in pointing them out to her more or less discerning grandchildren; she regaled us with all the ancient mythology connected with them. She played the wheezy little organ during summer church services in the old stone barn, and then, as treasurer, she carried the collection money home to count. You can bet not a nickel or dime went astray, even when the older grandchildren were allowed to help.

A privileged woman who helped to launch the YWCA in her town, she must have been a feminist without being aware of it. She was also the guardian of the family morals, so conscientious that she alienated some. This trait, which she shared with her mother, may have been responsible for difficulties in both their marriages: her father's departure and her own husband's infidelity.

I remember two of her adages, both aimed at me: "Brighten the corner where you are" (I was a prickly child) and "Don't hide your light under a bushel" (did she know of my poor self-image?). I haven't yet learned a balance between adding to the glow of home and hearth and shining my light on the world. She was a modest woman, my grandmother, but she shone through and brightened many lives. When she died, only her physical light was extinguished.

Seese's Sand Quarry Raspberry Jam

"Who wants to come berry picking?" asked my grandmother in a way that couldn't be refused. All the grandchildren visiting the summer home on the shore of Lake Winnipesaukee in New Hampshire would line up for empty sand pails and coffee cans. It was the annual pilgrimage to the sand quarry where raspberry bushes clustered. Starting out to please her, we'd get caught up in the treasure hunt, ignoring stabs and scratches but aware of her gentle teasing: "How many picker-eaters do I have today?" Even when a child with a very red mouth offered up just one pailful, she was happy to accept.

Later that day, we'd glance into the kitchen to see her next to her maid, Anna, tending large, steaming pots on the stove and pushing pulp through a great strainer. This was the only cooking I ever saw my grandmother do.

4 cups fresh raspberries
1 to 3 cups sugar, according
    to taste

This recipe makes 1½ to 2 cups of jam. You will need two large jam jars or several small ones.

Wash, rinse, and drain your jam jars. Put them in a deep pan and cover them with boiling water until you're ready to fill them.

Wash and drain the berries, then put them into a medium saucepan. Crush the berries with a potato masher or large spoon. Cook for 15 minutes or longer, until the berry juice is reduced. If you want to remove the seeds, push the fruit through a sieve or large strainer, then return the fruit to the saucepan.

Cook on low heat, adding sugar and stirring until it is dissolved. Bring the mixture to a boil. Adjust the heat, keeping the mixture at a low boil, and stir frequently until it thickens – about 45 minutes. During this time, add small amounts of water, if necessary, to keep the jam from burning.

Remove the saucepan from the heat when a drop of jam on a plate holds its shape, or when a jelly thermometer shows 214 degrees.

Skim off the foam and pour the jam into your hot, drained, sterilized jars. After the jars have been filled and sealed, invert the jars and let them stand for 5 minutes. Turn them right-side up and let them cool for 3 hours. Store the jam in the refrigerator.

I've Never Stopped Looking Up

Rebecca Peterson Bunnell
1882–1968

BY CYNTHIA STERLING RUSSELL

My grandmother moved in a sparkling cloud of her own making. She had a style and a radiance that took over a room when she made her grand entrance for tea or dinner – even at age eighty-four, when she majestically sailed into a restaurant on crutches, with her big straw bonnet and her beautiful smile.

She never lost her identity, even though she married early into a sea captain's family made famous in the China Trade of the 1880s. Surrounded by the legacy of the Sterlings, who were well known because they had arrived in the United States so early and given so much, she was a beacon in her own right.

I had the tremendous good fortune to be born in her shadow and to be inspired by her from my first days. We were close from my earliest recollection.

When I was two, wading in Long Island Sound, a crab tore off my toenail. "Big girls don't cry" . . . a trip to the doctor . . . gentian violet antiseptic spilling all over the rug (my parents expected me to do it all by myself). Granny cooed forgiveness, hugging me as she tossed the little rug into the wash. My parents might have wanted to push me into adulthood, but she was delighted with a toddler!

She loved all children and immediately set about improving them. There were dance classes on the back porch, art classes at the boatyard, horticulture lessons for the Boy Scouts she had hired to weed the garden. Totally self-educated, charming, beautiful, a fountain of energy, she lived a life of teaching and giving to others.

She was an inspiration to the town of Stratford, Connecticut, where her talents were widely recognized. She was asked to decorate the Yale faculty club. She fought to save the classic arboretum designed by Frederick Law Olmsted. She served on the board of the Shakespeare theatre. We dined with Nina Foch one night, entertained war brides and their children the next. Long before these skills were boxed in as professions – interior design, historic preservation, arts management – she excelled in them all.

The world she created doesn't exist anymore. She'd start the day with a French novel in her huge quilted bed; she'd serve afternoon tea (which she referred to by the French word *gout,* or "taste"); and she'd always follow a formal dinner with a gathering in the music room, where guests would sip coffee from the tiny, translucent cups brought back from Canton, China, by my great-grandfather.

My grandparents' life was one of rituals. Grandfather would take me up to the roof and teach me the constellations. Granny would settle into a cozy upholstered chair and embroider or mend with lovely colors, sharpening her needles on a little bag she had constructed with black emery sand from Barbados. Or she and I would stroll down the street in New Haven, and she would insist that we look up to note a gargoyle, or a lacy ironwork lattice, or some other architectural wonder. I've never stopped looking up.

In her last years, Granny fretted over the future of her beloved house, a 1790 Georgian New England homestead. When no one else was willing, I, the youngest, accepted her invitation to care for it. I had been the one who most adored her for her sociability and high ideals and relentless pursuit of beauty, education, and healing. I was grateful to become the steward of this house that was so important in her life.

Today, in this house, she is still in every corner. When I open a drawer her perfume escapes, as though she is just about to greet me, and I still find little scraps of paper with her thoughts, or recipes. . . .

Granny's "Indian Pudding"

My grandmother's kitchen — now my kitchen — holds many pungent memories for me. Good smells. People bustling about. Constant activity. After the end of World War II, she arranged parties for war brides to relieve their loneliness and isolation. (I babysat while the young mothers tried to socialize in English.) An Italian girl even moved into the house with her G.I. husband and their baby, living in an area off the kitchen. It was typical of Granny to invite them. After they arrived there was more activity than ever: quarrels, guests, crying, feasts.

It was a family tradition to make Indian pudding in the summertime; in fact, there is even an "Indian Well" park near the home, and our ancestral land was purchased from the Native Americans for a few dozen bushels of corn.

7 tablespoons Indian meal
　　(yellow cornmeal)
3 pints milk
2 eggs
½ cup molasses
½ cup sugar
2 tablespoons butter
1 teaspoon powdered ginger
1 teaspoon cinnamon
1 cup raisins

Preheat your oven to 350 degrees.

Gradually stir the cornmeal into 2 pints of the milk. Scald the milk, then let it cool. Add the remaining milk, then add the eggs, molasses, sugar, butter, ginger, cinnamon, and raisins. Pour this mixture into an ovenproof baking dish.

Bake uncovered for 3 hours, stirring occasionally. Check the pudding now and then to be sure it remains moist.

This traditional pudding is rich, grainy, and especially delicious with the best vanilla ice cream you can find. Serves 7 people.

Bertha Jarrett Rushmore
1884–1962

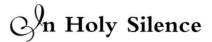n Holy Silence

BY SUSAN W. RUSHMORE

Grandmother Rushmore was a proper lady, thoroughly old fashioned, thoroughly Methodist. She believed in simple, unmovable principles: devotion to church, school, family. In her presence there was to be no swearing, drinking, dancing, or card playing.

Open-mindedness, to her, was heresy. Her mind was firmly closed; she knew what she believed, how she wanted to live, and she made no exceptions.

She was a New Yorker. In winter, she wore a long cloth coat; in summer, navy dresses with long sleeves; in every season, stout black pumps. She belonged to the Woman's Christian Temperance Union and the church sewing circle. She carried a handbag whenever she left the house, always wore a hat in public, and never went into the cellar or backyard.

She never spoke of herself. What little I know of her background I learned long after her death. Her mother died when she was young; she and her three sisters were raised by a maiden aunt. In an era when most married women did not work, she did, teaching school after her husband's antiques shop on Broadway failed in the Depression. He became a New Jersey farmer. Her teaching supported the family.

Ladies do not raise their voices, she told me, and, to my knowledge, she never did. She was polite, pleasant. It was her eyes that spoke – and, if you watched carefully, the tight muscles around her mouth. I knew when it was time to behave. So did my grandfather.

When I was old enough to walk down the road to her house, I went there for dinner on Wednesdays. She greeted me with a perfunctory hug. Had I done my lessons?

If I had, she sat with me anyway, watching me practice my penmanship. If I had not, I sat alone at the wooden rolltop desk until my homework was finished, knowing that she would check it afterward.

Supper was at five – no sooner, no later – in time to listen to *Bless This House* on the big radio. Like her principles, Grandmother's meals were formal and unvarying. They always began with a glass of tomato juice served on a small, thin china plate and always ended with coffee ice cream.

"Open-mindedness, to her, was heresy. Her mind was firmly closed; she knew what she believed, how she wanted to live, and she made no exceptions."

She was a quiet woman who never spoke ill of anyone. Only on her last trip to the hospital, thin and weak, her long cloth coat hanging from her frame, did she tell my mother: "I cannot go back to Charlie. I will go to my sisters. I have never been able to stand him."

Hers was a quiet household. Mine was not.

"I never spoke back to her," said my father, Grandmother's only child. "I may have hated her guts, but I never spoke back." His transgressions, excesses, and alcoholic rages cowed my mother and left unhealed wounds in his children. Learning of these, Grandmother ordered her son never to divorce. If he did, she threatened, she would never speak to him again.

He obeyed.

I fervently wish he had not. Multiple personalities, chronic anorexia, and agoraphobia are my legacy from him.

I have never been able to understand Grandmother's silent endorsement of his cruelty. Although I cannot pardon it, I must pardon her, for divorce was against her principles. And above all, she was a woman of principle.

But Grandmother gave me a great gift. From her silence, I learned to speak.

Grandmother Rushmore's Wednesday Casserole

Grandmother's food was, like her, pleasant and substantial and thrifty. Here is one simple casserole that I remember as being uniquely hers.

5 large potatoes
3 tablespoons butter
⅓ cup milk
1 teaspoon salt
Pepper
1 cup diced ham
   (boiled or baked)
¾ cup applesauce
Milk or cream for glazing
Paprika

Preheat your oven to 375 degrees.

Peel and quarter the potatoes; boil them until tender. Mash them with a potato masher or electric mixer until smooth.

With a fork, beat in the butter, milk, salt, and pepper. The potatoes should be slightly dry.

In a large casserole dish, layer half the mashed potatoes, then all of the ham and applesauce. Top with the rest of the potatoes, brush with milk or cream, and sprinkle with paprika.

Bake uncovered for 40 minutes. Serve to 4 to 6 people on Wednesdays (and on other days, too).

The Penny Jar

BY RUTH ANN MYERS

Charlotte Flemings Myers
1885–1953

I can't see a new copper penny without thinking of my grandmother. She kept a large jar in the skinny room she called "the pantry," and she filled it with bright new (only new) pennies for my brother and me. Every now and again I'll open my kitchen cupboard believing in my heart that Lottie's penny jar is waiting there for my day's leftovers.

The pantry had a deep soapstone sink where Lottie bent nearly double scrubbing vegetables, dishes, clothes, and (occasionally) me. I was the only granddaughter of this largely infertile couple, who after four miscarriages produced only my father. Lottie and James were rockbound laconic New Englanders who spoke only if they had to. James resembled Woodrow Wilson signing the League of Nations Pact, and Lottie was the only person I knew of, other than FDR, who wore pince-nez eyeglasses all her life. They were strict church-going Baptists whose lips never touched alcohol and whose greatest pleasure was taking Sunday afternoon rides in what my grandmother diffidently called The Machine. At the dinner table after church, she would say, "Go bring The Machine around, James." The Machine in those days was a 1937 Ford coupe with two jump seats for my brother and me.

They rarely traveled far from home. James was eager to return to England to visit old relatives' gravesites, but Lottie was content to stay home in the kitchen, read old copies of *National Geographic,* and save pennies for us.

They lived on in the same house where my father was born in Lowell, Massachusetts; we kept moving farther and farther away, finally landing outside Philadelphia. Our visits were sporadic and brief – mostly in the summer when their garden was in full pitch. She and I would sit on "the piazza," a large

"They were strict church-going Baptists whose lips never touched alcohol and whose greatest pleasure was taking Sunday afternoon rides in what my grandmother diffidently called The Machine."

screened-in porch, shelling fresh peas for James's dinner to be served at noon. I would be chattering disconnectedly about this and that, and Lottie would smile and offer monosyllabic comments. James would drive home in The Machine, eat in his three-piece suit, take a little nap, then return to his business having said less than four words. She always knew what he wanted and always provided it for him. I can still hear the silence of that dark dining room, broken only by the tick of a mantel clock and the ping of our silverware.

My father was the antithesis of them both: an alcoholic full of table-thumping rage or back-slapping joy, usually yelling or laughing too loud. But he had them come live in our home after James had a stroke and Lottie had severe dementia. Only then was I able to cook for *her.*

I often wonder if she was content with her life. I do know that, before she could no longer remember who I was, she loved me fiercely — and her chattering disconnectedly about this and that, at the end of her life, was her way of telling me so.

Lottie's Mincemeat Cookies

Her mincemeat cookies were my favorite. I never saw her make them, and I have searched for years to find a recipe exactly like hers. This isn't quite it, but it's close. Lottie would use a curly cookie cutter, making the finished cookies look very cheery in that dark dining room.

¼ pound (1 stick) butter
½ cup sugar
2 eggs
1 teaspoon vanilla extract
2½ cups flour
½ teaspoon salt
1 teaspoon baking powder
1 cup mincemeat

Cream the butter and sugar until fluffy, then beat in the eggs and vanilla.

In a separate bowl, sift together the flour, salt, and baking powder. Stir this into the creamed mixture until just blended.

Chill the dough for 30 minutes in the refrigerator. Remove half the dough at a time. On a floured pastry cloth or lightly floured board, roll out the dough to a thickness of about ⅛ inch.

Meanwhile, preheat the oven to 375 degrees.

Cut the dough into rounds with a floured cookie cutter. Depending on the size of the finished cookie, spoon from ¼ to 1 teaspoon of mincemeat into the center of each round. Place a second round on top and press the edges together. Prick the center of each cookie to allow steam to escape during baking.

Bake for 8 to 12 minutes, depending on the thickness and diameter of the cookies. Remove the cookies from the pan while they are still warm and cool them on a rack. Makes 2 to 3 dozen cookies.

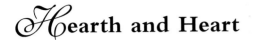

Hearth and Heart

BY LEA BERTANI VOZAR NEWMAN

Vera Citti Bollini
1885–1956

It is early in the morning, and I am a child standing in front of the huge cast-iron stove that dominates our kitchen. I have just made a mad dash from the unheated small bedroom that I share with my grandmother to the spot on the still frigid linoleum floor where she has laid out my clothes. I wrap the blanket on my shoulders tightly around me and huddle close to the innumerable opaque little windows that cover the stove's potbelly; I feel rather than see the burning coals encased within. This fire was banked the night before and rekindled early in the morning by my Nonna Vera, who lived with us and who, like the stove she tended, was at the center of our household.

She was a slender woman, fair-skinned, blue-eyed. As far back as I can remember, she wore her gray hair pulled back at the nape of her neck in a loose bun. Contrary to the stereotypical image of the boisterous, earthy Italian grandmother, she had a quiet, gentle demeanor, a serene smile, and an other-worldly air. I never heard her raise her voice, either in anger or in laughter. Her language was the Italian of Dante. She never learned English but spoke with the mellifluous vowels and soft consonants of the Tuscan dialect of her native village, Monte di Villa in Lucca.

Just about the time I was born, my grandfather died suddenly. I do not know the details, but I do know – because my grandmother told me over and over again – that she was devastated by her husband's unexpected death and that having me to take care of made it possible for her to go on living. He had been an enterprising, vigorous man in the prime of his life, and prosperity seemed finally to be within their reach. Together with their new son-in-law (my father), they had just bought a three-story building on the near-north side of Chicago, giving them some rental income and a flat large enough for both families to share. Now, with one of the wage earners gone, the family decided that my mother would go back to work sewing silk lampshades and my grandmother (who was less able to negotiate the outside world) would stay at home to cook and clean and take charge of the new baby – me. My earliest memories are of Nonna Vera's devotion. She was always there, stable, unchanging, selfless, every morning when I woke up, every night when I went to bed, and all night long since we shared a double bed. She had other grandchildren, but I was the one she lived with, and being an only child, I never had to share her with anyone.

"Her language was the Italian of Dante. She never learned English but spoke with the mellifluous vowels and soft consonants of the Tuscan dialect of her native village, Monte di Villa in Lucca."

By the time I was ten or so, the glowing potbellied stove was gone from our kitchen. But the warmth and comfort I associated with that stove remained; they had never been a matter of temperature, but simply of love. As a child, I knew, without ever thinking about it consciously, that I was loved and cherished. This feeling of security stayed with me as I grew up, allowing me to face life's tragedies with what might be called, in retrospect, a foolhardy confidence.

Nonna Vera and her unconditional love were an integral part of my life for many years, and never more poignantly than when, shortly before her death, I saw her hold my infant son as tenderly and lovingly as she had held me.

Nonna Vera's Spinach Frittata

During my grammar school years, I came home each day to a hot meal that Nonna Vera had ready for me minutes after I walked in the door. And as late as the 1940s, when I was commuting daily on the El to Chicago Teachers College on the south side of the city, my grandmother was still urging me to "mangia bene," still making sure I was well fed. During those college years, as I rushed around each morning madly trying to decide what to wear, which books to take, and what to do about my hair, Nonna Vera would gently insist that I sit down at the kitchen table and eat my egg and toast while they were still warm. No one has ever been as solicitous about my daily welfare. Today, when I see spinach frittata on a restaurant menu, I am immediately transported to the kitchen of my childhood, where I often watched my grandmother cook this favorite dish of mine. I occasionally try to recapture the experience by preparing it in my own kitchen.

2 tablespoons olive oil
1 small garlic clove
1 (10-ounce) package frozen
    chopped spinach, defrosted
    and drained
Salt and pepper
3 eggs
2 ounces mozzarella, shredded
2 tablespoons Parmesan, grated

Heat 1 tablespoon of the olive oil in a frying pan. Mince and sauté the garlic, then add the spinach and sauté until it is limp. (Add salt and pepper, if desired, but remember that the cheeses will add a lot of salt on their own.)

In a bowl, beat the eggs until the yolks are blended. Gently fold in the mozzarella and Parmesan. Pour the egg and cheese mixture into the frying pan over the sautéed spinach. Use a fork to separate the spinach and allow some of the egg mixture to reach the bottom of the pan. Leave this on medium heat until the eggs begin to set.

With a broad spatula, loosen the edges of the frittata and slide it onto a flat plate (with the cooked side on the bottom). Recoat the frying pan with the remaining 1 tablespoon olive oil. Place the frying pan over the frittata on its plate, then flip both the plate and the pan over. Remove the plate and return the frittata to medium heat. Cook until the entire frittata has set.

This frittata will provide two people with a light lunch. It is especially good accompanied by fresh Italian bread and a salad tossed with olive oil and wine vinegar.

$\mathscr{A}$ Woman in Her Own Right

Katharina Theodora Weidenbach
1885–1974

BY ERIKA KREIS OLMSTED

If my grandmother hadn't had a sense of mission bordering on the obsessive, my family would have been spared considerable discord. With her strictness and lack of diplomacy, Oma lost every popularity contest to Opa, my flamboyant, gregarious, fun-loving grandfather. His storytelling, his joking and guitar playing, his letting me join him in his drawing and painting sessions — all made him my favorite, as well as everyone else's.

Oma, too, had fallen head over heels for this charming man. With her characteristic determination, she simply got herself pregnant (my mother prided herself on being a "child of love") and married my grandfather when she was barely nineteen. The marriage was harmonious for many years until Oma developed her consuming interest in healthy, natural living. She felt compelled to boost the physical and spiritual well-being of all.

Opa endured her fanaticism with a sense of humor, but he needed an occasional escape from her nagging. He did not remain faithful to her, and this caused her much pain. He frequently left the house to smoke and drink, which she did not allow in her presence. (Even sipping a nice cup of coffee was enough to raise her eyebrows.) Sunday mornings usually started with reprimands against Opa for refusing to go to church. Pretending he had the grippe, he would stay in bed among piles of books. I would join him there and do my drawings, mostly portraits of him, while Oma prayed for us both during Mass.

But with Oma, I went to the nudist camp. And I owe her my lifelong delight in the aromatic air of health-food stores. She often took me to the Reform Haus for herbs, teas, cereals, nut butters, and magazines about vegetarianism, yoga, homeopathy, Dr. Kneipp's water cures, holistic healing, and much more.

Oma could always cure my colds by winding my legs overnight in water compresses. On principle, she refused to be treated by an "establishment" doctor. For weeks she bathed her infected right thumb in hot herbal solutions until things got so bad that a surgeon had to remove the tip. (She made other, less serious, mistakes: once she gave my baby cousin a full bottle of spinach juice!) Oma not only distrusted doctors' treatments, she also demeaned their judgments. When Opa died in his late eighties she questioned the medical examiner's diagnosis, maintaining stubbornly that Opa had succumbed to liver disease from his "drinking," although his consumption of alcohol had been moderate and merely social.

I can still see Oma doing her sewing, managing quite well without the tip of her thumb. Years before, she had made fashionable dresses and charming hats; she ran her own millinery shop when she was young. My first memory of Oma, in fact, is connected with an adorable pair of handmade, wine-red plush slippers. They were her welcoming gift to me when I came from America with my mother at the age of three, this time not to visit but to stay in Germany. Oma tended to make almost everything two sizes too large; clothing had to be sensible and long-lasting, and the deprivations of two world wars intensified her sense of thrift. Still, she created a comfortable – and even elegant – home. Sadly, she and Opa lost everything during the air raids that leveled most of Essen, the city of the Krupp steelworks.

But the delicate, determined little woman kept hanging in there, sustained by an indomitable spirit, by her ideals, and by the wisdom of philosophers and religious thinkers collected from various sources, including simple quotes from daily calendar pages.

My grandmother had wanted to be a schoolteacher. The realities of her life and time kept her a *hausfrau*. In retrospect, I see her as a self-taught naturopath.

Oma, I forgive you your rough edges. I am proud of your insights, your convictions, your pursuits. Today, slightly amended, they direct much of my own life. I admire you, Oma, for your openness to the early stirrings of the "New Age." You were ahead of your time. I raise my glass of delicious carrot-apple juice from my modern centrifugal juicer, and I salute you, my Oma.

Oma's Red Cabbage

Oma's concept of healthful food was most severe in her baking. She reduced the sugar and butter so drastically in her Sunday cakes that they were barely palatable. Her main dishes, however, were cooked with flair. Oma's red cabbage remains a family favorite. I include it in every Thanksgiving dinner.

2 onions, sliced

½ cup bacon fat, vegetable oil, or
   goose fat (at Christmastime),
   or ¼ pound (1 stick) butter

1 head of red cabbage, finely
   shredded

2 tart apples, cored, peeled,
   and diced

½ cup currant jelly, or
   2 tablespoons fruit juice

1 bay leaf

5 whole cloves

Salt and pepper

½ cup salt water or beef broth,
   if necessary

2 tablespoons wine vinegar

Preheat your oven to 350 degrees.

Sauté the onions in the bacon fat until they are soft. Add the cabbage, apples, jelly, bay leaf, cloves, salt, and pepper.

Schmor – which means cook slowly – for 2 hours in the oven. (My grandmother used a special clay pot for this. I use an iron casserole dish.) Stir occasionally and add a little salt water if it seems dry.

Remove the bay leaf and cloves, and stir in the vinegar before serving. This recipe serves 8 to 12 people.

Madeline Heiskanen Fiedler
1886–1972

When Grandma Got the Giggles

BY KAREN PHELPS

Song of My Grandmother

Grandmother, I invoke you.
Large, the placid oak leaf
Placid, the gnarled cedar
Gnarled, her veined hands
Veins, like a blue jay's feather
Blue, the sky overhead
Sky, the color of her eyes
Eyes, sparkling with laughter
Laughter, rich and endless
Endless, her love for me.
Grandmother, I invoke you.

My grandmother had pale-blue eyes the color of the ice in Finland, where she was born the youngest of fifteen children. The eyes changed in succeeding generations to a darker sky-blue in my mother and to a grayish-blue, the color of an overcast sky, in me.

Lena Heiskanen arrived in America not speaking a word of English. Her older brother, William, had settled in Wisconsin and sent $30 to his sister to follow. But when she discovered how cold it was out there, she decided to stay in the East. At nineteen, she was already her own person.

She learned how to cook in the kitchens of the wealthy – families like the Astors, on Long Island. Following one family to Westchester, she met my grandfather, Anton Fiedler, a carpenter from Austria hired by the prison in Bedford Hills that paid his passage over.

I grew up living less than a mile away from my grandparents, and my family often spent time at their home. I remember a house filled with laughter. When Grandma got "The Giggles," her body would go limp as she doubled up laughing, unable to stop until her eyes teared and she gasped for breath. It was impossible to look at her and not be stricken oneself. I have inherited her spontaneous laughter. There's no telling when or where The Giggles will strike me – in a movie, a class, a meeting, a fancy restaurant. My limbs become jelly, my face turns bright red, my eyes tear, and I laugh until my sides ache. We did our share of laughing together, Grandma and I, and she is with me still, whenever I get The Giggles.

But we had many quiet moments. Grandma loved to embroider. To me, it seemed like magic the way the needle and thread went through the cloth to form patterns. In her large rocking chair she'd embroider contentedly all afternoon: pillowcases, tablecloths, dresser scarves, and napkins. She'd encourage me to select the colors for birds and flowers from the rainbow of threads in the big tin by her side; on my next visit, she'd proudly show me the finished piece, as if to compliment me on my good choices. I have several of her beautiful pieces, but the most special are two horses done for my birthday when I was a horse-mad schoolgirl. She had chosen my favorites: Fury, the star of a Saturday morning TV show, and Trigger, the beautiful palomino of Roy Rogers.

My mother and aunt learned embroidery from my grandmother. So did my sister. I picked up embroidery only after my grandmother died. My first piece was an astrology wheel using every stitch imaginable. Painstakingly, I followed the complicated directions, feeling compelled to teach myself my grandmother's craft. She would have been impressed with the intricate design. The most difficult section included a two-inch circle of French knots in the center – a design especially difficult to make with bulky crewel thread.

"Her body would go limp as she doubled up laughing, unable to stop until her eyes teared and she gasped for breath. It was impossible to look at her and not be stricken oneself."

Her most cherished legacy to me, however, came many years after her death. For a decade I'd worn her engagement ring – a small diamond in a Tiffany setting – never expecting to marry. Then, at forty-one, I fell in love. How special I felt! My grandmother's wedding dress was retrieved from the attic. Her embroidery was incredible: dozens of roses in satin stitch and a bodice decorated in Queen Anne's lace made from hundreds of French knots. She had been a stocky woman with narrow shoulders and broad hips. My build was similar. As the sheer cotton material floated down around me, I held my breath. But the seventy-eight-year-old wedding dress was a perfect fit, an affirmation from my grandmother who had died twenty years before.

When I walked down the aisle, I felt my grandmother's spirit beside me and heard her blessing in my ear.

Grandma's Pussy Feet

Grandma passed the torch to the next generation when she taught me how to bake our family's two favorite cookies. With an oversized apron wound around me, I learned these recipes from the consistency of the dough, not from the measurement of the ingredients.

Pussy feet and almond half-moon cookies have become my Christmas traditions. When I shape the dough, I remember my grandmother's instructions as though she were peering over my shoulder, whispering in my ear.

The Cookies

2 egg whites, beaten
1 cup sugar
2 to 3 cups walnuts, ground fine
   as cornmeal (use 3 cups if
   you're using a blender to chip
   the nuts)

The Icing

2 pasteurized egg whites
Confectioners' sugar

Preheat your oven to 350 degrees.

Beat the egg whites, then add the sugar. Stir in 2 cups of walnuts. If the dough is too soft and sticky, add more nuts until it can be easily rolled by hand into grape-sized balls. The amount of nuts will vary with each batch of cookies. Make sure you buy enough nuts, just in case.

On a greased cookie sheet, place three balls of dough close together, like a cat's paw. Repeat until you have filled the entire cookie sheet. Bake until the cookies are tan in color, about 15 minutes. If the cookies go flat, add more nuts to the next batch.

For an optional icing: cream 2 egg whites and confectioners' sugar until the icing is the desired consistency. After the cookies have cooled, dab some icing onto the center of each. Makes 2 to 3 dozen cookies.

Grandma's Almond Half-Moon Cookies

Because these cookies use egg yolks and the pussy feet use egg whites, we always made both recipes on the same day.

½ pound (2 sticks) butter or
    margarine
½ cup sugar
2 egg yolks
1 cup ground almonds
3 to 4 cups flour
¼ cup confectioners' sugar
¼ teaspoon vanilla extract

Preheat your oven to 350 degrees.

Mix the butter, sugar, and egg yolks. Add the almonds, then add 3 cups of the flour. If the dough is too soft, add more flour.

Form the dough into half-moon shapes about the width of your index finger. (Too thin and they'll burn; too thick and they won't cook.) Place the half-moons on a greased cookie sheet and bake for 10 to 15 minutes.

On a plate, mix the confectioners' sugar with the vanilla. Roll the cookies in the sugar as soon as they are finished baking.

This recipe will make about 3 dozen cookies.

Grandma's Finnish Pancakes

These light, thin pancakes are the Finnish version of crêpes suzette. They are quick to make, and most cooks have the ingredients on hand. My mother made them as a special treat in the middle of the winter when we wanted something different for dinner. Grandma made them on Halloween when we were too excited and rushed to eat a regular meal.

2 eggs
½ cup milk
½ cup flour
1 teaspoon baking powder
½ teaspoon salt
1 teaspoon sugar
Butter or oil for oiling
    the pan

Beat the eggs well, then add the milk, flour, baking powder, salt, and sugar. Mix until there are no lumps and the batter is the consistency of cream.

Butter a hot, medium-sized frying pan. Ladle in just enough batter to fill pan. Turn the pancake over when the top is full of bubbles and the bottom looks cooked. (Because these pancakes are thin, they cook very fast.) Serve with preserves or powdered sugar.

This recipe makes 4 to 5 pancakes. To make 15 to 20 pancakes, increase both the milk and the flour to 1½ cups, but keep all other ingredients the same

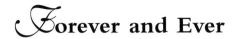

Forever and Ever

BY TAKAYO NODA

Hatsu Nakamura
1887–1974

Asking My Grandmother

I asked her happily, "Do you like my new dress?"
She smiled and said "Yes" warmly,
Then kissed me on my forehead.

I asked her softly, "Do you like my white hat?"
She looked into my eyes and said "Yes" sweetly,
Then kissed me on my left cheek.

I asked her slowly, "Do you like my dress-up shoes?"
She put her hand on my knee and said "Yes" gently,
Then kissed me on my nose.

I asked her hastily, "So, do you like me very much?"
She stretched her arms around me and said "Yes" lovingly,
Then held me very tight for a long, long time.

My paternal grandmother, the matriarch of my family, tormented my young and beautiful mother. I often heard my mother crying at night. Her tears filled the darkness and seeped into my bedroom, leaving me with pain and sorrow and fear.

But in times of sadness, my maternal grandmother held my wounded heart in her soul. She showed me how beautiful it is to love and be loved. She taught me to dream and hope with the light of the sun, the moon, and the stars. After all these years, I still dream and hope with this same light that ignites my creativity over and over again.

When I was very young, she taught me how to fold origami. Her fingers were slim and beautiful, the short nails polished a pale pink. I wanted to touch her hands because they were so warm and loving. I still see my grandmother's hands when I fold the paper.

She had a profound love for me, and I was the one who was special to her. But she was special to many.

She lived in Japan all her life. She graduated from Japan Women's University in Tokyo with an English degree in 1908. While she was a student she married my grandfather, who was also a university student, and they had the first of four children. (My grandmother did not have a married name; my grandfather took her name instead, a common practice in Japan when the wife is an only child and the husband has older brothers.) During her university years, she developed a strong interest in European culture through her English professor, a woman she visited in England after World War II when the professor was ninety-five and my grandmother was seventy.

She dedicated her life to women's and children's rights, working first to enact a law, which was passed by the Diet in 1937, to protect women and children. After World War II, she established a charitable institution in Tokyo to assist the Japanese women and children who had escaped from Manchuria after their men had been killed there during the war. When my grandfather died in 1952, she joined the Japan Widows Organization and subsequently became its president. In the last segment of her life, she convinced the government to build a nursing home in the southern island of Japan. She became its director, living and working there until she died. For her dedication to the cause of women's and children's rights, she was awarded the Medal of Honor from both the Tokyo government and the federal government.

She cared about people she didn't know and would never meet. She nurtured their well-being and saved their spirits. She also nurtured my young, fragile soul with her deepest love, giving me the strength to see and feel the beauty of nature and life.

You made me the artist I am, Grandmother. Thank you very much for all you did for me with your greatest love. I love you very, very much forever and ever.

Grandmother's Pork Tenderloin with Ginger and Soy Sauce

This is a quick dish for busy people. My grandmother did not often have time to cook but she sometimes prepared this dish for us. When we smelled the mixture of soy sauce and fresh ginger, we knew she was cooking and we knew it would be delicious.

6 tablespoons soy sauce

3 tablespoons Japanese sake or dry white wine

3 tablespoons fresh ginger, grated

1 pound pork tenderloin, thinly sliced (⅛ to ¼ inch thick)

3 tablespoons vegetable oil

2 medium onions, thinly sliced

Flour

Make a marinade by mixing the soy sauce, sake, and grated ginger.

Use a cleaver to flatten the pork slices, then place them in a large noncorroding container. Pour the soy mixture over the pork.

While the pork is marinating, heat ½ tablespoon of the vegetable oil in a nonstick frying pan. Add the onions and cook them until they are almost tender. Remove the onions and set them aside.

After the pork has marinated for about 30 minutes, take it out of the container and place it on a paper towel to soak up the excess moisture. Sprinkle flour lightly over the pork, then remove the excess flour.

In the nonstick frying pan, heat 1 tablespoon of the vegetable oil and cook the pork over medium heat until both sides are fully cooked and golden in color. (Cook a few pieces at a time, adding more oil as needed.) Remove the cooked pork and set it aside. In the same frying pan, cook the onions again, on medium heat, until they are golden and coated with the pan juice. Be careful not to burn the onions.

Arrange the pork and onions side by side on a plate. This dish serves 4.

he Pocket Girl

Evdoxia (Eva) Nechkin Andreeff
1887(?)–1974

BY MICAELA NECHKIN WOODBRIDGE

My grandmother was four foot ten and had lovely legs. When she was young they called her "the pocket girl" because she was so small, and men drank champagne from her slipper. A playbill from Harbin, Manchuria, dated December 30, 1912, lists her in the lead role as Cinderella. We called her "Babi," short for *babushka,* the Russian word for grandmother.

Babi grew up in Odessa, but would always explain that she was born in Siberia of Russian parents; God forbid someone should think she was Ukrainian. Her father worked for the railroad, furnishing the interiors of passenger cars. Fleeing the social unrest in Odessa, Babi followed the Trans-Siberian Railroad to Harbin, Manchuria, where her only son (my father) was born in 1907. My grandfather – who fancied pigeons, gambling, and other women – deserted them seven years later, leaving Babi to support herself and her child by working in the railroad office.

When Bolsheviks took control of the railroad in the mid-1920s, Babi immigrated to western Canada with her second husband, a former officer in the White Russian Army. "The Reds were coming," she said, "and then nobody would have nothing." The Reds had killed her twelve-year-old nephew just because he belonged to some youth organization. For many years I envisioned a copper-skinned Mongolian horde sweeping over The Steppes just as Babi rushed onto the boat.

In Canada, Babi taught herself to speak, read, and write in English. She spoke with a heavy accent that never improved. When my sister Ann and I tried to teach her, for example, that a "beet" was not a "bit," she would answer contemptuously, "Beet – beet! for me der's no *dee*-fer-r-rence!" After all,

English was a corrupt and miserable language compared to Russian, in which each letter stood for just one sound.

But Babi read English very well. Having studied Shakespeare's plays in Russian, she took great joy in reading them in English. We shared Steinbeck and Hemingway, Balzac and Proust, Tolstoy and Dostoevsky. For my high school graduation, she gave me the complete works of George Bernard Shaw in three large volumes, but she took them back and read the whole thing – plays, introductions, and all – before I had my turn with them.

I spent more time with Babi than with anyone else in my family. She made me think a lot, and to me she seemed the soul of wisdom and objectivity. I discovered the limits to her broad-mindedness only when I gave her *The Catcher in the Rye.* "Don't geef me no more dirty books," she said.

When my father was overseas in World War II, Babi took over the household so my mother could work. Sometimes they argued, and I would find Babi crying. "She is your mother, and I would not say some-ting bad about her," she would sob. From this I was to understand that my lazy mother had cruelly used my poor Babi, who only wanted to do everything for us. To this day, I'm not sure I've sorted out the myth from the reality.

Babi was my conscience, more so than either of my parents. Her love was – and probably still is – the core of my motivation. Every piano recital, every "A" report card, was an occasion for great rejoicing and sweet rewards. When I was hurt or disappointed, I cried in her lap and she cried with me. But her tears weren't only for me. She cried every year on the anniversary of her husband's death. She cried for her poor oppressed Russia. She cried for anyone who suffered or was hungry. Before I was old enough to go to school, I would secretly lead railroad bums home from the freight yard, knowing that Babi would feed them a hot meal. In later years I heard the expression, "There but for the grace of God go I." The words weren't familiar, but the concept, I knew, was something I had learned from Babi.

Babi's Deep-Fried Lamb Pockets *(Tcheburiki)*

It was a family occasion when Babi made one of her Russian meat-in-pastry dishes. First, she would mix the meat and make the dough. Then, as she rolled out the dough, my sister and I would cut out the discs and assemble the pockets. There were three varieties: one boiled, two fried. The best of all was tcheburiki, *which I offer here.*

I have included some refinements, for which I thank my dietitian sister, Ann Patrick. However, in the original recipe, Babi writes, "I never measure all that ingrediance, just by taste, more or less anything does not spoiled." George Bernard Shaw would have understood.

The Filling

1 pound ground lamb (use a
    good cut: leg or shoulder
    is fine, with a small amount
    of the fat ground in)
1 stalk celery, very finely
    chopped
6 scallions, very finely chopped
A few sprigs fresh dill, very
    finely chopped
½ cup water
Salt and pepper

The Dough

3 eggs
¼ to ½ cup water
½ teaspoon salt
½ teaspoon baking powder
4 to 5 cups flour
Melted fat or vegetable oil
    for deep-frying

For the filling: combine the meat, celery, scallions, and dill in a large mixing bowl. Add the water, salt, and pepper. Mix lightly with a fork and set the filling aside.

To make the dough: first beat the eggs, then add the water (Babi used the egg shells to measure a volume equivalent to 3 eggs), salt, and baking powder. Gradually add the flour until the dough can be rolled. Knead the dough on a floured board until it is nice and springy.

Divide the dough into quarters and roll one quarter at a time into a thin sheet. Using a large-mouthed jar or lid (about 4 inches in diameter), cut discs out of the sheet.

Place a scoop of meat on each disc. Fold the disc in half and pinch tightly around the edges, making a fat crescent. It takes a bit of practice to get just the right amount of meat – be sure you don't stretch holes in the pastry. The edges must meld into a seamless flange to hold in the meat juices. If the pastry becomes too dry to make a good seal, use your fingers to dab a little water on the lower edge before closing.

Lay the *tcheburiki* on a floured board and cover them with a damp dish-towel. When all are made, heat several inches of fat in a deep frying pan or kettle. Deep-fry the crescents until they are golden brown. Serves 4 people.

Back in the Garden of Eden before they invented cholesterol, we would hold a hot crescent in a paper napkin, bite off the top, and pour in melted butter. Today, we enjoy *tcheburiki* just as they are.

Babi would always keep count of how many she had made, and how many each person had eaten. "You ate only five! Eat some more!" I could never refuse.

A Legacy Found in Letters

Mary Suldane Candice
1887–1982

BY NOEL CANDICE HORN

It would never have occurred to Mary Candice that she could establish her own identity. Mary was defined by her generation, her role in life determined by the era. Daughter. Spinster. Wife. Widow. At the turn of the century, my grandmother was stranded by convention on an island of limitation.

But Mary's spirit could not be bound. Using her pen, the essential Mary built a bridge of words with details of her days and memories of her years. Letters connected her to a world she couldn't reach in any other way.

Writing at her kitchen table, Mary created sacred space in an ordinary place. Her letters were filled with the magnificent and the mundane, the celebrated and the sorrowful. She wrote of past happenings and future possibilities, always with astute observations. During the quiet hours of early morning, the small, white-haired woman of few spoken words shared herself generously on paper. She wrote to family, to far-flung friends, and to people who were strangers until her letters found them.

Mary's letters led me to the riches of writing. After I married and moved thousands of miles away from home, she and I shared our lives through our correspondence. Today, rereading more than one hundred of her letters, I've discovered another woman between the words, a woman I now see through the lens of my own life's journey. Though the details of our lives differ, the substance is the same. Our stories tell of a woman's way in the world.

When she was eighty-nine, Mary wrote one of her last letters to me. She shared her astonishment and pleasure at having helped bring a book to publication. The book, which had been an incomplete history of an early Catholic settlement on Chicago's West Side, would not have seen print without Mary's

vivid memories and vibrant letters. She had lived in that neighborhood, taught Sunday School at Madonna Center, and worked with the center's founders and earliest benefactors. Mary was honored at a gala reception that marked the debut of the book, part of a history project on Jane Addams's Hull House.

I was forty when Mary died. Soon after, I was widowed. How grateful I am that she never knew of her first-born grandchild's experience. Her letters had revealed heartache over her own widowhood at sixty. Though we were from different worlds, some truths are bitter constants. Like her, I found myself cast away to an island, confined there by other people's perceptions and expectations.

As I slowly built a new life, I understood that her letters were foundational to my efforts. Pen and paper would provide my passport to a new world. We were bonded by family ties, Mary and I, but something much deeper and truer linked us in spirit.

Mary laid the groundwork for my exploration of writing. Her letters demonstrated the importance of detail and description. They taught me that each experience holds meaning and that story is all.

Eventually, I moved beyond my own letter writing, and articles I submitted found publication. Like Mary's, my spirit soared.

My grandmother fed my heart, my imagination, my creativity, and my soul. Her legacy has proved life-giving as well.

Mary's Bean Soup

Mary was three when she arrived at Ellis Island in 1891. She never forgot the lessons in community that the trials of steerage had taught her. Throughout her life, her remarkable generosity of spirit reflected what she had learned on that passage.

Her days were centered in her kitchen, the heart of an Italian household, from which she generously provided nourishment through food, words, and love. Here, from her letter of November 11, 1977, is a recipe for hearty bean soup, one of her favorite dishes.

1 pound dried navy beans
2 onions
2 stalks celery
1 (6-ounce) can tomato sauce
2 large carrots
1 cup cooked rice
½ small Savoy cabbage
Salt and pepper

"My dear Noel Ann,

I found myself very busy the other morning after telling Florence [my aunt] to buy one pound of navy beans for me. You'll never guess what I did with them! I counted them! Can you guess how many navy beans are in half a pound? I counted one thousand and twenty-five beans but didn't win a prize. I did get to look them over pretty carefully before I washed them. I took some onions out of the basket where we keep them in the dark, taking the ones about to give birth (one was about to have twins!). I chopped them and also cut up two stalks of celery in fine slices. Florence had tomato sauce left over so I added several tablespoons to give the pot some color. I also cut up two large carrots. Everything went into the pot and was covered with water to simmer for about an hour. Florence had rice partly cooked and some Savoy cabbage too. In they went. Believe me, it was a treat to have all of those goodies stewing away, much better than any of the beef sold in the supermarkets today. I dolled up the pot with some salt and pepper, not too much, and had some Italian bread on hand. This makes a mighty fine supper dish and can take any other vegetables you want to add. The more the merrier. Try it some time and let me know how you like it."

Serves 6 to 8 people.

Notes from Underfoot

Maria Arcangela Barbara Ferrarese Savino
1888–1957

BY BARBARA MARIE GRAVINESE

All I have to do is inhale deeply, and in the bottom of my lungs is the air of my life with her, the sweet, spicy scent of a basil, rose, and mint garden.

I have been told that my grandmother sailed alone at the age of twenty-seven to join her husband in America. The impetus behind this departure from her birthplace in Gravina di Puglia, Italy, was an overbearing mother-in-law. Grandma embraced life in New York with characteristic tenacity and vigor. Early on, her husband died. She remarried. Her first son died. She mourned deeply.

My grandmother was vital to my life in my early years. When I was about one year old, my mother and older sister and I went to live with my grandparents in their brown wooden house in the Bronx. The trauma of my parents' recent divorce drove my mother to seek refuge in work and in friends. In her virtual absence, my life with Grandma began in earnest. Until her death when I was ten, she was the center of my life.

Although there was little common language spoken between us, I remember our communication as most satisfactory. We spoke some of each other's language, but for the most part, she spoke Italian to my English.

Attached to her apron, I sailed kite-like through my grandmother's daily life. Together we made red wine in our cellar. We toasted our health with shot glasses of olive oil sent in small wooden kegs from Grandma's property in Italy.

Every day Grandma cooked, cleaned, and sewed at her treadle machine. Her feet, driven by an internal music, carried her along a road that she alone traveled. We could always count on her return.

Her cooking was miraculous. She commanded high authority over the elements. Volcanoes of white flour rose from the kitchen table as she fearlessly poured water into the center of a crater she had made with her fist. Then, slowly, she lowered her hand down into the water, touching the flour at the bottom. Her fingers wriggled fish-like as they transformed the flour and water into dough.

Every morning she bathed, and I stood behind her while she combed and braided her long white hair, crowned her head from ear to ear, and fixed the braids firmly with tortoise-brown hairpins.

Every night she bathed us, washed our hair, patted us with baby powder, and in her raspy voice sang us to sleep. Memory draws me back to the rumble of snoring from her bedroom. On her dresser was a flickering, blue votive candle; shadows moved across the walls, animating the portraits of heavenly saints slaying nightmare demons.

And so the minute hand of my life with her moved on, and I will always remember.

"Attached to her apron, I sailed kite-like through my grandmother's daily life. Together we made red wine in our cellar. We toasted our health with shot glasses of olive oil sent in small wooden kegs from Grandma's property in Italy."

Grandma's Frittata with Parsley and Cheese

Grandma indulged my shy but persistent self, but her small black leather shoes were always one step ahead of me. I begged to eat the frittata before it was cooked because it smelled so good. How I tried to convince her that it was ready when it was still a gelatinous pool simmering in olive oil! She always made me wait, and it was always worth waiting.

6 large eggs

¼ cup pecorino Romano, grated

1 tablespoon dried unseasoned bread crumbs

1 large garlic clove, minced

1 tablespoon Italian parsley, minced

½ teaspoon freshly ground black pepper

½ teaspoon salt

1 teaspoon cold water

¼ to 1 cup olive oil, according to taste

1 medium onion, cut in half-moon slices (not too thin) or diced

Break the eggs into a bowl. Add the cheese, bread crumbs, garlic, parsley, black pepper, salt, and cold water. Mix thoroughly with a fork.

Generously cover the bottom of a frying pan with olive oil; heat on a low flame. Add the onion slices and sauté them over medium heat until they begin to brown. Immediately pour the egg mixture into the middle of the oil. Turn the heat down a little and cook without stirring until the edges begin to pull away from the pan (about 5 to 10 minutes).

Once the edges begin to pull away, use a wooden spoon to fold the edges of the mixture toward the middle of the pan. If the mixture is sticking, add a little oil around the edges.

As the egg begins to set, it will remain in the center. Pat it down and shape it into a thick circle. Add a little more oil at the outer edges whenever necessary.

With a spatula, loosen the frittata and turn it over. Continue cooking for 5 to 10 minutes over low heat, then slip the whole frittata onto a large plate. (It tastes good in pieces, too!)

Serve with beets and onions dressed in a light vinaigrette, and with boiled potatoes seasoned with black pepper, parsley, and olive oil. Frittata can be reheated, eaten at room temperature, or served cold. Serves 3 people.

Note: This recipe is quite versatile. Try adding different ingredients to the egg mixture, such as spinach, zucchini, mushrooms, tomatoes, sausage, and various cheeses.

Grandma's Baked Haddock with Tomato

On Friday nights a meatless dinner was in order, and this recipe was a favorite of mine. Soon after it goes into the oven, a magnificent aroma fills the house.

Whenever Grandma cooked, I tried to orchestrate her time-worn movements to my liking. I'd dance around her demanding more colored sprinkles on the Christmas cookies, more carrots in the soup, and more cheese and parsley in the baked haddock.

4 to 5 (6-ounce) fresh
   haddock steaks
4 to 5 ripe plum tomatoes,
   coarsely chopped
2 tablespoons Italian parsley,
   coarsely chopped
2 medium yellow onions,
   sliced
2 tablespoons pecorino
   Romano, grated
Freshly ground black pepper
2 tablespoons olive oil
1 tablespoon cold water
Salt

Preheat your oven to 350 degrees. Rinse the fish in cold water.

Layer half of the tomatoes, parsley, onion, cheese, and black pepper in a baking dish. Drizzle 1 tablespoon of the olive oil on top.

Next, arrange the fish steaks on top of the cheese. Then, layer the remaining tomatoes, parsley, onion, cheese, and black pepper over the fish, followed by 1 tablespoon olive oil. Sprinkle the cold water over the top, then salt to taste.

Bake for 30 to 45 minutes, or until the onions are slightly browned. Delicious with green beans, crusty Italian bread, and red wine. Serves 4 to 5 people.

Note: Ingredients and proportions can be modified to your taste. For example, you can substitute canned tomatoes for the fresh plum tomatoes, or you can use codfish or center-cut shoulder lamb chops instead of haddock.

Making Do

BY H.H. PRICE

Lillian Maud LaGrange Hemenway
1889–1974

My paternal grandmother became my mother for a few years, beginning in 1947. I was seven years old and she was in her late fifties, the age I am now. When I meet my reflection in a mirror I sometimes see Gramma, and for a moment I carry on an emotional dialogue between the child in me who depended on her, and the adult in me who understands what she must have faced.

Gramma was a strong, Vermont country lady who managed a large family as well as her share of the big dairy farm she ran with Grampa. By the time I came to live with them they had only a subsistence farm, which they husbanded on little or nothing. It is a good thing Gramma knew how to "make do," because within three months the key people in both her life and mine were gone.

My loss came first. It happened swiftly, during blackberry season. My father had placed me with his parents because he and my mother were warring beyond repair. Two weeks later, my mother traveled 200 miles to get me. She and Gramma fought. After two days and nights of arguments and phone calls on the old-fashioned crank phone, two sheriff's deputies removed my mother from the back porch of my grandparents' small farmhouse in a struggle that still reverberates in the thud-and-screech part of my inner ear. Gramma had won. My mother was kept in a mental institution until I was a teenager and knew her not.

The setting for both my loss and gain of "mother" was in Gramma's village, where the foothills of the Green Mountains – *les verts monts* – pour into French-speaking Canada. Gramma's claim to the territory went back to her maternal grandparents, who settled there when it was still a forest, and she held on to it with the tenacity that gives Vermonters their reputation for stick-to-itiveness. She was the only one of twelve children to live all her life in her ancestral village, and die there, too. Good for Gramma! Her progeny have a sense of place, something that cannot be bought or manufactured.

Shortly after I became Gramma's little girl (the final remnant added to her family quilt), Grampa died. I was making paper chains for the Christmas tree when he forced out his last word from their bed upstairs, a guttural call for "Lillian." There we were, alone, Gramma and I. My father worked and lived away. My only sibling, a restless adolescent boy, was constantly running away. My mother had been put away. And Grampa had "slipped away." I knew how much Gramma missed him because I tried to fill up the potholes in her daily course.

Gramma and I went at the task of "making do" with life. She pumped her treadle sewing machine and sang revival hymns, hung laundry on the line as if it were an art, kept the wood cookstove burning for food and heat and heart, and slept back-to-back with me for warmth and company. Now that I am as old as she was then, I cry to think of how lonely she must have been.

If Gramma were here, she probably would not allow me to cry too long. She had a fierce but ladylike sense of humor, and she told me the kind of stories that nowadays they call "oral history." We might be playing two-handed canasta or doing up the dishes when she would launch into some tale about her sisters, or about our ancestral village when it was a premier mineral springwater spa. One story, from the early 1900s, combines the two. The spa business had spawned a dozen hotels, some the size of oceangoing ships, but by the turn of the century they had dry rot and were languishing because the mineral-water business had dried up. Lillian and her sisters were all young women then, dressing in long, pastel, tight-waisted frocks and wearing their hair wound atop their heads like teacups on saucers. When many of the hotels mysteriously burned down one summer, people ran all over the territory to see the blazing sights. Gramma laughed about this free but fiery entertainment, and I imagined her and her sisters — all country ladies — lifting their skirts to dash about, still balancing their "cups and saucers" as if attendance at these events were by invitation only.

When Gramma was dying, thirty years after Grampa died, the oxygen tube in her nose was so uncomfortable she asked me to take it out. Gramma had never asked anything of me (except to join my stepmother's church), but I could not do this for her; she would have died. She died anyway. I cried so hard I thought the emotional explosion would surely bring her back. I was thirty-four, with children the age I had been when she took me on. How could I live without her?

After we buried Lillian on a slope overlooking the village, the family went back to one of my aunt's for food and company. I was called upstairs by Gramma's daughters to go through her few possessions. What a privilege! In the end, I *was* one of Gramma's girls. She had "made do" with me, too.

Gramma's Rag-a-Muffins

Gramma always used a pet name, something from the countryside vocabulary, to call me inside or wake me up or set me straight. It might be Peanut or Punkinhead or Sweet Pea, depending on her whim and my ways. My favorite nickname was Rag-a-Muffin, and it was my favorite food, too. She whipped it up the way she did everything in our world of scarcity, "making it from scratch" or "pulling it out of thin air."

She passed on her recipes through conversation, and I can hear her now, telling me how to make these treats.

Leftover unbaked dough
　　(from raised bread,
　　biscuits, raised doughnuts,
　　or piecrust)
Butter
Maple syrup, brown sugar,
　　or white sugar mixed
　　with cinnamon

"Take the leftover dough and roll it out into a broad piece. [Do this on a floured board. Gramma wouldn't have thought it necessary to mention this – nor would she have given me a baking temperature, or told me to turn the oven on. The oven would already be on from baking the pies or bread; part of 'making do' is not heating up an oven twice. But if you're starting with a cold oven, you'll want to turn it on about now, to 350 degrees.]

"Spread the dough lightly with butter, then with Vermont maple syrup (that's the first choice, naturally) or brown sugar, or white sugar with cinnamon, and roll it up like a newspaper.

"Cut generous 'snails' [about 1 inch thick] off the roll and put the cut-sides down onto a lightly greased pan. Bake the rag-a-muffins in a moderate oven until golden brown. They will surely please some rag-a-muffin child, of which there is no scarcity these days."

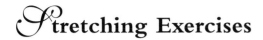tretching Exercises

Elizabeth Boehm Richter Godecker Rendler
1891–1989

BY NORA RICHTER GREER

Whenever Grandma visited our house, the stretching began – the stretching of dough, that is, for the crust of her savory strudel. To my girlish eyes, the movement of her hands seemed like a magic trick. She'd plunk down a ball of dough in the middle of the kitchen table, which had been spread with a cloth and sprinkled with flour. With her strong fingers she would pull and pull, moving the clump around in perfect rhythm, never breaking a hole in the dough, until it covered the table's entire surface. She'd then quickly spread the filling over the dough and, using the cloth, roll it up into a cylindrical shape. Soon the aroma of baking strudel – a smell I will forever associate with my grandmother – would fill the house.

You could always sense the strength in her solid, stocky fingers, even when they were throbbing with arthritis. Elizabeth worked those hands hard every day of her life, first on the family farm in Austria, then as a housekeeper in Budapest, Vienna, and Chicago. She pinned the diapers of five children – and lost one of them in infancy. She assembled radios in a Zenith factory during World War II, baked breads and cookies in a bakery she owned with her second husband, and crocheted yards and yards, maybe miles, of tablecloths, afghans, and other finery. Yet through all the years, through good and bad, the stretching of strudel was a constant for her.

If I close my eyes, I can still hear Grandma's thickly accented voice, her unique combination of German and English. Whenever I asked her about her life – what it was like to move to Chicago as a teenager, knowing only two other people there, or to lose my grandfather in 1940 to tuberculosis – Grandma would tell me that life was about hard work and survival. You can't let disappointments get the better of you, no matter what the circumstances. You just keep stretching and stretching.

"You could always sense the strength in her solid, stocky fingers, even when they were throbbing with arthritis. Elizabeth worked those hands hard every day of her life."

Elizabeth Boehm Richter Godecker Rendler stretched as long as she could. She lived independently until it was no longer possible – well into her nineties. She witnessed nearly a full century, a journey that took her from a farm without electricity in the Old Country to the wonderment of man walking on the moon. She loved, and outlived, three husbands. Her life, like her strudel, was stretched to its limit. And if she maintained a somewhat unsentimental, pragmatic relationship with her grandchildren (we were, after all, expected to behave with a certain dignity), she would undoubtedly be proud that we too – her nine grandchildren, seventeen great-grandchildren, and three great-great-grandchildren – are stretching today, each in our own way.

Grandma Rendler's Apple Strudel

To economize during the Depression, Grandma often served soup and strudel (the strudel containing cheese or cabbage) for dinner. In fact, strudel became a staple for the family.

Grandma Rendler's strudel is versatile. Try filling it with apples, cherries, cheese, or even sauerkraut. Patience is needed with this recipe, for it may take some practice to conquer the stretching technique without breaking holes in the dough. (If you get a hole, just pinch it together and continue stretching.) If you prefer, you can use a food processor to mix the dough. Slowly pour in the liquid, then mix or pulse until smooth. This cuts the mixing time in half and eliminates the kneading.

The Dough
(for two 24-inch pieces)

1 egg
2 tablespoons vegetable oil
1 teaspoon vinegar
½ cup warm water
2 cups flour
¼ teaspoon salt
¼ pound plus four tablespoons
   (1½ sticks) butter, melted

Combine the egg, vegetable oil, vinegar, and water. Warm the liquid gently. Meanwhile, mix together the flour and salt. Make a hole in the center of the flour and pour the warm liquid into the hole. Mix this with a wooden spoon.

When the dough becomes stiff, knead it on a floured surface, adding more flour as necessary, until the dough is smooth and elastic. Divide the dough in half, rubbing each half with melted butter. Cover each half with a warm bowl and let it rest for at least 30 minutes.

Cover your kitchen table or countertop with a sheet or tablecloth. Sprinkle flour in the center. Place half the dough on the flour, then roll it into a circle about 1 foot in diameter. Brush the circle with melted butter.

With lightly floured fingers, begin stretching the rolled-out dough. To do this, place your hands beneath the dough and gently pull away from the center. (Grandma always stretched the dough by herself, but beginners may find it easier to stretch with two or three people.) When the dough is paper thin and about 24 inches in diameter, it is ready for the filling.

By now, the edges of the dough will have become thick. Remove these thick edges, then sprinkle about 3 tablespoons of melted butter over the stretched dough.

The Filling

10 medium tart apples
½ cup raisins
½ teaspoon cinnamon
½ cup plus 4 tablespoons sugar
1 cup crushed cornflakes
½ cup chopped walnuts
6 tablespoons butter, melted,
    for brushing on the dough
Confectioners' sugar (optional)

To make the filling, first peel and core the apples, then cut them into thin slices. Next, plump the raisins by soaking them in warm water for 10 minutes. Drain the raisins and squeeze out the water.

In a separate bowl, mix the cinnamon and the ½ cup sugar, then add the apples, raisins, cornflakes, and walnuts. Mix well.

Divide the apple mixture in half. Set one half aside and spread the other half over the surface of the dough. Sprinkle with 2 tablespoons of the sugar.

Preheat your oven to 375 degrees.

Using the cloth beneath the dough, gently lift one side of the dough. Roll up the dough and place the roll in a lightly greased baking pan, seam-side down. If your pan is too small, cut the strudel in half and use two pans.

Now, repeat the process: Roll out the second piece of dough, stretch it paper-thin to about 24 inches in diameter, and sprinkle with 3 tablespoons melted butter. Spread the remaining filling over the dough, sprinkle with 2 tablespoons sugar, roll it up, and place the roll in a lightly greased baking pan.

Bake both rolls for 25 to 35 minutes, until golden brown. Brush with leftover butter twice while baking. Cool, cut, and serve the strudel with a sprinkling of powdered sugar or a scoop of ice cream.

Strudel may be frozen. When ready to eat, simply thaw the strudel and gently heat it in a warm oven. Makes 12 to 15 servings.

y Guiding Light

Epifania Gennarina LoPorto
1892–1967

BY KATHLEEN LaPLANTE

My grandfather, who did not believe in God, went to a convent to pick out a wife. He wanted a "pure woman," I learned as a teenager. Never mind that he turned out to be a bigamist, which meant that in the eyes of the Church my grandparents were never married. This was a true cross for my grandmother to bear – excommunicated through no fault of her own. I always wondered why Grandma, a devout Catholic, never took Communion!

After they were married fifty years, the Pope gave them a special dispensation. Did that make it all right? Between Grandma and God, perhaps, but maybe not between Grandma and Grandpa. Throughout their fifty-nine years together, Grandpa never passed up an opportunity to challenge her faith, to which she never failed to reply, "Epifanio, you make-a me so mad!" (They had many differences, but they had this one odd similarity: They shared the same unusual first name.)

Because I came into Grandma's life when she was entering the years of wisdom, I am guilty of thinking of her as always capable, always doing the best thing. But I wonder what it must have been like for a sixteen-year-old girl, raised in an orphanage run by Catholic nuns, to marry a stranger twelve years her senior. And then to leave her homeland, come to America knowing only his family, and by age seventeen have her first of six living children. She later lost a set of twins at birth. What did she have to fall back on? She did not have a mother. She did not have a grandmother. She had been sheltered from the world. (As a child, she had not even known what she looked like, because there were no mirrors in the convent. The girls went to a pond to try to see their reflections.) What she had was God, and this sustained her all her life.

Women today do not have the same agendas as our grandmothers did. My grandmother's life was about survival, about getting by and keeping it all together. She lived a life totally devoted to the family she created; it made up for the family she never had while growing up.

I will forever be amazed that someone of such humble origins could possess her knowledge and expertise. She knew all the Italian operas. She was a superb seamstress. She was an accomplished chef in the restaurant that she and my two uncles created in 1946. She had vision – her ideas, and in one case her hard work, were responsible for two successful businesses in upstate New York. She worked hard all her life, often in blatant defiance of a body that, in the end, simply wore out. Her days started at 5:00 A.M. and often ended well after midnight. I do not know how she did it, with her body in almost constant pain from arthritis and other ailments.

She used to be tall, but by the age of seventy she was barely five feet, most of it in a hump on her back. She had always been a proud woman, and this deformity embarrassed her. Once, in a corset shop, the saleswoman kept referring to "the problem" and Grandma kept apologizing, as if it were her fault that she was difficult to fit. And I? I said nothing. It was painful for me, hearing someone talk to Grandma as if she were a freak. I hope she knew I didn't think of her that way.

Whenever anyone asked her about retiring, Grandma would say, "When-a I'm-a seventy-five-a." We constantly fought with her about doing too much. Even in the end, when she became suddenly ill while working in the restaurant, she insisted on finishing the lobsters she was preparing for customers. During that night, Grandma had a stroke that would claim her two weeks later – one day past her seventy-fifth birthday. She left a void in this matriarchal family – and a legacy of love.

I think of her often. Every day, almost. Her scents were of starch and Jean Naté and vanilla and flour and bleach and cold cream. I think of her while ironing, when the hot iron sears the starch and releases that smell of freshness. I think of her when I smell fresh bread or apple pie baking in the oven, or spaghetti sauce simmering on the stovetop. I see her asleep in her chair, her hands still clutching the knitting needles or crochet hook. I'd give anything for one more trip to Louie's Silk Shop to pick out material for just one more dress; Grandma always knew which fabrics were the finest.

Whenever I hear an Italian accent, I am transported back to those wonderful, safe years of my childhood and early adulthood. I can still hear her say, "My dear, it's-a always-a darkeest before the dawn," or "You can-a do-a these-a thing." Her magical, singsong voice, the wisdom of her years, and her constant, unconditional love were the steadying forces in my life. She is always with me.

Grandma's French Pancakes (Crêpes)

When I was little and staying with her for the summer, she sometimes woke me in her Italian/Bronx accent: "Katarina, come on-a get aup. I make-a you pan-a-cakes theese-a morning. I make-a theese yust-a for you." And I'd scurry out of bed for the best pancakes ever.

I watched her pour the milk and eggs over a mound of flour and then whisk them up. She took a small, long-handled black frying pan and placed it over the gas flame. I stood beside her, just tall enough to see into the pan as the butter bubbled and sizzled. I watched her pour the thin batter, then quickly twist the pan from side to side to coat the bottom. When one side was done, she turned the pancake over to finish the other side. After she put it on my plate, I poured on lots of Log Cabin syrup. As I began eating that first pancake, I was already thinking of a second, and a third! But every time, I'd realize halfway through my second serving that my eyes had been too big for my stomach. With regular pancakes I could eat three, maybe even four. But with Grandma's pancakes, the first one filled me right up! I didn't know it then, but what my Italian grandma called "pancakes" were really French crêpes.

1 cup flour
1½ cups milk
4 eggs
¼ teaspoon salt
¼ pound (1 stick) butter

Beat the flour, milk, eggs, and salt until smooth. Cover and refrigerate the batter for at least 2 hours. Stir the batter well before you begin the pancakes.

For each pancake, melt ½ tablespoon of butter in a medium-sized shallow pan over medium heat. Stir the batter once or twice, then pour just enough batter into the pan to cover the bottom. Tilt the pan to coat it completely. Cook 2 minutes, or until the batter is set and the bottom is slightly browned. Turn the pancake over and cook about 30 seconds longer.

Grandma's French pancakes may be served with syrup, powdered sugar, or preserves. The recipe makes approximately 16 pancakes, so be sure everyone's very hungry.

Etta Berthel Bowen
1892–1975

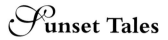unset Tales

BY SHEILA DeSHIELDS

Granny slowly eased out of her rocker, spread newspapers on the pale-yellow linoleum in her parlor, and set up her large easel. She moved haltingly, like a turtle easing along the bottom of a pond. She and I then sat on metal folding chairs in front of a tightly stretched canvas. She wanted a woman fishing. I wanted a sunset. She mixed bold reds and yellows while I stroked blacks for elms, blackjacks, and oaks. She outlined the silhouette of her woman rowing to shore. With the tip of my thick brush, I flicked reds and yellows over the tiny woman, her hat, her pole, her rowboat.

After Granny set down her palette, she moved back to her rocker and settled into it. Surrounding us, on the papered walls, were row upon row of her original oil paintings. She pointed to one. "Princess, see the woman's portrait?" she said, cocking her head to one side. "That's your great-grandmother by the Big House on our plantation. . . . I always liked the veranda there. Shady, with lots of plants to hide in. We left the plantation in a covered wagon when I was eight. Never did return to Texas."

She took my hand and placed it on her lap, a soft bulging belly. I breathed in deeply, smelling a hint of cinnamon mingled with the snuff buried in the deep pockets of her petal-thin cotton apron. Her piano-playing fingers threaded with mine, holding me to her.

Granny rocked for a while and then said, "I remember now. Mama, Papa, and I entered Oklahoma Territory for the first time on an afternoon in 1900. Wait now, let me see. . . ." Her voice drifted off. Minutes passed with only the sound of the fan humming. A window's filtered light framed her unmoving face in late-afternoon reds and golds.

Softly, she said, "It's the first time I jumped from the wagon into the ocean of prairie grasses. You remember the story, princess. Tell it to me." And she leaned back in her sea-blue cushioned rocker and closed her eyes.

I sat up tall as a persimmon shoot and closed my eyes, too. "It's 1900," I began. "I'm lost, can't find my mama. The red soil grinds under my stiff shoes. The golden grasses stretch further and further over my head. Lost, I cry out to my mother, 'Under, under!' Mother says, 'Hush! Run like a coyote, and the rip-ples of grass will help me find you.' I'm thrashing the grasses that have swallowed me. My white bon-net bounces off my head, the ties choking me like snakes. I hear a scream deep inside myself, and then outside, too. Mother's there. She crushes me to her shoulder and carries me back to the wagon. She's whispering, 'Hush now, child, hush.'"

The creaking rocker slowed, stopped. Granny's eyes opened in tiny slits. She patted my hand, then groped around in her pocket until she pulled out her silver snuffbox. "Bass are striking this time of day," she said and took a dip of snuff.

Granny's Cinnamon Dough Strips

We spent many afternoons together, my granny and I. She told me all her stories – how she lived on a plantation in Texas until the Great Galveston Flood; how she taught from the age of sixteen in one-room schools around Ada, Oklahoma; how she married at the age of twenty-eight and then, alone, raised seven children during the Depression.

When I think back on that slow-moving afternoon decades ago, I remember my grandmother's hands, her scent, her paintings. But one thing more is fresh in my mind. Before I left, she offered me some cinnamon strips. I accepted, for food was as important as stories in my grandmother's house.

I understand that women all across the country made this recipe, in one way or another, using up every scrap of leftover dough. It isn't a difficult recipe – Granny was not known for her cooking. Perhaps it was difficult for her, *though; she had diabetes and couldn't eat these sweet things herself, yet she continued to make them for everyone else.*

Leftover piecrust or
   cobbler dough
Cinnamon
Sugar

Preheat your oven to 350 degrees.

On a floured surface, roll out the dough to a thickness of ¼ inch, then cut the dough into 6 x 1-inch strips.

Place the strips on a greased cookie sheet or pie pan, then sprinkle a little cinnamon and sugar on top. Bake for about 10 minutes, or until the strips are light brown and puffy.

The Darkness Behind Her

Bella Ordansky Schneiderman
1892–1977

BY JOAN LEDERMAN

Until I saw some on a greeting card yesterday, I had forgotten that Gramma Bella had huge and droopy breasts. After all, she did nurse three daughters. I remember her earthiness, her sweat, her verbal gutsiness. I remember her kitchen and how it centered the home, before and after meals, with women working, chatting, and harboring the angst of life. And I miss everything about her but the beads of sweat on her upper lip when she kissed me.

One summer night several years after she died, I began to relive memories of her touch. I was on a Russian research vessel docked in Woods Hole, Massachusetts. Surrounded by vodka and unfiltered cigarettes, I was watching a Russian film about gypsies. In one scene, a woman approached the wound of a man with her hand trembling as if she were receiving his pain. She took the pain into her hand and flung it far from both their bodies. At that moment I remembered my gramma. Whenever I had a headache or a wound, her touch was attentive, sensing, purifying.

She was a visceral type who would not tolerate animals as pets, but would squeeze as many family members into her house as she could. She worked, hoarded, and saved. She was generous with food, with caring hospitality, and — when it came to her family — with money. (But she wouldn't let my grampa buy records; he had to sneak them into the house.) She made her wishes known, but talking back to her was allowed, even necessary.

I wonder why she wouldn't talk about her passage in steerage from Russia when she was fifteen. Her many sisters had preceded her to the United States, leaving Bella and her mother behind until they, too, left Minsk for the uncertain trip to America. I wonder why she didn't chat more casually when she showed me how to sew on buttons. She listened, but did not offer much story.

I sensed darkness behind her. Her intelligence wasn't from accumulated fact so much as from a strong sense of knowing. She was concerned with the here and now – and with saving for the future. She stored food on her body, and I remember her communicating a fear of going hungry. Her attentions focused on eating, bathing, shopping, cleaning, and bossing people around. She took tea in a glass next to a small plate with a sugar cube that she sucked; this was contemplation time. I like to think of her shoveling coal into the furnace, as I've been told she did, though I don't remember seeing it. I feel related to her when I notice how much I like to work.

The summer cottage that she and my grampa had at Rockaway Beach gave me an opportunity to live by the ocean, as I do again now. After eighteen years away from coastal living, I landed in Woods Hole, where I could anchor my senses to the familiar smells of honeysuckle, salt air, and blue snowball hydrangeas. Here I again find happiness in the water, trust in intuition, and physical robustness. The sounds of rolling waves collage into layers of association that include the rumbling sound of my gramma drowning in the fluid in her lungs. Hers was the first human death I witnessed. She was ready.

"I sensed darkness behind her. She was concerned with the here and now – and with saving for the future. She stored food on her body, and I remember her communicating a fear of going hungry."

Gramma Bella's Sweet and Sour Stuffed Cabbage

My grandmother's health problems included stomach cancer and a tricky gall bladder, so maybe her cooking is not to be emulated. But she meant well, and even allowed my father to joke about the heaviness of her food. I joked, too, saying that of all the dishes I didn't like (and the list was long), I liked this one best. Actually, with my substitutions, I now love it.

1 large head of cabbage
1 tablespoon vegetable oil
2 onions, chopped or sliced
2 (28-ounce) cans tomatoes
2 teaspoons salt
½ teaspoon pepper
1 pound lean ground beef, or tofu mixed with sunflower seeds (see note below)
1 egg
4 tablespoons onion, grated
3 tablespoons uncooked rice
3 tablespoons water
3 tablespoons honey
¼ cup lemon juice or cider vinegar
¼ cup raisins

To soften the leaves for folding, freeze a head of cabbage, then remove it from the freezer, cover it with boiling water, and let it stand for 15 minutes. Remove the leaves carefully, setting aside 12 or 18 depending on the size of the leaves and the number of servings you want.

Heat the oil in a deep, heavy pot and lightly brown the chopped onion. Add the tomatoes, then add 1 teaspoon of the salt and ¼ teaspoon of the pepper. Set this mixture aside.

Combine the beef, egg, grated onion, rice, water, and remaining salt and pepper. Spread a scoop of this mixture on the inner side of a cabbage leaf, in an oblong shape across the length of the stem. Starting with the stem-end, roll the cabbage leaf once. Fold the sides of the leaf toward the center and continue rolling. You might want to secure the leaf with a toothpick, but be careful not to lose the toothpick later in the sauce.

Gently place the cabbage rolls in the tomato sauce, cover the pot, and cook on low heat for 1 hour. Add the honey, lemon juice, and raisins, then cook for 30 minutes longer.

This recipe serves 12 as an appetizer (1 per person) or 6 as a main course (2 or 3 per person).

Note: Vegetarians can substitute 1½ pounds tofu, mixed with ¼ cup chopped or ground sunflower seeds, for the meat. Increase the rice and water to 6 tablespoons each, and reduce the first stage of cooking time to 30 minutes.

A Very Tall Lady

Lauretta Polk Baker Downing
1892–1979

BY LYDIA L. ENGLISH

I come from a long line of working women. Every day my grandmother would get up at 5:30 A.M. to prepare to go to work. After bathing, she would brush and comb her long hair until every hair was perfectly in place. She would lotion her skin from head to toe with glycerin and rose water, and put the final touches on her face with powder, rouge, and lipstick. Grandma wouldn't dream of leaving the house, for any reason, without these preparations. I loved to touch her skin; it was so soft, especially her hands with their beautiful high veins. I loved her fresh smell and her smooth style. She was soft, dignified, and fierce. Young and old loved her, and nobody I ever knew messed with her. She had a quiet way of letting people know where the boundaries were. She was very fair, but she usually got her way. My grandma was a tall woman, and she was only five feet one inch.

Grandma always dressed up to go to work: She wore beautiful hats and gloves and carried a large tapestry bag. My grandmother worked in a downtown Chicago office building of fancy women's shops. When she got to work, she would take her freshly washed and ironed uniform out of her tapestry bag and put it on. She always wore a string of real pearls and pearl earrings with her uniform. Grandma was the matron in the Women's Lounge where she emptied ashtrays, cleaned toilets, and wiped makeup off the sinks, but she was a lady first. Grandma had a cheerful smile and a kind word for everybody, and she carried out her duties with great charm.

As a child I never saw Grandma's work as menial. I was proud of who she was, and she was proud of me, too.

My grandmother taught me the first principle of self-esteem – it does not come from outside, it comes from within.

Grandma was integral to my everyday life. She lived upstairs from us on the second floor. Until I was fourteen years old, I called on my grandma every evening from 5:00 PM until 6:00 PM. She was a stickler for manners and formality. At 4:40, she came in from work. At 5:00 sharp, I would climb the stairs and knock at her door. I waited until she said "come in" before opening the door, and then I said, "Good evening, Grandma, how was your day?" She invited me to sit at the kitchen table where we would discuss our family history and the events of our days.

Over and over, I would ask my grandmother to tell me stories of my great-great-great-grandmother, who was stolen from Guinea, West Africa, when she was a little girl. I reveled in her courage and wondered how a child could possess the strength to survive both a kidnapping and a gruesome transatlantic passage. Upon arriving at the port of New Orleans, my great-great-great-grandmother was purchased by some people from Arkansas, where she bore twenty-two children as a slave breeder. She was allowed to keep only two of them, a boy and a girl. The girl, Alice, became a skilled artisan – a loomer – traveling by horseback from plantation to plantation to thread looms for making fabric. She became skilled at dodging the white patrollers ("paterollers" in slave dialect) who were deputized by local communities to curb runaways, and who might maim, rape, terrorize, or even kill her.

I never tired of these stories. They gave me strength and courage, and a profound compassion for those who struggle in their lives. My grandmother represented these women who were my ancestors. They were strong women. They were smart women. They were good women. They were beautiful women. Resilient and steadfast in the face of overwhelming odds, these women affirm in me that hope, perseverance, and determination will always carry me through. My grandma was my connection to the past and my source of hope for the future. I had always felt that Grandma was my best friend, and now I know that she was my most steadfast mentor and my tallest role model.

Grandma's Hot "Biscuits"

As I reflect on the beauty of my grandmother, I can hear her lilting whistle as she bustled around the kitchen, and I can smell the comforting aroma of her delicious hot biscuits baking on a Sunday morning. We called them "biscuits" though, strictly speaking, biscuits are made with baking powder. Since these are made with yeast, most people would call them rolls.

1 cup milk

3 tablespoons vegetable shortening

1 heaping tablespoon sugar

1 envelope (1 tablespoon) active dry yeast, dissolved in ¼ cup warm (not hot) water

1 teaspoon salt

1 egg, beaten

2 to 3 cups flour

1 tablespoon butter, melted

Scald the milk, mix in the shortening and sugar, and allow the mixture to cool. Stir in the yeast water, then add the salt and beaten egg. Stir in 2½ cups of the flour and blend well.

Set the dough aside to rise in a warm place. When the dough has doubled in size, knead in the rest of the flour, if needed.

Roll out the dough to a thickness of ½ inch. Use a cookie cutter or the mouth of a drinking glass to cut the dough into rounds. Brush each round with melted butter. Place the rounds about ½ inch apart on a cookie sheet and let them rise.

Meanwhile, preheat your oven to 400 degrees.

When the dough has doubled, bake the rounds for 20 to 25 minutes until golden brown. Serve them hot, with butter and jam. Makes a dozen biscuits.

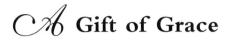

A Gift of Grace

Grace Louise Powers Bowen
1892–1979

BY DONNA LEE BOWEN McDANIEL

My father's mother adored me, her one and only grandchild. We were a good pair. She needed someone to fuss over and I needed to be fussed over. My own sweet mom cared for me too, but for most of her life she needed someone to mother her more than she needed to be a mother. Nana, whose name was Grace, was indeed the source of grace in my otherwise emotionally impoverished life.

Because of the war and other hard times, my parents often lived in the same house as my grandparents, and thankfully so, for there I could enjoy my grandmother's unconditional love. To Nana, no one in the world was smarter or more beautiful than I was. When, in my middle twenties, I wrote home from my teaching post in Japan about how beautiful the women were, Nana fired back a letter chastising me for denigrating myself by comparison.

Grace Louise herself was beautiful by everyone's account. In my most vivid picture of her, though, she is ready for bed, corset undone, silver hair loosened from Swedish-style braids, face gleaming with Pond's Cold Cream.

She was one of five strong and striking half-Swedish sisters who grew up in Chicago. None had the chance to finish high school, and all worked hard throughout their lives within their happy or not-so-happy marriages to rather thoughtless men. When my grandfather lost a prospering string of gas stations in the Depression, he and Nana moved back to his home state of Rhode Island. There she cooked, cleaned, and supervised the help in their seafood restaurant jutting out into Narragansett Bay, and in an old hulk of a hotel facing the water.

And then the war came, and both her husband and her son – her only child – went to sea. Nana said little of the agony she must have felt listening to the news day after day. I saw her cry just once, after a phone call on Christmas Eve reporting that her nephew's plane had crashed into a Japanese carrier. She hugged me in her lap while the tears streamed down her face.

Growing up, for me, was having Nana scrub me, buy me treats, and write me letters when she was away. But mostly, it was having her do what she did best – cook delicious food. She took enormous joy in taking my plate from the warmer (never a cold dish!) and turning it 'round and 'round in a dishtowel as she sought the precise place to set it down before me. In her pleasure she sounded like a hen clucking over her chick.

Through most of my years, Nana was there to cluck over me. And, in the realization of her greatest dream, she lived long enough to see me have some chicks of my own. What a joy I had in making her sweetest dream come true.

"And then the war came, and both her husband and her son – her only child – went to sea."

Nana's French Fries

On Sundays, we'd have Nana's leg of lamb. Other evenings, Nana often served quahog chowder, a common dish for us Rhode Islanders during wartime meat rationing. Best of all, though, were the French fries that Nana made in their White Nook Restaurant, located at the end of a wharf in Jamestown, Rhode Island. The wharf disappeared in the hurricane of 1938, but the White Nook's Blue Willow dishware survived in bits and pieces, worn smooth by the tides and buried in the sands of the same beach I would watch over, years later, as a lifeguard.

These fries, so hot, so thin, so crispy, were tipped out of the fryer and into a brown paper bag, one order at a time. I would beg for a fry as Nana prepared a customer's order. She often gave me more than one.

4 large Idaho potatoes
Peanut oil for deep-frying
Salt

Cut the potatoes lengthwise into long strips about ⅜ inch thick. Rinse the strips in cold water, let them sit for about 10 minutes, then dry them thoroughly in cloth towels.

In a deep-fat fryer or heavy pan, heat the oil to 365 degrees. Place the fries in the oil, one layer at a time. Don't crowd them. You may need to cook them in two batches.

Fry the potatoes until they are tender and golden brown, perhaps 15 or 20 minutes.

Remove the fries from the oil and place them in a brown paper bag. Salt them to your liking, then shake the bag until the oil is on the bag instead of the fries. Release the fries only when the bag is translucent. (If a second batch is cooking, keep the first batch warm in a 200-degree oven.)

Don't fail to cluck over any chicks – young or old – who are lucky enough to eat these with you. Serves 6 to 8 people.

Strong Hands, Warm Heart

Aniela Pitenska Konior
1893–1995

BY DIANALEE VELIE

When I recall the sweet, warm aroma that filled the house as I was growing up, I am reminded of my grandmother and her large, strong, able hands. Strong, patient hands that cooked and cleaned and loved and lasted and told us our own hands could tackle any job from baking bread to building bridges. When my hands are strong and busy and my heart is light, I know my grandmother, Babci, is with me. She has taught me, with her own calm strength, not to fear the unknown. I see her hands guiding me always along the rails of life's bridges, bridges I can build and cross. I know my own hands inherit that intensity. I know I can do.

We grew up on the babkas that Babci made in Brooklyn. Babkas, fresh from the oven, were eaten with gusto. We toasted stale slices and spread them with jam. Slices that were too stale became bread crumbs for cooking. Any leftovers we gave quickly to the birds. My memory flies, like those birds, to a fire escape in Brooklyn and to the babka crumbs I held out in my hands as a toddler. Now, in the woods of my Connecticut backyard, both the babkas and the birds have followed me, securing a tender place in my heart. My soul fills with love for Babci as I replenish my bird feeders and scatter my own babka crumbs on the ground.

Without ever trying, Babci taught us to make babkas. My mom and I learned by watching and helping her, then one day making babkas on our own. I can't help but wonder who taught Babci to cook, as I can't help but wonder who taught her to love. I am sure neither came easily.

When her mother died in Poland, her father married a woman with daughters of her own. Unwanted and alone at age eight, little Aniela was put on a ship to America. Her final destination was a city of unknowns, an uncle and aunt she

AT GRANDMOTHER'S TABLE • 171

had never met. Good-byes, I am sure, were in her heart. Good-byes to the farm she loved and the horse she thought was her own.

In Massachusetts, at work in a garment factory, her hands learned to use needle and thread. Did she go home after work to help cook the meals? Is it there that she learned to knead those babkas, or did she recall the recipe with an ache in her heart for her missing mother? Is there a cookbook written on the soul? Did they love her dearly here in America, or tolerate her as a family burden? Whenever I tried diplomatically to ask that question, she only shrugged and said with a smile and a tear, "Life is beautiful when you are busy being."

At fourteen she met my grandfather and started to sew her own wedding gown. At sixteen she married him and my family was founded and headed for Brooklyn. I look at the timid smile on her face in her wedding photograph and it is not the strong, self-assured smile I saw at the end of her long life. But her hands were the same. They were the hands of a doer. They were the strong and capable hands that my mother, daughter, and I possess. We are doers. We can do! We know how to make Babci's babkas, and we know we can do whatever else life calls upon us to do. At one hundred and two years old, my Babci continued to restore my soul. I was still her Dinusha. (This diminutive Polish nickname some-how made me feel taller.) My strong hands assured Babci that her babkas were here to stay. Both the hands and the babkas are a gift, a legacy, of simple strength.

Babci's Babkas

When that sweet, warm aroma fills my own kitchen, everyone knows that Polish bread is in the oven. Babkas are crusty on the outside and dense on the inside. They can be served with breakfast, lunch, or dinner. Better yet, this same recipe can be rolled thin, filled with poppy seed or prune filling, then popped back in the oven for a sumptuous dessert. (Babci made her own filling; I use canned.) See which flavor you like best, and remember to save the last precious crumbs for the birds.

1 quart whole milk

½ pound (2 sticks) butter, softened

1 cup sugar

2 envelopes (1 tablespoon each) active dry yeast, dissolved in ¼ cup warm (not hot) water with 1 tablespoon sugar

1 pound raisins

1½ tablespoons salt

5 eggs

12 to 14 cups flour (about 3½ pounds)

1 tablespoon milk

Scald the milk and remove it from the heat. When the milk is lukewarm, add the butter and allow it to melt. Then, slowly stir in the sugar. While this mixture is still lukewarm, add the yeast water, the raisins, and the salt. Move the mixture to a very large bowl.

Beat 4 of the eggs and stir them in slowly, alternating with the flour.

Knead the dough until it comes away from the sides of the bowl. Then, cover the bowl and let the dough rise until it has doubled.

Punch down the dough and put it into 6 small loaf pans (or place 4 large lumps on cookie sheets). Let the dough rise again until doubled.

Preheat your oven to 400 degrees.

Brush the tops of the babkas with a mixture of 1 egg and 1 tablespoon milk. Bake for 10 minutes, then lower the oven to 350 degrees and bake for 30 minutes more. Think of the strong hands that made this as you enjoy it. Makes 6 small loaves or 4 large rounds.

Note: Much depends on the weather. Make sure the dough rises in a place free of drafts; on days that are cold, rainy, or damp, allow more time for the dough to rise.

The Stranger I Loved

BY KATHERINE KOMNINOS WILDER

She will always be a mystery to me, my Grandmother Komninos.

I do not know her first name. In fact, I know her only through one of my father's precious few photographs from "the old country," as he called his native Greece. Was she stern like her pose, or lighthearted and fun-loving like my father? This woman with the huge, black eyes, this clear-featured woman whose face speaks of experiences I'll never know about, has had a profound effect on me.

As a child I used to stare at her image, seeing so much of my father in it, longing to hear the tone of her voice, to know if she ever sang when she worked in her whitewashed home in Piraeus, the port of Athens, the way my father sang in the kitchen of his New England restaurant halfway across the world. She saw pictures of me, too, in my father's letters to her. What did she think of her strawberry-blonde American granddaughter, named after her own precious raven-haired girl, Katina? There was never a chance to find out, because sometime during World War II, when I was still a toddler, her letters stopped coming.

I'm glad she didn't live long enough to know that her son, a teenage merchant seaman who jumped ship in America to look for gold in the streets, would die at forty-three. But I wish she had known that he lived to realize many of his youthful dreams. My father always wore a white carnation in her memory, but spoke little of her except to tell me how she sold her silver to send him to school. Later, I understood why he was unable to talk about her. When I was of an age to comprehend, my mother told me how Grandmother died: she starved to death during the Nazi embargo of Greece, along with her husband and hundreds of thousands of their countrymen. At least Grandmother didn't have to witness her daughter's grief for the twelve-year-old son who would years later step on a long-forgotten land mine.

Although I never met her, I know a few things about Grandmother Komninos. She was of tough stock. She survived the Turkish takeover of Smyrna and, with husband and children, made her way to the other side of the Aegean to safety. She raised three children: John, who was so tall and handsome he became a King's guard; Charles, my dad, who dared to adventure the seas and the New World; and Katina, dark-eyed and elegant, after whom I am named.

I am probably older now than my grandmother was when she died, and, as I age, I look often at her photograph. I have come to recognize a quiet joy in her eyes and am willing to bet that, in spite of the hardships she knew, this stranger who was my grandmother was fully able to dance in the moment and laugh generously with the spirit of life.

Grandmother Komninos's Green Beans Halki Style (*Fresca Fasolia me Lathe*)

Grandmother Komninos must have been a good cook. After all, her son was known through-out New England for his culinary arts, and he must surely have come by some of his talent through her. In daydreams I picture her patiently pressing out her own phyllo — paper-thin and delicate — and, like my father, seasoning each dish according to aroma, never needing to taste.

2 pounds whole string beans, fresh or frozen
½ cup water
2 medium onions, chopped
¼ cup extra virgin olive oil
2 (14½-ounce) cans diced tomatoes (about 4 cups)
3 tablespoons fresh parsley, finely chopped
Salt and freshly ground pepper
Pinch of cinnamon

Steam the beans in the water until they are tender but still crisp. Drain off the water and set the beans aside.

Sauté the onions in olive oil until they are translucent. Add the tomatoes, parsley, salt, pepper, and cinnamon. When this is hot, add the beans, cover, and remove from heat. Serve the beans hot. This makes an excellent side dish for 8 people.

Grandmother Komninos's Baked Rice Greek Style (*Pilaffe tou Fournou*)

Today, I have my own version of the Komninos recipes. I refer to them as "Americanized Greek cooking" because I use less oil and must find substitutes for some of the ingredients. Still, whenever I cook "old country," the heady tang of chicken avgolemono or the tongue-tickling sweetness of baklava brings me to the kitchen I was never privileged to visit. There I stand right next to my strong and handsome Grandmother Komninos, helping her ready the table for the return of her beloved family — and mine.

2 (10-ounce) cans beef consommé, chicken stock, or vegetable stock
1½ cups water
12 whole cherry tomatoes or 4 plum tomatoes, quartered
¼ cup extra virgin olive oil
½ teaspoon dried oregano
1 teaspoon garlic powder
1 medium onion, diced
4 garlic cloves, minced
2 cups uncooked long-grain rice

Heat the consommé and the water in a large pot.

Dip the tomatoes in olive oil and sprinkle them with oregano and garlic powder; set the tomatoes aside.

In a large skillet, sauté the onion and garlic in the remaining olive oil until they are translucent. Add the rice, stirring often. Cook until the rice is golden.

Pour the rice mixture into the heating liquid. Bring it to a boil, cover, reduce the heat, and simmer for 15 minutes.

When the rice is cooked, remove it to a large baking pan. Top with the tomatoes and bake at 375 degrees for 30 minutes, or until the tomatoes wrinkle. Serves 8 to 10 people as a side dish.

Grandmother Komninos's Baked Meatballs (*Keftedes sto Fournou*)

Because I watched my father cook up so many wonders in his restaurant kitchen, it's not hard for me to imagine my Grandmother Komninos doing the same in her own kitchen all those years ago. They say that of all the senses, smell is the most powerful. If that is true, I have been present in my grandmother's kitchen many times through the aroma of this recipe, even though I have never physically been there at all.

The Meatballs

1 medium onion, diced
2 garlic cloves, minced
2 tablespoons extra virgin
    olive oil
1 pound lean ground beef
½ cup dried bread crumbs
1 egg, beaten
2 tablespoons dried mint leaf
Salt and pepper
Juice of 1 lemon

The Sauce

2 tablespoons extra virgin
    olive oil
½ to 1 small onion, minced
2 garlic cloves, minced
1 celery stalk, chopped
1 (32-ounce) can crushed
    tomatoes
1 teaspoon dried oregano
1 small bay leaf
Pinch of cinnamon
Salt and pepper
1 tablespoon margarine

To make the meatballs, sauté the onion and garlic in the oil until they are translucent. Stir in the ground beef, bread crumbs, egg, mint, salt, and pepper.

Form the meat mixture into balls about 1½ inches in diameter (the size of golf balls). Place the meatballs on cookie sheets and bake for 20 minutes in a 350-degree oven. Turn them over and bake for another 20 minutes, or until they are brown.

Meanwhile, make the sauce. In a large pot, heat the olive oil and sauté the onion, garlic, and celery for 3 to 5 minutes. Add the tomatoes, oregano, bay leaf, cinnamon, salt, and pepper. (Do not overseason the sauce – it should be smooth and mild.) Cover the sauce and bring it to a boil. Reduce the heat and allow the sauce to simmer while the meatballs are baking.

When the meatballs are done, remove them from the oven and drain off any fat. Squeeze the lemon juice over the meatballs and let them sit for 15 minutes.

Remove the bay leaf from the sauce and add the meatballs. Stir in the margarine. (Do not use butter.) Serve hot as either an appetizer or main dish. These meatballs make great leftovers, too. Makes 4 to 8 servings.

Note: When making the sauce, you may wish to replace the onion, garlic, and celery with ¼ teaspoon onion powder, ¼ teaspoon garlic powder, and 1 teaspoon celery powder.

Just the Two of Us, Spirits Together

Pauline Oldham Harrison Lange
1895–1960

BY PAULA E. KAUTZ-LAPORTE

I fell in love with my grandmother at the age of four. She picked me up in her shiny green 1951 Ford and drove away. The tears flowed until she stopped and treated me to a chocolate ice-cream cone. Grandma's mission was one of mercy, but I didn't understand. Sure, Mom was about to have a baby – she had three of us already – so what was the problem? There was no problem. It was the beginning of the most wonderful time of my life.

Grandma's house was tantalizing with its baby grand piano (which Grandpa played each evening), its sun-drenched breakfast nook, and Great-Grandma's quiet little bedroom and bath behind the kitchen. Even the upstairs bedrooms were special. One had a small balcony, another had its own hallway, and Grandma's had its own spacious bathroom. The attic and cellar were spooky, both of them large and dark with mysterious corners and closets. Why, Uncle Fred's duckling tumbled behind a huge chest in the cellar and disappeared forever.

For a month I explored, and hid, and giggled, and ate Franco-American canned spaghetti for lunch. It was heaven on earth, and I was the angel. Even when I went to kindergarten with a neighbor and had a delightful time finger painting while my grandparents searched frantically for me, I still had wings when I bounced off the school bus.

Grandma was my sunshine. She warmed my soul and brightened every day. She used to stick out her tongue to tease me, and I would always smile.

I was eight years old when my mother told me that Grandma had died. I didn't see her when she was sick; I didn't go to the hospital where she lay in a coma, afflicted with brain tumors; I didn't go to her funeral. I wish I had seen her through all of it.

In my childhood dreams I continued to have precious visits with my grandmother. We would hang out together in her secret room, her bathroom transformed. Just the two of us, spirits together. Sometimes other relatives (Grandma had six children) would be outside, but we never appeared to them. We hovered about the upper walls of the brick house and watched them.

As a young woman my dreams changed. One dream took place in the hospital. I stood in a long corridor: walls and doors, that's all there was. Down at the far end Grandma called to me. I went to her room and looked in. From her bed she said, "It's okay, it's me. I'm dead." Another dream took place at the little house I was then renting. I was standing on the front stoop when Grandpa and Grandma drove up in the green Ford. They stopped, and Grandma looked at me with her laughing, dimpled smile. We both knew she was dead, but she had come to visit me. The emotions were overwhelming. Sobs of joy and sobs of sorrow.

I wish Grandma had had an equally wonderful relationship with her own grandmother, but she didn't know her. My grandmother was the love child of two domestic employees of Mr. and Mrs. Edgar Levy. (Mr. Levy was comptroller of New York City at the time.) Mrs. Levy's mother, a Mrs. Harrison of Tennessee, lived with the childless couple and adopted the baby. Pauline was very fond of "Uncle Edgar," and he in turn gave her love, a comfortable life, and an excellent education. Nevertheless, she carried with her all her life the stigma of having been adopted and the embarrassment of knowing she was "illegitimate."

At the age of thirty, Pauline resigned from her job as a Wall Street secretary to marry Fred Lange and start a family. As Grandpa said, they both knew what they wanted and they wanted the same thing. They must have had a happy home – full of family, friends, and music.

When I was thirty-three and expecting my first child, I wanted the child's middle name to be Sunshine. When I finally realized that Grandma was my sunshine, my daughter's middle name became Pauline.

Grandma's Pineapple Upside-Down Cake

Pauline never cooked a great deal. She grew up in a home where the cooking was done by domestic employees, and when she was a mother of six, her mother-in-law cooked for the family. Pineapple upside-down cake, however, was one of Grandma's weaknesses, and so she made it often. Just as her dimples were passed on to my mother and then to me, Grandma's upside-down cake has been handed down through the generations. I recall bubbling the butter and brown sugar when I was ten. As a child of modern conveniences, I used a yellow cake mix. (Today, if I'm pressed for time, I still use one.) Grandma and Mom used a simple one-egg cake recipe.

The Topping

1 (20-ounce) can sliced
   pineapple, packed in juice
¼ pound (1 stick) butter
1 cup packed brown sugar
1 (6-ounce) jar maraschino
   cherries

The Batter

1 box yellow cake mix

OR

1 egg, beaten
6 tablespoons butter, softened
1¼ cups sugar
1 teaspoon vanilla extract
1¾ cups flour, sifted
2½ teaspoons double-
   acting baking powder
1 teaspoon salt
1 cup pineapple juice or milk

To make the topping: drain the pineapple juice from the pineapple slices, setting both of these aside.

Melt the butter in a good-sized, well-oiled (or nonstick) ovenproof skillet. Add the brown sugar, cooking slowly and stirring constantly until the sugar is dissolved and the mixture is bubbly. Remove the pan from the heat. Place one slice of pineapple over the sugar in the center, then arrange a large circle of slices around it. Place a maraschino cherry in the hole of each slice.

To make the batter: preheat your oven to 350 degrees.

Prepare a yellow cake mix according to the directions on the box, but substitute pineapple juice for the water or milk. (If you are making the batter from scratch, cream the egg with the butter, sugar, and vanilla, and set this aside. In a separate bowl, combine the flour with the baking powder and salt. Alternately add the pineapple juice and the dry ingredients to the creamed mixture. Beat for about 2 minutes.)

Pour the batter over the fruit in the skillet. Be careful not to fill the skillet more than two-thirds full, or the cake may spill over the sides as it rises.

Bake the cake for 30 minutes, or until the cake shrinks from the edges and is firm in the center. Remove the skillet from the oven, place a serving plate on top, hold on tightly, and quickly turn the skillet and plate over. Leave the skillet over the cake for 5 minutes to let the topping coat the cake. Serve warm or save for later.

Adele Margaret Blow Chatfield-Taylor
1895–1977

 World Opens Up

BY ADELE CHATFIELD-TAYLOR

My parents were quite sure their second child would be a boy, so when I was born and turned out to be another daughter, they were unprepared. Their first-born had been named after my mother's side of the family, so for me they looked to my father's forebears. At first, the story goes, they asked my paternal grand-mother if they might call me "Adele," after her. She said no. When they considered "Adelaide," after her estranged sister-in-law, Grandmother capitulated. I became Adele, and we became linked for life.

She had sixteen grandchildren (eight of them granddaughters), very seldom assembled at the same time. With several she had special relationships, and ours was about art. She called each one of us darling, as she did almost everyone else, but when she and I were having an extra nice time, she called me lamb, or occasionally lamb-pie.

When I spent time with her it was usually just the two of us, which for me (one of six siblings) seemed eerily quiet and intoxicating. She could draw and paint watercolors, she wrote many letters each day, and she seemed to keep up with concerts and exhibitions around the world. (When she was older, she always went away for the winter, with or without my grandfather.) She read and looked around constantly, usually at paintings or furniture or buildings. Besides our name, we had one huge thing in common: a love of architecture, especially old houses. She spent much of her time rebuilding and restoring historic houses. I drank it in.

I grew up in Virginia, and she was a Virginian, too, the descendant of a family that settled there in 1609. But she had grown up in Illinois (in La Salle and Chicago) and in Europe, and was completely different from anyone I had ever known before, or have ever known since. Her manner was dear but rather grand.

By the time I came around she was a tall, matronly version of the beautiful, out-doorsy blonde she had been as a bride. In my day, she was dressed either in lavender taffeta or a gray tweed suit. She had that generational accent that has since disappeared from the world, except in certain old movies. Her voice was high-pitched and formal, and what she said was formal, too; in a word, she was old-fashioned. But everyone I knew then was old-fashioned, so it was more than that. To me, she seemed slightly foreign. I was fascinated by her.

Later, when I was older and living in New York City, she would come to town and stay at the Cosmopolitan Club. She would get me a room there, too, thereby finessing the questions of exactly where I lived, exactly who I lived with, whether or not I had curtains – and how she could avoid expressing her opinion about any of these things. She never asked me whether I *wanted* to move across town for the weekend but simply informed me of the arrangements she had made, and I stepped out of my life and back into hers. Her world seemed quite unreal to me by that point, but still enchanting. We visited every museum, shopped on Fifth Avenue, and went to the theater twice a day to see the likes of *La Plume de Ma Tante* or *Nude with Violin*. Looking back, I find this arrangement inspired. It was the sixties, and she knew I might just have spent the night in jail for political protesting. Our activities kept us occupied. Anything more confrontational would have meant certain anguish for one or both of us.

"A sunbeam passed through the little garnet-colored globe and, piercing the crystal, made it fiery red and alive, revealing specks of dust churning lazily in the air around it."

She was a connoisseur of food. Not that she cooked. She rarely entered the kitchen with an apron on, but she planned all the menus, did all the "marketing" (as she called it), and oversaw every detail.

Her diaries shed light on her domestic affairs and her dealings with food. I inherited ten years of these volumes, each bound in soft, dark leather and mono-grammed with a gold AC-T in the lower right-hand corner. Every day she wrote a few lines about the weather, the health of the household, any travels, and news from those who dropped in or called. She systematically recorded every detail of her entertaining, too – the date, who came to the party, where they sat, and what she served.

In her earlier diaries, she and Grandfather were just moving to Washington, eventually to a lovely house at 22nd and S Streets, NW, at the top of Decatur Place. (This was the first roof over my head. I was born in the last days of World War II, and my mother and I spent a lot of time with my grandparents while my father was away in the Coast Guard.) The New Deal was in full swing, and my grandparents were both involved in public life – Grandfather having shocked his conservative Lake Forest friends by accepting a deputy cabinet post from President Roosevelt, and Grandmother cofounding and helping to steer the National Women's Democratic Club. In Washington, a great deal happened over dinner, and because Grandmother had style, I suspect that an invitation to dine at their house was not a bad thing.

My earliest memory of color was in that house. A red crystal paperweight lay on my grandmother's desk. It was part of a magical transformation that occurred every morning when a sunbeam passed through the little garnet-colored globe and, piercing the crystal, made it fiery red and alive, revealing specks of dust churning lazily in the air around it. (Only later, when I visited Stonehenge, did I again see an equivalent alignment of light and the elements.) The sunbeam then passed on; the specks and the fiery red vanished and the paperweight became a garnet lump again. It happened silently and inevitably every morning, in the days before I could talk. Grandmother watched me watching it, while she watched it, too. I have always thought that this was her way of welcoming me into the world as a kindred spirit. And what a world! For me, in that cozy, silent upstairs room, with curtains and thick rugs, a ticking clock, and Grandmother nearby working on her letters and books, it was the birth of color and magic and art.

Grandmother's Thursday Night Soup

By the time I began to pay attention, meals had become a formal routine only on special occasions. I'd visit Grandmother on Nantucket during the summers, when she was down to a staff of one, Ethel. On most days the household stuck to a simple cycle. After break-fast, Grandfather packed up his easel and paintbox, and drove out to the moors to spend the day painting Poot's Pond over and over again. Grandmother walked her corgi, Stranger, to Charlie's on Main Street to do a little shopping, and any grandchildren in res-idence took off for the water or for work. Lunch varied, but dinner was usually at home, for no more than four people, served in the dining room as the sun sank in a luminous summer sky and as the centerpiece — a pitcher of zinnias or limp white roses — went from a blazing intensity to a dusky glow.

If you stayed through a Thursday evening, when Ethel was off, whatever you'd had for dinner during the week would make another appearance, whether it was lamb chops, lima beans, bluefish, or corn on the cob. Delicious the first time around, these leftovers could hit any extreme the second time. Invariably, everything went into a soup and, admirably, the logic of whether it all went together never entered Grandmother's mind. Her soup du jour was a wholly artistic enterprise.

Cooked leftovers: red (such as beets, tomatoes, or cherries); white (such as chicken, potatoes, or coconut); or green (such as spinach, peas, or broccoli)

1 (10-ounce) can cream of celery or cream of mushroom soup

Salt

Curry powder

Dry sherry

Hard-boiled egg yolk

1. Open the refrigerator door.

2. Remove anything that is red, white, or green.

3. Place the contents of one can of cream of celery or cream of mushroom soup (Grandmother used only S.S. Pierce) in the top of a double boiler, remembering to put water in the bottom. Add a can of milk or water, if you like. Turn the burner on, and slowly stir the soup until it is hot.

4. When the soup is bubbling, add either the red, white, or green leftovers.

5. Consider adding all three.

6. Season with salt, curry powder, and dry sherry.

7. Garnish with crumbled hard-boiled egg yolk.

8. Serve to grandchildren, any number. Proclaim delicious.

The Woman Who Loved Ships

Em Turner Merritt Nickinson
1896–1973

BY EM TURNER

She was the real thing: a Southern gentlewoman with a French twist in her white hair and a passion for elegant clothes. But my grandmother was something more – she was also a ship's agent and head of a stevedoring company, a businesswoman directing the off- and on-loading of cargoes. She was a legend on the docks of Pensacola, Florida, for her mastery of profanity. But she also loved a good drink, her twelve grandchildren, her cook, the memory of her naval-officer husband, pretty shoes, and ships.

Children find it easy to synthesize all contradictions into a single image or experience. It is as adults that we later try to make sense of the individuals, try to find out what drove them. I have spent many years trying to understand my grandmother, and I know that I will never quite get there. The feeling I have for her is a blend of awe, respect, fear, envy – and, yes, love. If there is an afterlife, I'm putting in my request now for a long chat, because I want to know more than I learned in the eighteen years we walked the same earth.

We called her the Poor Old Lady (our first lesson in irony), which soon became "Poyady." The name originated when my oldest brother, Ben, asked her to dance with him one night after she had been on the docks all day. He was about five at the time. Poyady replied, "Oh darling, I can't. I'm nothing but a poor old lady." Falser words were never spoken.

Her passion for the sea was natural. Shipbuilders named Merritt had lived in Scituate, Massachusetts, for nearly two centuries before one came south in the 1820s to New Orleans and then to Pensacola. He never went back. His descendants continued to make their living from the sea as ship brokers. My grandmother's father followed the tradition, running a shipping agency in partnership with his brother-in-law. The stevedoring business started as a sideline but soon became the moneymaker.

Poyady went to work in the family business as a stenographer during World War I so that she wouldn't have to spend the war knitting socks. On the death of her father and his brother-in-law, her mother gave Poyady effective control of the company in 1945, saying "Em's the one with the brains." Em proceeded to run the business until 1971, two years before her death. She had the big office at the back of the Merritt and Company Ship Agents building on Palafox Street, the big boulevard leading to Pensacola's port. Smoking Kools, she would sit behind the enormous mahogany desk, with nautical maps on every wall of the room, plotting and planning how to load cargoes bound for the Philippines or Brazil.

I never knew her to cook so much as an egg. For all the housewifely arts she depended on her friend, cook, and housekeeper, Margaret Sims, who kept Poyady and her family fed, clean, organized, and on time for forty-two years. A rail-thin black woman who wore a tired gingham dress, apron, and slippers in the house, Margaret did her job in her own way and on her own terms. She would not under any circumstances cross the long bridges between Pensacola and Pensacola Beach, where my grandmother had a beach house so that her grandchildren would come for long visits. I remember many times taking trays of Margaret's biscuits, neatly cut out and ready to bake, and packing them into my grandmother's blue Nova convertible. Big bowls of *gaspache* sat on our laps. Margaret stayed at home to preside over the town house, a small bungalow that my grandmother and grandfather had built on East Pensacola Bay in 1925.

At the beach we'd pile out, unload the car, and then the grandchildren would disappear to the water, where we splashed and played until Poyady appeared with the other grownups. Floating barrel-shaped in her flowery green bathing suit, she was hard to picture as the elegant dresser, or the hard-bitten businesswoman, or the proud grandmother who gathered us around her like petals in a black-eyed Susan.

My grandmother was far more complex than I understood at the time, and some of her is still a complete mystery to me. A member of one of Pensacola's old and distinguished families, she was entitled to join the Daughters of the American Revolution and the United Daughters of the Confederacy, but she never did. Directing the dockworkers – mostly black men – as they loaded and unloaded ships, she didn't have time for such nonsense. As the wife of the commander of the Naval Air Station during World War II, she lived at the Naval Air Station. Neighbor ladies could not understand why she motored off every morning to work. The opinion of her neighbors, however, never bothered her.

> **"Floating barrel-shaped in her flowery green bathing suit, she was hard to picture as the elegant dresser, or the hard-bitten businesswoman, or the proud grandmother who gathered us around her like petals in a black-eyed Susan."**

She was not just a businesswoman, though. My grandmother gave her lunch hours to the Red Cross, the USO, and the League of Women Voters. She felt a strong sense of responsibility toward the black longshoremen of Pensacola. But she was no idealist. She once told me she had no use for women's liberation: she had never needed it, she said. What she meant was that hard work and determination had gotten her where she was and would serve as well for other women. Perhaps partly as a result of this feeling about self-reliance, she voted staunchly Republican in national elections in her later years. But she was a registered Democrat so she could vote in local elections. Another contradiction? Not entirely. The South had virtually no Republican candidates at the time, because of its long-lasting grudge against Lincoln. Poyady understood the complexities of life.

Was she a woman of conscience? Yes, on personal and civic levels. But she was a creature of her time and place. She would not have felt comfortable dining with a black person. Yet when Pensacola's lunch counters were opened to black customers during the civil rights movement, it was partly due to her intervention with other businesspeople, as her daughter, another Em Turner, recalled. When she died, black as well as white workingmen gathered around her closed coffin, rugged men in working clothes surreptitiously wiping their eyes. I can still see it because I hadn't expected it; this part of her life was something the grandchildren had known little about.

The relationship between Margaret and my grandmother was certainly one of respect and, there is good reason to believe, of deep affection. They were two very strong-willed women, and they disagreed often, but our grandmother's commitment to Margaret was unquestioned. How did Margaret feel toward Poyady? I would not presume to guess; it would be impertinent – not to mention impossible. But she died only a few months after Poyady did.

Was my grandmother a tender woman? Not to me. When she died, I was still going through an awkward and unattractive adolescence. She wasn't impressed and she let me know it. But we did have one conversation that I remember with gratitude. The summer before she died, I told her I was tired of having to explain my name. "Just wait," she said. "When you're about thirty, people will start trying to explain it to you." And they did.

When I was divorced a dozen years ago and had to choose a new name, a new identity, I couldn't see myself inventing a totally new name (Rosie Fields?) or going back to my father's surname (Chitty – a name rich in history but tiresome to have to spell constantly). I kept finding myself at the name I shared with Poyady, with my aunt, and with my great-aunt (the one who was still climbing on her roof to repair it at eighty-five years old – but that's another story). I kept finding myself at Em Turner, my original first and middle names. By choosing to keep her name as my own in full, I am not celebrating the parts of her I cannot share – the old-South parts – I am celebrating the brave, pragmatic iconoclast that she was. When we have that talk, I hope she gets the compliment.

Our Family's Bread Salad *(Gaspache)*

My grandparents hired Margaret Sims early in their marriage, and I associate many unique tastes, most notably the one that follows, with her capable, long-fingered hands. Margaret used to say that she had never been ashamed of any of her children, either her African-American children, all adopted, or the white children she raised in our family.

Pensacola, called the City of Five Flags, has an ancient Spanish heritage and, of course, a long association with the sea. Although it shares some elements of its culture, such as Mardi Gras, with New Orleans, Pensacola has its own traditions. One of the most particular ones is gaspache *(not* gazpacho, *the soup, which is a New Orleans dish).*

Gaspache has a close analogue in Italian cookery. Except for the use of mayonnaise instead of olive oil, gaspache *is essentially the same as the Italian bread salad* panzanella. *Gaspache, however, uses an ingredient difficult to find outside of Pensacola: ship's hardtack, a rock-hard, twice-baked bread. (Stale Italian bread may be substituted, but be sure to use a coarse, airy bread, not a fine-grained one.) This recipe is adapted from our family recipe, used by Margaret and included in the* North Hill Cookbook *(North Hill Preservation Association of Pensacola, Florida, 1981).*

6 hardtack loaves
   (or 1 stale Italian loaf)
Mayonnaise thinned with oil,
   water, or vinegar
6 firm, ripe tomatoes, thinly
   sliced
2 to 3 cucumbers, peeled and
   thinly sliced
Salt
1 green pepper, sliced
1 mild onion, thinly sliced

If you are using hardtack loaves, soak them in cold water until thoroughly soft (about 2 hours), then squeeze the water out of the bread with a cloth or with your hands. If you are using Italian bread, do not soak; simply cut it up and proceed to the next step.

In a large serving bowl, arrange a thin layer of bread, followed by layers of mayonnaise, tomatoes, and cucumbers. Sprinkle a little salt over each layer. Continue layering the ingredients until the bowl is full. Garnish with sliced green pepper and thin slices of mild onion. Chill thoroughly before serving. This recipe serves 6 to 8 people.

Note: Homemade mayonnaise adds a special touch to this wonderful recipe.

A Stitch in Time

BY COLLEEN J. MILLER

This morning, as I smoothed the thick, green flannel sheets on our bed, I remembered lying in a small narrow bed at my grandmother's, fingering her soft, much-washed flannel sheets, getting cozy under the blankets, and talking to her as I drifted off to sleep.

All through my childhood, I had a bag packed and ready to go to my grandmother's apartment across town in Burlington, Vermont. I loved being with her. She treated me like an individual, told me I was beautiful, and showed me off to her friends. Once a year, she and I would board the bus from Burlington to visit her hometown of Montreal.

We always had an adventure in Montreal. My mother was horrified to learn that on one trip I toured a working crematorium and received a lovely collection of funeral ribbons. Another time we saw Kateri Tekakwitha's bones in a glass box. She was on her way to becoming a saint, but I didn't think she would have liked her bones in a box, with blue ribbons tied on them. And I didn't understand why they had Brother André's heart in a jar. I saw lots of interesting things with my grandmother.

Montreal was my grandmother's city. She was the youngest daughter of a Swedish family who had immigrated to Montreal on a boat from Riga, Latvia. Her parents, Pauline and Johan, had met another family on the boat – the Johnsons – who settled in Barre, Vermont. My grandmother was sent to Vermont to spend summers on the Johnsons' farm, and there she fell in love with the youngest son, Victor, a tall, handsome Swede.

She spent the war years in Montreal. In 1914, she saw 4,000 troops of the Black Watch Regiment as they marched to bagpipes into troop transports, and she was there when the 180 survivors returned. She cried, fifty years later, telling me about their return.

She married Victor after he returned from the war. Unfortunately, his lungs had been damaged when he was gassed in the trenches of the Ardennes. He died in 1930 of lung disease, leaving her with a small son at the start of a worldwide depression. Looking back at her life, I remember a strong, hard-working woman who was careful not to waste anything. In her later years she enjoyed the butter and sugar she had missed through the Depression and during wartime rationing, but she never seemed concerned with material items. She didn't mind a chip in a mug as long as the cup of tea was strong.

When I got old enough, I would go alone to visit her. I would get off the bus by Greenblott's Market and walk down the block to her apartment, my small suitcase bumping against my leg. I would drag the suitcase up the slanted steps to her apartment, excited to be visiting. It was a small apartment, just four rooms. The square kitchen held her pride and joy, a black Singer sewing machine with gold letters that sparkled in the sunlight. The kitchen table and chairs were black with gold stencils, as if to match the sewing machine. Over the years, I spent hours sitting beside her, my legs wrapped around the rungs of my stool as she patiently showed me how to run that machine. I would study her – gray hair bound in an invisible web of netting, old-fashioned hairpins, gray stockings, serviceable black shoes, elbow skin that was so soft to touch, as soft as the flannel she used to make me a nightgown. She taught me how to make a potholder, an apron; eventually I graduated to making clothes.

Her favorite expression still echoes in my ear: "Use up, wear out, make do, or do without." Old flannel was used for the lining of potholders. Scraps of every material were sewn into quilts for her grandchildren. Years later, we would spread our quilts out and look delightedly for pieces from the dresses, night-gowns, and doll clothes that she had made, once upon a time, for each of us. Her life shines through in those quilts – her ability to use every last scrap, and to give from a love that never ran out.

My Grandmother's Rice Pudding

My grandmother couldn't cook; my father thought that military food was good compared with hers. She would put meat and vegetables in a pressure cooker, cook it a while, then serve it. Before she died she gave me her pressure cooker. It sits in my cupboard to this day, still wrapped and tied with a string. I think of her whenever I open that door. I've never used the thing — never understood how to use it — but I miss that bland mixture of carrots, potatoes, and lamb.

Just as she wasted nothing when she sewed, she wasted nothing when she cooked. She used leftover rice to make the best rice pudding, plump with raisins. I serve it to this day.

2 eggs

½ cup sugar

¼ teaspoon salt

2 cups whole milk

1 teaspoon vanilla extract

2 cups cooked rice

Raisins

1 teaspoon nutmeg

Preheat your oven to 350 degrees.

Beat together the eggs, sugar, and salt. Scald the milk, then add it to the egg mixture. Add the vanilla, rice, and a handful of raisins.

Pour the pudding into a shallow 1-quart casserole dish and sprinkle nutmeg on top. Set the uncovered dish into a pan containing an inch of water.

Bake until the top of the pudding is slightly brown (about 1 hour), or until a knife comes out clean. Serve the pudding warm, with ice cream. Yields 4 servings.

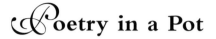

Poetry in a Pot

BY STELLA EHRICH

Eva Michaelson Isaacson
1896–1978

Grandma Eva could have been envious of Grandpa Abe. He was a poet, although he earned his living by other means, and in my most vivid memories he is sitting in front of the big black typewriter, hunting and pecking his thoughts and dreams. Sometimes he wrote prose: philosophical short stories that reflected his yeshiva upbringing in Russia before the turn of the century. More often he wrote poems: long epic verses that contained any detour or contortion he could devise in order to create a rhyme. His Russian-language base did not produce concise lines in English, but his experiences as an immigrant made for fascinating reading.

He had a new poem or story to share at every family gathering, and his readings were a regular Sunday afternoon event. At these times, my grandmother seemed content to stay smiling in the background, dressed in her homemade apron, happily cooking in the kitchen.

Was she jealous? Not a bit. She explained to us proudly that she put her poetry into her cooking pot. And we all loved it.

I had the good fortune to live down the street from her, on an oak-lined avenue in the same Mississippi town she had come to as a bride in 1918. Cooking with her was a magical time for me, a time when I learned our family history as well as the recipes that had been passed down from generation to generation. She made me feel indispensable as I kneaded bread for her on Fridays after her own hands became too arthritic to work the dough. But it was I who felt privileged to be in *her* company, for my mother's mother was a happy, loving person who made each of her grandchildren feel as if they were the center of her universe.

I loved to hear the stories of her upbringing in Maine, in the home of Hasidic parents who had emigrated from the same Russian village where my grandfather was born. She told me of her courtship with my grandfather, in a rowboat on a lake in Maine. He had spent his first ten years in America traveling with the Barnum and Bailey Circus, taking tintype portraits as a sideshow attraction. When the circus went to Mississippi, he happened to meet an old friend and study partner from his yeshiva years in Radiscovitz. Ready to settle down, Abe the adventurer was easily persuaded by his Russian friend to marry and bring his bride south.

In those days, there were people in Clarksdale, Mississippi, who had never seen a Jewish woman. They would brush past her on the street, closer than necessary, trying discreetly to lift the skirts of her long dresses to see if Jews indeed had hoofs like the devil-people they were rumored to be. The first Jewish male born in our town caused a lot of excitement among the locals, who tried to see if there were signs of horns budding on his head. After all, Michelangelo's Moses had horns, and the adult Jewish males always wore hats. Who knew?

In the first year of her married life, my grandmother suffered greatly from loneliness. The heat and humidity of the Delta summer were suffocating. Every day she cried. And every day she wrote to her parents, never missing a day until – one year and 365 letters later – her father wrote that she must stop. Her letters were so regular, he said, that if she missed a single day she would cause them endless worry until the next letter arrived. I imagine she felt stunned at first, with the severing of this postal umbilical cord, but without her constant attention to correspondence, she began to devote herself to her life in Mississippi.

And devote herself she did. Eva was the glowing center of our family life. She embraced each daughter, son-in-law, and grandchild with the wisdom of acceptance. She met with open arms the first non-Jewish bride to marry into our family, exclaiming, "Ah, God has sent me an angel!" Because of her, my cousins became like brothers to me, and my aunts became like sisters. She bound our family together with tenderness, and those bonds remain strong long after her passing. She fed us more than her poetry in the pot, more than her wonderful cooking. She fed us love.

Eva's Honey-Nut Cookie Squares *(Teiglach)*

Every time I take out one of her recipes, I feel her presence again. But I had a problem sending one of these recipes out into the world. "My grandmother would die *if I ever told anyone her* teiglach *recipe," I cried to my husband.*

Wisely, he pointed out, "But, Stella, your grandmother is already dead." And so, because her family tree has flowered in so many parts of the globe, I decided that her favorite recipe belongs out there too, a secret no more.

Grandma's recipe for teiglach *was a secret shared only with her daughters and grand-daughters. It was the jewel in her culinary crown, and it made her shine at every baby naming, bris, bar mitzvah, bat mitzvah, and wedding in Clarksdale, Mississippi. Each and every Jewish woman had her own special recipe for important occasions. She would appear with her contribution in the basement kitchen of our little synagogue, where enormous trays of pastries were carefully compiled and arranged in the grand Southern tradition. Outside catering was never considered, no matter how wealthy the host or how momentous the occasion. Everyone knew that the best feast, the most delicate and delectable, could only be put together by the women of Temple Beth El, each contributing her prized heirloom, her secret family recipe. This is my grandmother's.*

Step 1

2 cups flour
2 teaspoons baking powder
¼ teaspoon salt
⅛ cup sugar
3 eggs
¼ cup vegetable oil

Combine the flour, baking powder, salt, and sugar. Make a well in the center and break the eggs into it. Scramble the eggs lightly with a fork, then add the oil. Gradually pull the flour into the center, mixing until a dough is formed. Add a few drops of water if dry flour is left in the bowl.

Knead the dough until it is smooth, then lightly oil the surface. Allow the dough to rest for 20 minutes.

Preheat your oven to 350 degrees.

Divide the dough into five equal pieces. Use your hands to roll each piece into a long snake, about ½ inch to ¾ inch in diameter. Sprinkle flour on a cutting board, dip a knife into the flour, and cut the rolls of dough into small nuggets, about ½ inch wide.

Bake the nuggets on an ungreased cookie sheet for 20 minutes, or until they are light gold in color.

Step 2

1 pound honey
1 cup chopped pecans
Sugar
Powdered ginger

Using a heavy pot (a pressure cooker without the lid, for example), bring the honey to a boil over medium heat. Lower the heat and add the baked nuggets. Stir often with a wooden spoon to keep the sides and bottom of the pot from burning. Make sure that the honey doesn't boil over. After 30 to 50 minutes, the honey will begin to coat the nuggets. Continue cooking and stirring until all the liquid is gone and the honey hangs in strings from the sides of the pot.

Remove the pot from the heat and stir in the nuts. The honey will be quite thick; it will cling to the nuggets and harden as it cools.

Turn the mixture out onto a wet wooden board and use a wet wooden spoon to pat out a 15-inch square approximately 1 inch thick. Cover the top with generous amounts of sugar and ginger.

When the *teiglach* has cooled, cut it into 2-inch squares using a heavy knife (tap the knife gently with a hammer or wooden mallet), or break the *teiglach* into pieces with your hands. The *teiglach* will be crunchy, sticky, and somewhat dry. Makes 20 to 25 pieces.

Note: If you like, you can do Step 1 of this recipe on the first day and Step 2 on the second.

The Gift of Knowledge

BY KATHERINE QUIMBY JOHNSON

Daphne Craig Quimby
1896–1993

"What's that?" I point to small orange and yellow flowers growing on the shady bank. "Jewelweed," Grammy answers, "also called touch-me-not. I'll show you why." She strokes a seedpod. . . . It explodes! I yelp and jump into the dirt road. She shows me how to find fat, ripe pods. Pleased with this new skill, I pop one after another. Still curious, I inquire, "Is it edible?"

Grammy remembered this walk as proof of my precocity. "Imagine a four-year-old using the word 'edible!'" she would say, as she told the story yet again. (The answer to my question was "No.")

Grammy and I enjoyed each other's company. We shared an interest in the world around us and a delight in knowledge. A grade-school teacher before her marriage, Grammy Quimby was a natural instructor who also loved to learn. At age ninety she asked if I knew what hermeneutics was. (I did.)

Daphne Craig Quimby equated education with status. A Ph.D. and a professorship were worth more than riches. Discussing politics (with those who agreed with her!) and quoting poetry were her idea of the high life. Once an avid Red Sox fan who could rattle off batting averages and win-loss ratios, she relinquished this interest in her eighties, believing it unintellectual.

How she came to revere academia is a mystery. One of eight surviving children (a sister died in childhood of diphtheria), Daphne Craig grew up in the remote northeast kingdom of Vermont. Her father, son of "the tallest man in Glasgow" (Scotland), taught her to dance the Money Musk. The family farmhouse burned when she was young, forcing them to rent housing. Frugality reigned, but apparently her parents also valued education; Daphne was able to graduate from high school before going out to work.

Silence covered any disappointment. She and her husband moved to California in the 1920s, where he worked as a paperhanger and painter. During the Depression they moved back to Vermont to farm, just when everyone else headed west. She never said why. Many years later, she was thrilled when my two cousins went off to college. But when one dropped out, she never mentioned it.

I was a clumsy, bookish girl, most comfortable in the classroom. Eventually I went away to graduate school, pursuing a doctorate in German. Grammy couldn't have been prouder. At last, a scholar in the family! She was interested in my studies, no matter how obscure the topic, and she was a touch envious – "Young women today have so many opportunities!"

Illness ended my aspirations; I lacked the stamina for publish-or-perish. But I vowed to finish my dissertation. My husband and I moved back to Vermont, bought a house, had a child. I started a garden, did research, wrote three chapters.

The last time I saw my grandmother, in March 1993, she had two questions: "How's your thesis coming along?" and "Have you started your tomatoes yet?" She died that August, shortly before her ninety-seventh birthday. In the following weeks, I canned tomatoes and sauce. I even made tomato paste. Work on my dissertation grew difficult, then impossible. Academic jargon wasn't what I wanted to write. I mailed my letter of resignation, knowing what Grammy would have said. Nothing.

Grammy Quimby's Potato Chip Cookies

Grammy liked to serve unusual cookies. She kept several varieties in her freezer so that she would always be able to offer guests a selection. This recipe is one her grandchildren enjoyed.

¼ pound (1 stick) butter
½ cup plus 1 tablespoon sugar
1 egg
1 teaspoon vanilla extract
2 cups flour
¾ cup finely crushed potato chips
½ cup chopped nuts

Preheat your oven to 350 degrees.

Cream the butter, sugar, egg, and vanilla. Mix in the flour and potato chips, then stir in the nuts.

Roll the dough into 1-inch balls. Place the balls on a greased baking sheet and flatten them slightly.

Bake for 16 to 18 minutes, or until the cookies are golden brown. Cool on waxed paper. Makes 1½ dozen cookies.

&t All Comes Out in the Wash

BY KERI PICKETT

Josie Lou Lydia Walker Blakey
1897–1998

In the nursing home, a worker kissed my hundred-year-old Grandma on the cheek and said, "Hello, Miss Josie." My grandmother surprised me. Always upbeat and positive, she said grumpily, "Why did she call me *Miss* Josie?" Then her face brightened. "Well, maybe she didn't know my B.B."

Grandma's husband was never far from her thoughts, even after five years without him. They'd been married for sixty-four years. Grandpa used to say, "That means we've spent twenty years together in bed." Josie was the most upbeat person I've ever known. She was my role model for her selfless commitment to her family, her quick wit, and her deep respect for her lifelong love – B.B.

Josie Lou Lydia Walker and Bernard Buckner Blakey married late in life, compared with the norm of 1929. Both were considered spinsters, she at thirty-two, he at thirty-four. Their courtship is the stuff of legends, and indeed it continues to be one of the great romantic stories of our family. It happened this way: B.B. had been engaged to Josie's former roommate but had broken off the engagement, then regretted doing so. Josie, always the do-gooder, began writing to each of them trying to get them reunited.

Josie's work as a traveling minister had taken her from Kansas to Kentucky, and there a preacher became interested in her. She wasn't at all interested in him, however, so she wrote to B.B., asking him to send her blank sheets of paper in envelopes marked "personal," because all her mail came to the preacher's box and she wanted him to think she had a "beau." This started a daily exchange of love letters through which my grandparents revealed their thoughts, dreams, and desires. One year and more than seven hundred letters later, they married.

Josie hesitated three months before saying yes to B.B.'s proposal. In part, she didn't want to saddle him with her college debt. When they were married, Josie had exactly one dollar to her name, a dollar she promptly gave to her husband. "I married her for her money," B.B. would joke.

Like most people, I have many treasured family photographs. But unlike most people, I am a professional photographer. I began casually photographing my grandparents as a natural result of spending time with them. I visited often, loving their company, and sought to reflect their love for one another, and their passion for life, in my photographs.

I had long heard about my grandparents' postal courtship and romantic marriage; these were folklore in our family. After Grandpa died, I finally looked into the big box of letters from their year of getting to know each other. I was so moved by their budding love that I wanted to celebrate it, make it known to everyone. So I paired my photographs with their love letters in a book I called *LOVE IN THE 90s: B.B. and Jo. The Story of a Lifelong Love. A Granddaughter's Portrait* (Warner Books, 1995). In this book we see letters beginning with "Sweetheart O'Mine" or "Lovely Lady Love" or "Pal of My Heart" or "My Own True Love." The letters reveal my grandparents opening their hearts to each other, talking about their days, their hopes for their home-to-be, their eagerly awaited life partnership, and their love. Grandma loved the book because she thought it could help people. All she ever wanted to do was help others.

Many people have asked me what happened in between my grandparents' courtship and life in their nineties. Three months into her marriage, my grandma found herself pregnant. She had given up her career as a minister in order to start a family, but what looked like a bright future took a bleak turn as the Depression changed everyone's lifestyle. My grandpa lost his hardware store and took a job collecting money from Phillips University students for their college education. This was my grandmother's alma mater. Grandpa often arranged for the students' families to trade goods and services in exchange for tuition, and his ingenuity is credited with helping the university survive the Depression. In his twenty-seven-year career with Phillips, Grandpa extended loans of one million dollars – and all of it was repaid.

"When they were married, Josie had exactly one dollar to her name, a dollar she promptly gave to her husband. 'I married her for her money,' B.B. would joke."

Josie and her B.B. learned to live well with little, during the Depression. But they had so much in every other way, through all their years. They never walked down a hall without her arm through his. She always laughed at his jokes. He couldn't sit next to her without touching her. Even late in life, they were frequently taken for honeymooners.

Near the end of her life, I continued to learn something new and wonderful about her whenever we were together. I liked to cuddle with her in the residence where she lived. I'd read to her from the old letters, and she'd tell me stories about her early days with Grandpa. I even asked her how old she was when they stopped making love. Her answer: "We never stopped making it! We made it up to the very end."

Her own end was quiet. She died as beautifully as she had lived. My mother and I sat on either side of her, holding her and singing "Swing Low, Sweet Chariot" to her. In the first verse, we sang, "My sweet Jesus, waiting there for me." Then, for the second verse, we sang, "My sweet B.B., waiting there for me." And with that, our sweet Josie died.

Josie's Ham Hock and Bean Soup

Grandma's family had been very poor. She remembered picking a hundred pounds of cotton a day as a child, and playing with dolls made of corncobs. But even during the Depression, when she bought the family's food on credit, she was happy to share what she had. People would come to the back door asking for a hot meal, and they always got it from Grandma.

Many times, what brought them was the aroma of Grandma's washday soup. She would start up a big pot of ham hock and beans when the light was blue and soft and the day was young. Her three kids then hauled out the wringer washer and the week's laundry, and everyone pitched in. The old washer gave everyone a workout, because all that washing and wringing had to be followed by hanging, retrieving, and folding. Load after load they worked as the soup cooked on the stove, until the orange sun marked the end of the day.

Happiness for Josie came from hard work and nurturing and love. Life is not unlike her washday soup. You put in all your ingredients, then you let them simmer and blend, stirring only occasionally. With this method, you can walk away and let your soup/life cook on its own, knowing that what you're making is based on good ingredients so it's bound to turn out great.

1 pound dried white
    navy beans
1 pound smoked ham hock
2 onions, chopped
Salt and pepper
Kombu seaweed (optional)

If you want a soup with very little meat, ask the butcher to give you a ham hock that would have gone to someone's dog.

Soak the beans overnight to soften them. Drain away the water.

Put everything in a pot. (This granddaughter's recipe calls for a piece of Kombu seaweed to help with the gas and to add nutrients.) Add water to an inch above the ingredients. Bring the soup to a boil, then turn it down to simmer. Now, go work on your chores.

If you're both cookin' all day, it would be a good idea to add water both to yourself and to the soup pot.

Behind Her Smile

Emma Dott Chow
1899–1983

BY JOANNE CHOW WINSHIP

Privacy is a power. This is what my grandmother instilled in me. She was small, quiet, and calm, with a coy smile that said, "No matter how much you ask, I won't tell." Also with this smile, known as The Look, she controlled much of our behavior. The Look implied expectations to work hard and achieve.

Her father was a doctor and dentist; her mother, a student of the piano at the Chicago Conservatory of Music. Their life in America started in the late 1800s in Chicago, where they had the first of nine children. Soon they journeyed to St. Louis and then to California. Hard times followed with the death of Emma's father, leaving fifteen-year-old Emma (the second oldest) to help her mother raise the family. They survived to produce more doctors and professionals.

Emma was proud of this early start into California history, and she did not allow anything to intrude on this pride. Family matters were private, withheld even from family members. Maybe this caution reflected a time when the Chinese avoided possible immigration problems by revealing as little as possible about their family origin. She never talked about her arranged marriage, nor did she show emotion at the death of her mother, which was quickly followed by the death of a son serving in World War II. She dutifully continued to help her family, taking in a brother or two, a teenage niece, and her eldest son with his family of five. Through all this, never a raised voice or a sign of frustration, only that smile to hide the difficulties and to remind us of our heritage.

Too often, we allow our pride to wrap us in a veil of loneliness. I wonder if my grandmother had wanted to talk about the tensions around her illegitimate grandson or the complexities of her brother's homosexuality. Because she was proud, she was alone with her emotions.

But she gave of herself in every sweet way. Her home was always available for a family game of canasta or mahjong, a meal of enchiladas, or a long stay. She volunteered at the First Chinese Baptist Church where she was the financial secretary. Although she never went to college, her intelligence and perfect English helped her husband's wholesale produce business to flourish. The top priority in her life was her family: her remaining son, daughter, and eight grandchildren.

With nostalgia I recall the simple pleasures of riding in her Packard, helping her shake down the grapefruit tree, or watching her deftly roll up her long, thin white hair and pin it close to her head as she had done in exactly the same way every day of her life. I never did learn what was behind her smile. Maybe it was her determination to get on with the living of life, and to avoid dwelling on what can't be changed.

Emma's Enchiladas

Emma loved cooking for a crowd, and on Sundays after church we usually gathered at her house for lunch. While things simmered on the stove we would peek into her refrigerator. Seeing so many ancient leftovers crammed into the far reaches of the old icebox, we would tease her about being so frugal. And for a little lady, she sure ate a lot. She loved good food. Yes, we had Chinese food too, but remember, we were in the heart of the San Joaquin Valley, heavily influenced by Mexican cooking. One of Emma's most popular dishes was her beef enchiladas; her special touch was to use shredded beef, not ground beef.

Meat Filling

3 tablespoons vegetable oil
1 (3- to 4-pound) rump or
  chuck pot roast, boned
2 teaspoons salt
¼ teaspoon pepper
1 cup water
1 small onion, chopped

Preheat your oven to 350 degrees.

Place the vegetable oil and the meat in a heavy Dutch oven or a large, heavy pot. Brown the meat well for 7 or 8 minutes on each side.

Season the meat with salt and pepper, then add the water and onion. Cover tightly. Bake for 4 to 5 hours, until the meat is tender and can be flaked away with a fork. Periodically check the meat, keeping ½ inch of liquid in the Dutch oven at all times. Once the meat is cooked, shred it into thin ½-inch strands and mix in the cooked onions.

Vegetable Filling

2 tablespoons vegetable oil
1 medium onion, diced
1 large green pepper, diced
½ cup chopped black olives
¼ teaspoon salt
Hot sauce (optional)

Enchilada Sauce

¼ cup vegetable oil or
    shortening
¼ cup flour
¼ cup tomato paste
1 teaspoon chili powder, or
    more to taste
2 teaspoons salt
¾ teaspoon cumin
½ teaspoon garlic salt
4 cups water

Assembly Ingredients

⅛ to ¼ cup vegetable oil
12 corn tortillas
½ pound Cheddar, grated
½ pound Monterey Jack, grated
½ cup cilantro, avocado, or
    guacamole (optional)

To make the vegetable filling: heat the oil and sauté the onion and green pepper. Add the olives and season with salt and hot sauce, if desired. Set the filling aside.

Next, make the enchilada sauce: heat the oil, then stir in the flour and tomato paste. Add the chili powder, salt, cumin, garlic salt, and water. Boil for 20 minutes, or until the sauce thickens. Pour one-third of the sauce into the shredded meat mixture.

To prepare the tortillas: heat ½ to 1 tablespoon of the oil in a skillet. Lightly sauté both sides of a tortilla until it is soft and flexible. Repeat for each tortilla, adding a little oil to the skillet each time.

When the tortillas are ready, mix the meat and vegetable fillings, then place a scoop of this mixture in the center of each tortilla. Roll up the tortillas and place them side by side in a 9 x 12-inch baking dish.

Pour the sauce over the rolled enchiladas and cover them with grated cheese. If you have extra sauce, pour it over the cheese.

Bake at 350 degrees until the sauce is bubbling and the cheese has melted. This may take 20 to 30 minutes. Garnish with cilantro, avocado, or guacamole before serving. Serves 4 to 6 people.

Helen Sweeten Layton
1899–1984

 **Old Sweetie**

BY M. KATHERINE LAYTON

My paternal grandmother, Helen Sweeten Layton, is as close to me now as when I first looked to her for sanctuary from my chaotic family. True to her name, she still sweetens my life.

My family was a raucous bunch of pranksters led by my father. Nothing was sacred or off-limits unless shared privately with Gram, a sympathetic listener. Always eager to help me find interests I could call my own, she helped me start my own little petunia patch by our back porch, and she gave me my first "first editions" of cherished books (now part of a sizeable collection). An avid reader, Gram proudly supplied me with books as if she were writing them herself, inscribing our names in her meticulous script.

In her fifties, she appeared to live a privileged life, sheltered by Powie, my grandfather. I later learned the more complete story. A letter written by my father in 1937 described how Gram had gone to work as a beauty operator in Wilmington, Delaware, when the family cigar business, F.W. Layton & Son, Inc., began to falter. My father began college at New York University that year. She worked on her feet from 8:00 A.M. until 7:00 P.M. during the week and until 10:00 P.M. on Saturdays. Only after their three children were out of college did my grandparents enjoy the prosperity I witnessed, with Gram wearing tailored suits, white gloves, a fox-fur stole, and hats with veils.

The men in the family called her "dizzy" when she adored Harry Truman or stayed out weeding her gardens in the pouring rain. Dizzy or not, she humbly allowed them the ultimate say, but I knew that her acceptance of male authority was not agreeable to her. On Thanksgiving Day, when I was ten, this fact was impressed upon me. Gram was in her kitchen, juggling her serving bowls and steaming pots, wiping away the perspiration from her flushed face with a lace hanky that she kept tucked into the waistband of her starched apron. My grandfather, father, brothers, uncles, and male cousins had assembled in the living room to watch football while "the girls" prepared the table. During halftime, when Powie decided it was time to eat, he took his place at the head of the table and bellowed, "Helen, sit!" My heart jumped. She shoved the cut-glass cranberry bowl into my hands and sat like an obedient dog — man's best friend, not his equal. Loyal as the family pet, she never turned on him. But I saw her bottom lip quiver at his harsh dominance. When I started to speak up for her, my mother put her hand on my shoulder and said, "Never mind." I did mind, though. Since then, I have tried to be courageous with my freedom: to be true to myself, for my own sake and for the sake of the sacrifices Grandma Layton had to make.

Gram and I discovered our inner resources by the same route — when we found ourselves financially strapped as single women. In 1963, after Powie died, she began to exercise the independent spirit she had held in check during forty-five years of marriage. A penniless widow, she was now doing the same things I was doing as a penniless teenager: babysitting and wearing hand-me-down clothes. Like me, she delighted in driving to visit friends. We both named our cars: mine was "White Fang," a Ford station wagon, and hers was a little Vauxhall she called "Vauxie." She flirted with the widower next door, and shed her flowered dresses and matching costume jewelry in favor of baggy pants and loose shirts. When my father tried to rein her in, I was astounded to see her stand up to him and say, "You are not my boss!"

Even struggling to make ends meet, she never lost her ability to foster grace, using an embroidered cloth in the bread tray, or placing a nosegay of violets by a guest's plate. She had a gift for making others feel special.

Unfortunately, she did not sustain her mental clarity into her last years, and as her house and gardens collapsed, so did her mind. The last time she recognized me we were driving to visit her sister. I was horrified when she drove off the paved road into her field of violets, churning them under the tires. I tried to take the wheel from her but she stubbornly pushed me away. We bounced along in the field for several miles before she found the paved road again. My father took her car keys from her that day. Within months she couldn't remember the names of flowers anymore.

Grandma Layton's Violet Jam

Feeding folks was a great pleasure for my grandmother, although if she had to choose between her kitchen and her gardens, the gardens always won. Preparing food was a way of showing her love for others, but gardening was a way of cultivating love for herself.

She admired a field of violets for its fruitfulness as well as its beauty. Her recipe for violet jam appropriately combines food for both body and soul.

She sent me this recipe soon after I moved to Vermont as a newlywed in 1970. I was raving to her about the neighbors who inspired me to make gooseberry and crabapple jellies and dandelion wine; we fried the surfeit of squash blossoms from the garden and ate our home-baked bread with freshly churned butter that a farmer brought to us in glass jars. Not to let the Garden State be outdone, Gram sent me her recipe for violet jam. You need an abundant field of violets if you want to make a large quantity.

1 cup well-packed violet
    blossoms (be sure that no
    pesticides were used on
    the violets)
¾ cup water
Juice of 1 lemon
2½ cups sugar
6 ounces liquid fruit pectin

Wash five 4-ounce jelly jars and scald them in a pot of hot water. Leave them in the hot water until you are ready to use them.

Use a blender or hand mixer to blend the violets, water, lemon juice, and sugar. Blend well until the sugar dissolves and the liquid turns lavender. Set this aside.

In a saucepan, boil the pectin for 1 minute. Meanwhile, use tongs to remove the jars from the hot water. Set the jars upside-down on a clean cloth.

Add the violet mixture to the pectin and return to a boil, stirring constantly with a whisk. You may want to remove the excess flower pieces that collect on the surface. Work quickly so that the jam does not set.

As soon as the jam begins to boil, ladle the hot liquid into the hot jelly jars, leaving ¼ inch of space at the top. After the jars have been filled and sealed, invert the jars and let them stand for 5 minutes. Turn them right-side up and let them cool for 3 hours. Store the jam in the refrigerator.

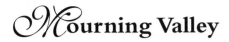# Mourning Valley

Mabel Vannoy Reynolds Perkins
1899–1985

JEANNETTA P. HOLLIMAN

"Mourning Valley?" I ask my dad.

"Mourning Valley," he repeats. "Like a valley of mourners. That's how I fixed it in my mind."

All these years I had thought the church my grandma attended was *Morning Valley Baptist Church.*

Mourning Valley. Marytown, West Virginia, in McDowell County.

Across the river from Marytown is the place where I was born and where the Perkins clan resided: Twin Branch, West Virginia, on the banks of the Tug River. At the time, my mother tells me, only two black families lived there, the Perkinses and the Evanses.

"Only *two* black families?"

"That's right," my mother says. "Everybody else was white. But we went to church in Marytown, which was mostly black. You remember Marytown?"

Yes, I do remember. *I am three years old, walking through the tunnel with sisters from the church, on our way to Marytown. Easter Sunday morning. Talking fills the darkness. Someone holds my hand – Grandma, Mama, or Aunt Joann.*

Grandma and Granddaddy were married in Marytown in 1915. At the Mourning Valley Baptist Church, I presume. Grandma was sixteen; Granddaddy, twenty.

Mourning Valley Baptist Church. I think I am dreaming, but I am not. This morning I have gone to the valley of mourners. Last night my friend Gilda died. *(But it is spring. The flowers are blooming.)* Today, reality sets in.

Grandma was born in early spring – "when the leaves come out and the flowers start to bloom," she used to say. She was born in North Wilkesboro, North

Carolina, on the R.J. Reynolds Plantation. She migrated to Twin Branch with her younger sister Grace in the early 1900s, to lighten the load on their mother Fannie's shoulders.

I was born in the middle of winter, 1950; I lived in Twin Branch until 1954. (Jones and Laughlin Coal Company had shut the mines down, so my daddy moved us to Youngstown, Ohio, trading coal mines for steel mills.) From the time I could walk until the time I left Twin Branch, I was my grandmother's shadow.

"I followed underfoot as we did our chores – fed the chickens, gathered eggs, prepared meals – barely a word whispered between us. Yet, I knew what to do and what to say and when. In her silence, in her presence, I learned to be still."

I like shadows. When I was three, I'd sit with Grandma in a dimly lit room in her house, watching her make dolls from scratch. Shades drawn. Sunlight blocked from the room. The room filled up with shadows. She'd hum old spirituals; I'd rub my hands up and down her arms, lulled by her song. I felt safe in the shadows of that room. In the shadow of my grandmother. *Under Angel wings.*

Daddy said Grandma loved the 91st Psalm. She lived by it. *He that dwelleth in the most high shall abide under the shadows of the Almighty.*

It is spring, and I am mourning. Shadows comfort me still.

I have lived in Columbus, Ohio, for the past twenty-four years. For nearly that long, I've taken morning walks at Schiller Park in German Village, a historical neighborhood in the city. Last week along my walk I stepped onto the bridge to cross the pond, and I stopped. The golden weeping willow tree and yellow daffodils beneath it caught my eye. Two springs ago I longed for Grandma and the stillness of my childhood. I wanted a sign that she was with me, that she had me under her wings. My eyes fell upon this same spot: an island in the middle of the pond – a still-life framed forever in my mind. I knew then that she was with me. That she had sent the gust of wind to turn my head so I could see: *I am here, my child, I am here. In the tree that weeps golden tears and in the flowers of early spring, I am here.*

She is with me now, in the valley of my mourning. Tears flow like the rivers of my birthplace. Twin rivers. Daddy told me that's how Twin Branch got its name. "Twin streams branch out – on opposite sides of the mountain – and flow to Tug River in the valley below."

Grandma flowed like the river and smelled like the earth after a springtime rain.

Grandma went to the valley often and took me with her. We climbed mountains together, too – to the top, where Granddaddy grew golden fields of corn, and I ran up and down the rows.

Grandma was a quiet woman. Big-boned and tall. Skin the color of honey. "Indian blood," Daddy said. (Cherokee, I think.) She wore cotton dresses and two fat braids that fell over her shoulders and hung below her breasts. Salt-and-pepper hair. She had seer's eyes. I followed underfoot as we did our chores – fed the chickens, gathered eggs, prepared meals – barely a word whispered between us. Yet, I knew what to do and what to say and when. In her silence, in her presence, I learned to be still.

"She had unbelievable faith," Daddy told me. "It was like she *lived* with God." He shook his head, bewildered.

I am bewildered by Gilda's death. It was too sudden. Too soon. I miss her.

This morning I remember what Grandma taught me, and I am still. It's 8:30 A.M. I raise the shades to let the sunlight in. I stand facing the sun, which has risen over my backyard. My magnolia tree has blossomed and more daffodils are blooming. A flock of birds fly east. It is spring, I am reminded. In my heart, it is winter, and I wait.

For He shall give his Angels charge over thee, to keep thee in all thy ways.

In the meantime, I promised my sons I'd bake biscuits this morning. The smells of Grandma's kitchen come back to me: fried apples, cooked and waiting in the pan; coffee percolating on the range; hoecakes baking; and chicken frying for breakfast.

Our Family's Hoecakes

Traditional Southern hoecakes were made with cornmeal and cooked on the blade of a hoe. Our family recipe calls for no cornmeal, tastes like biscuits, and is baked in the oven. Perhaps "hoecakes" is a misnomer, but that's what our family has called this recipe for generations. My mother tells me that hoecakes are also called pone bread.

2 cups flour
2 teaspoons baking powder
1 teaspoon salt
½ cup lard or vegetable
    shortening
⅔ cup buttermilk or
    sweet milk (whole milk)

Preheat your oven to 425 degrees.

Mix the flour, baking powder, and salt in a bowl. Cut in the lard with a knife until the mixture is coarse and crumbly, then stir in the buttermilk. "Work that up" (knead the dough) on a lightly floured board for about 30 seconds.

Separate the dough into 3 pones (oblong pieces). Place each piece into a 9 x 13-inch ungreased baking pan. Pat each piece into ½-inch (or so) thickness, 1 to 2 inches apart. Bake for 15 to 20 minutes, or until golden brown. Break the pones into 12 servings.

Leah Waxman Wendkos
1900–1979

The Charleston Dancer

BY DORRI OLDS

I didn't know my grandmother when she won prizes dancing the Charleston. I remember Granny lying on the dark green sofa in my parents' house when I was eight and she was seventy. With her head in my lap, she would drowsily hand me her comb and say, "Do my hair, Dorri." And I would comb her short white hair. She'd brush her soft, wrinkly hand across my face and call me *shana punim* (Yiddish for "pretty face"). She was part of the old world and the new, speaking Yiddish and dancing the Charleston. It was her parents who had made the daring leap into the new world, each arriving in the United States at the age of thirteen (her mother from an obscure village in Austria, her father born in Germany and raised in Lithuania).

When I was eight, I knew nothing of Granny's past. I was only concerned with the present. I loved sitting next to her at the big wooden dining table. I never heard anyone chew a bagel so loudly. Her false teeth clanked, then down went the bagel bites with a bellowing gulp of coffee.

I loved visiting Granny and Pop in Philadelphia. They had a sofa as soft as a down pillow and I'd sink a million miles into it. Granny always put dishes of hard candies by the door. I'd pop a coffee treat into my mouth with my right hand, while my left hand snuck a stash into my pocket.

During the day we'd go to the museum, to stores, out to lunch. For Granny, a sandwich was always on rye with mustard. When I ordered mine on white with mayonnaise, she'd look at me incredulously and slowly shake her head.

At night we'd play Scrabble. I thought Granny should have been famous; she was impossible to beat. Then afterward we'd watch TV. She loved Pop with all her heart, but she loved Kojak, too — she thought he was the sexiest man alive.

And when he said, "Who loves ya, baby?" she'd clutch at her heart, sigh, and wink at me. The racier she was, the more thrilled I was.

She loved to dish the dirt on people. I loved to listen and laugh. She had a salty tongue, a quick wit, and a funny saying every two seconds, like "With one *tuchas* you can't dance at two weddings." Or, when she didn't like someone, "May he fart in his grave!"

Remarkably, she kept her keen sense of humor despite a life full of tragedy. First she lost her favorite brother when an illegal whiskey still blew up in his face. Then she lost both her sons – Buddy to his second heart attack at forty-three, Carl to suicide at fifty-six. But when she lost her husband of fifty-seven years, she deteriorated rapidly. She changed. I changed. We became two angry wildcats. She thought I was spoiled. I thought she was selfish. I was pissed at her for growing old.

I know she loved me though, and I bet she's looking over my shoulder right now, pen in hand, ready to correct my grammar and serve up a wisecrack.

Granny's Cinnamon Buns

I spent a lot of time in the kitchen with Granny. She loved sweets and so do I, and my great pleasure was to help her bake — and help her taste. One day I watched her pare an apple for pie. She held the knife toward her thumb and I held my breath, sure she was going to cut herself. I could see an indentation on her thumb where the knife touched it, but her hand never slipped. She turned to me and said sharply, "Don't you ever cut an apple like this. You could cut yourself. Do as I say, not as I do!" That tone of voice meant business — and I listened. Even today, in my own kitchen, I wouldn't dream of paring an apple the way she did.

My favorite goodies were her soft, fresh cinnamon buns. Glazed with brown sugar and maple syrup and decorated with perfect walnut halves, they were more beautiful and more delicious than any I have seen in the finest bakeries. They had just the right amount of sweetness. One was perfect; two were too much. When tempted to overdo something in life, I often think about this lesson in moderation I learned from Granny's cinnamon buns.

3 cups flour

½ plus ⅛ cup sugar

¼ teaspoon salt

1 envelope (1 tablespoon) dry active yeast, dissolved in 2 tablespoons warm (not hot) water with ½ teaspoon sugar

¼ pound plus 4 tablespoons (1½ sticks) unsalted butter, softened

½ cup milk, scalded

2 eggs, beaten

½ cup mashed potatoes

3 tablespoons brown sugar and/or maple syrup

24 walnut halves

2 teaspoons cinnamon

½ cup raisins

Combine the flour, the ½ cup sugar, and the salt. Mix in the yeast water and set this aside.

Melt the ¼ pound butter in the scalded milk. Add this to the flour, then add the eggs and mashed potatoes. Mix well, stirring until the mixture comes away from the bowl. Refrigerate overnight.

Butter the muffin pans generously. Pour a little brown sugar or maple syrup (Granny used both) into the bottom of each muffin cup, followed by an upside-down walnut half.

Roll out half the dough on a lightly floured board. Spread 2 tablespoons soft butter over the dough. Then spread 1 tablespoon sugar, 1 teaspoon cinnamon, and ¼ cup raisins. Roll the dough up tight and slice it into 1-inch thick pieces. Repeat this process for the other half of the dough.

Place the buns in the muffin tin, set them on top of the stove, and cover them with a towel. Let the dough rise until doubled, about 45 minutes.

Preheat your oven to 350 degrees.

Bake the buns for 25 to 30 minutes. Take the pans out of the oven and let them stand for 1 to 2 minutes before turning them out onto brown paper. This recipe makes 24 delicious cinnamon buns.

One More Question

Helen Theresa Jasinski Michalski
1902–1988

BY CHRISTINE MAY ROBLEE

"I'm giving you my pearls. I don't wear them anymore. I got them when I was in my thirties, now I'm in my seventies. That is the only thing that I got and I hope you will like it and keep as a keepsake," read the note that accompanied the little box holding my grandmother's double strand of pearls. It has been more than twenty-five years since they arrived, along with Gramma's best wishes for my future and an apology that she and Grampa couldn't make the trip to California for my wedding. The pearls are yellowed now, the rhinestones and silver tarnished and dusty, but when I hold them I can hear her raspy voice, slightly tinged with the Polish accent so prevalent in the working-class Milwaukee neighborhood where she was born, the same neighborhood where she grew up, married, and raised her own family.

Helcha, as she was known to her friends in that comfortable neighborhood, loved to tell her grandchildren about the "old" days in Milwaukee. Memories of horse-drawn carriages and sleigh bells right out of a Christmas carol. Stories of the ten brothers and sisters who shared her life. Sweet tales of the navy man she loved and how he returned from the sea to marry her in 1922. Stories, funny and sad, of my mother and aunt, whom they raised in this very house on the double lot near the airport. Reluctant reminiscences of the two babies they lost but couldn't forget.

I spent many hours sitting at her Formica dinette, listening to her stories while she prepared the day's meals. She never missed a beat as she talked and worked, all the while coaxing her little parakeet to answer her. It was clear that even though she was fascinated by the many changes and inventions she had witnessed in her eighty-six years of life, she never lost her love for the old things, the old ways. The big copper kettle for bathing the kids, the keys used by the girls for their roller skates, the tree in the backyard where Grampa would sit tending his "worm garden," the handmade afghans and blankets on each of the beds.

The house by the airport has been sold and moved, and Gramma and Grampa are both gone. But the bedspread that Gramma made for me when I was eighteen still adorns my bed, and the pearls wait in their little box for the day when I will give them to my daughter. I will tell her the story of how they were given to me, and I will pass on some of Gramma's stories as well. But I won't be able to tell her how Gramma came to have the pearls. What stories did they bring when they came into her life?

Isn't that always the way? No matter how many afternoons, how many years, how many stories, there's always one more question left unanswered. One more story left untold. I don't mind. I'm lucky that so much of my loving and generous Gramma lives on, not only in this double strand of pearls and in my beautiful bedspread, but in my heart and in the rich family history she shared with me all those afternoons ago.

"The pearls are yellowed now, the rhinestones and silver tarnished and dusty, but when I hold them I can hear her raspy voice, slightly tinged with the Polish accent so prevalent in the working-class Milwaukee neighborhood where she was born."

Gramma's Chicken Soup

Each Christmas, as my family made the journey from California to Milwaukee in our cramped and stuffy car, a sweet anticipation made the trip bearable. We knew we'd have snow, a real treat for us fair-weather kids. There'd be a big Christmas tree with lots of presents, and Gramma's homemade chicken soup simmering on the stove no matter what time of day or night we arrived. It welcomed us, warmed us, and made a faraway place feel like home. When I was eighteen, Gramma taught me how to make this special soup, and whenever I need to feel comforted I make a big pot to keep me company.

Gramma's chicken soup is a "kitchen sink" recipe — you use anything and everything you have; you don't shop in order to make it. In the old days, every homemaker worth her salt always had at least one chicken on hand, either in the yard or in the freezer, and most of the vegetables could be found in the refrigerator or taken from the backyard garden.

1 chicken, cut into pieces to fit the pot (skin, bones, giblets, and neck included)
2 to 4 carrots, diced
2 stalks celery, diced
1 to 2 onions, diced
Potatoes, turnips, and other vegetables as desired
1 bay leaf
Salt and pepper

Place the chicken pieces in a large, heavy pot, along with 1 or 2 carrots, 1 stalk of celery, an onion, a bay leaf, salt, pepper, and enough water to cover the ingredients. Cover the pot and bring the contents to a boil.

Simmer for 1 to 2 hours, or until the chicken begins to fall off the bone. Skim the scum from the top until the broth is clear. Remove the chicken pieces and set them aside.

The chicken fat will accumulate at the top of the pot. You can skim off the fat for a leaner soup, but the soup tastes best if you leave the fat in the broth.

Cut up more celery, carrots, and other vegetables and add these to the pot. If you like, you can add small pieces of the chicken, too. Simmer until all the vegetables are tender. (Or simmer all day long – the soup will taste even better.)

Remove the bay leaf, then add more salt and pepper if needed. Serve with homemade egg noodles or with rice. Makes 8 servings.

Note: Save the chicken pieces you removed from the pot. Pat them dry and fry them in butter until they are brown. Serve the chicken with mashed potatoes, bread, and gravy made from your soup stock. This was Grampa's favorite chicken meal.

Anna Maria Giovanni Riello
1904–1985

Abbondanza

BY SHARON LLOYD SPENCE

Grandma and Mamma disagreed on everything important: religion, money, sex, men. They were friends only in their affection for food, *abbondanza* portions of it.

A budding ballerina, I lived among two headstrong earth mothers. The more I struggled to become lanky and lithe, the more they plied me with veal, mozzarella, lasagna, and other temptations, every meal created from scratch and served with wide-eyed expectation.

At Mamma's table I could usually escape with "gotta go do my homework." At Grandma's table I was held captive as her special guest. Bending over my left shoulder, she ladled out buckets of minestrone, mountains of garlic eggplant, and, always, sugared *chiacchiere* for dessert.

"Eat, Sharon-a eat!" she commanded in a husky Neapolitan accent. Her pendulous breasts were pressed firmly against my back; her breath was sweet with tomato sauce and oregano. When I dared to leave a morsel on my plate, she shook her head sadly, as though the Pope had died, and fondled her pink rosary beads. "What-a can I do?" she would sigh. "You're gonna be a stream-a-line."

"But Grandma," I tried to comfort her, "I can't dance if I'm fat."

Of course it was hopeless. I never left Grandma Anna Riello's house without several new pounds accumulated from the best meals of my life. . . .

After Grandma passed away, her soul went to live on the mysterious mountainous island of Sardinia. She waited many years for my visit.

Driving into the deserted coastal town of San Giovanni, I see her standing outside a restaurant, wringing her hands over my lateness. At first I don't recognize her slightly slimmer form. But there is no mistaking those eyes, shiny dark-brown as a newborn puppy's. Her eyebrows still meet thickly in the middle; her face is as lovely as ever, a desert of wrinkles engraved by time. Delicate gold-hoop earrings set off her elegant Roman nose and her gold-toothed smile. She still wears her hair pulled neatly into a tiny bun.

"We were exploring the Roman ruins of Tharros and got lost," I explain from the car window. Grandma opens her side-yard gate, gesturing us to park there. Two dozen cats, crouching low in the yard, scatter to their corners as we drive in. Grandma grabs my face, kissing me fiercely on both cheeks. Her breath is sweet with tomato sauce and oregano.

San Giovanni is little more than a dozen white wooden houses on three gravel roads. It's September. Tourists have left and residents have not yet moved home for the winter. Grandma Riello owns a restaurant now, and we are her only guests.

Twelve tables are arranged in a white stucco room decorated with huge woven baskets, gourds, giant salad bowls, oversized wooden forks and spoons. Sunshine dapples the handwoven cloth on the table where Grandma seats us.

Excited as a young bride, she serves our first course: delicate slices of smoked mackerel floating in homemade olive oil, with shredded lettuce and sliced egg on the side. Magnificent.

A whole mullet poached with fresh thyme arrives next. Grandma carefully scrapes away the fish skin with the skill of a heart surgeon, as though hurting the perfect fish would be endangering us as well.

Enjoying the succulent fish, I hear the clank of metal being stacked. Grandma glides out of her kitchen with a tray of fresh silverware. She moves our used plates to another table, then places clean plates and cutlery before our amazed faces. Apparently the meal is just beginning. More is coming, much more. *Abbondanza!* Grandma smiles and speaks quietly in Italian.

"What is she saying?" I ask my girlfriend Lucia.

"She's made your favorite spaghetti sauce," Lucia laughs.

That afternoon we consume enough food for all of Sardinia: spaghetti with sun-dried tomato sauce; ravioli stuffed with ricotta, parsley, and egg; a bread loaf called *panetina* stuffed with artichoke, olives, peas, and capers; a second mullet cooked in Vernaccia wine, lemon, and olive oil; eggplant stuffed with meat and egg.

Grandma tells me the name of each ingredient, each dish. She knows I speak no Italian. Standing behind my left shoulder, pressing pendulous breasts against my back, I hear her silent command. "Eat, Sharon-a eat!"

Grandma Riello's Spaghetti Sauce

Anna Maria Giovanni came to America as a teenager to marry Joseph Riello. She brought her zest for life, her curiosity, and her recipes.

Grandma spent many happy hours in her small backyard garden, growing tomatoes and fresh herbs. The result was a heavenly spaghetti sauce I can smell to this day.

1 pound fresh plum tomatoes

2 celery stalks

1 whole bulb garlic

1 red onion

3 tablespoons extra virgin olive oil

½ cup dry red wine

½ cup fresh basil, shredded

1 tablespoon fresh oregano, chopped

Salt and pepper

Chop the tomatoes and celery into chunks. Peel and slice the cloves of garlic. Skin and slice the onion into thin rings.

Sauté the celery, garlic, and onion in the olive oil until the onions are translucent and the garlic is soft. Add the tomatoes and wine and cook for 5 minutes. Then, add the basil, oregano, salt, and pepper.

Simmer the sauce over low heat for 30 minutes, stirring occasionally. Let this stand, covered, for another 30 minutes.

Reheat the sauce before serving over hot spaghetti. This sauce will freeze well for future meals. Make enough for your granddaughter to take home. Serves 4 people.

Turning Bitter into Sweet

Esther Widem Shinder
1905–1981

BY T.J. BANKS

The comfortably shabby Colonial farmhouse where my grandmother Esther lived was a haven to all of us, especially during those long, muggy summer days that squeezed the sweat and energy right out of us. It was always cooler under the gargantuan weeping willows, listening to Esther tell stories about her child-hood. About her strict Russian father teaching her the Hebrew alphabet. About her embittered stepmother, also Russian-born, making a drudge out of her. About her protective older brother, Max, enlisting in the Canadian forces during World War I and dying in France. And about Josie, their equally poor Christian neighbor in North Canton, Connecticut, making her the one pretty dress she'd had as a child.

Sometimes, too, Mama (as we all called her) would complain about the early years of her marriage and about the bossiness of her strong-willed czarina of a mother-in-law. And because my grandmother clung fiercely to her loves and her hates – long after the people who sparked them had died – her stories had a vividness that made the world I could see and touch seem washed-out by comparison. Born in New Jersey, she had somehow managed to pick up an Old Country accent that only added to the colorfulness of her talk.

Now, when I think back on those stories that she spun for me out under the willows or in her cool, shadowy kitchen, I'm amazed. Not by the harshness of her life, marred by poverty, by loss (her mother had died on Staten Island when Esther was barely two), by her stepmother's abuse (you could, my own mother swears, see scars on Esther's scalp from the woman's hair pulling), by her father's aloofness, and by a marriage that brought her only more hard work instead of the freedom she'd sought. No. What amazes me is how – despite all those things –

she managed to keep alive within her a talent for loving and giving that I've seen in few other people. "I don't know why people complain about their mothers-in-law," my dad would say. "Mine'd give you the food right out of her mouth and the shirt right off her back."

The food right out of her mouth. Esther gloried in feeding people. She brought coffee to the men working on the road in the winter, carried a snack to a neighbor helping with a sick cow on Christmas Eve. "I know this is your holiday," she told the latter, trotting out to the frigid barn with her homemade cookies, despite her severe arthritis.

By physically feeding others, of course, she emotionally fed herself – fed the hungry, motherless child inside her, the skinny, sad-faced little girl who'd wanted so very much to love and be loved. For a woman who'd grown up with precious little nurturing, she had a tremendous need to nurture everyone and everything: children, grandchildren, friends, neighbors, even flowers and houseplants. And now, when I find myself making a pie or stew for a helpful neighbor or putting out leftovers for a stray cat, I know it is Esther working through me.

She didn't have much use for recipes – that would have meant following directions. No, she simply added sugar, salt, or whatever felt right to her at that moment, like a poet rummaging among her favorite words. Cooking was a form of creative expression for Esther, an outlet for all her pent-up energy and warmth. A way of making something out of nothing, or, at least, out of very little.

In a sense, that's what she did with her life. She was no Pollyanna: she could bear a grudge with the best of them and never glossed over the poverty and unhappiness she'd known. But she turned around and took the love for which she'd had little outlet early in life, and she stirred it into her soups and fruit compotes. And she kneaded it into her light, flaky piecrusts, and she poured it over the fruit within, just as she poured love into everything else in her life, turning bitterness into honey-sweetness.

Very-Close-to-Esther's Apple Pie

Mama could take a little lukshen *(egg noodles), some chicken (with the greasy skin hanging from it), a few carrots and potatoes, and her usual Zen mixture of seasonings, and concoct a chicken soup to end all chicken soups. She made a jelly roll that melted away on our taste buds like a dream. Her apple pies were her greatest triumph, however: the apples, which came from the side-yard orchard, were small, wormy, and mouth-puckeringly sour. But with a little poetic license, Mama created pies that were just the right side of sweetness. The apples lost their sourness but not their* tam *(flavor).*

There was, of course, no carefully written-out recipe. (Who had time for that?) But in the years since her death, I've found one that comes very close. It's a Swedish apple pie — not really a pie at all, since it has no crust; then again, this makes it all the more appealing for those of us who rank among the crust-making challenged.

7 firm, tart apples
1 to 2 teaspoons cinnamon
1⅛ cups sugar
¼ pound plus 4 tablespoons
    (1½ sticks) butter, melted
1 cup flour
1 egg, beaten
1½ cups chopped nuts
Salt

Preheat your oven to 350 degrees.

Peel, core, and slice your apples. Fill a 9-inch pie pan two-thirds full with apple slices. Sprinkle the cinnamon and ⅛ cup of the sugar on top.

Combine the remaining 1 cup sugar with the butter, flour, beaten egg, chopped nuts, and salt. Spread this mixture over the apples.

Bake for 45 minutes, or until the pie is golden brown. Serves 6 to 8 people.

I think Esther would've liked it.

Concepción Garza De León
1905–1988

Her Hands Always Warm

BY ALBA DE LEÓN

My mother's mother, Abuelita Concepción, lived in the little town of Nogales in the state of Nuevo León, Mexico. Each summer my family traveled what seemed to me a very long distance from San Antonio to Nuevo Laredo and on to Nogales. We stopped only to buy the brightly colored La Joya sodas, in a little town whose name I can't remember, right after we crossed the border. (There was nothing like those sodas we found in Mexico!) We stayed all summer long. Just as I was starting to feel Mexican, it was time to come home.

My grandmother was a big woman who always wore dark colors because she was in mourning for my grandfather. I never knew him; he died before I was born. He had been a soldier, I believe in the Mexican Revolution, but I don't know what side he fought for. (If he had been my father's grandfather, he would have been on the side of the Mexican Indian.)

It was hard to tell whether my grandmother was a happy or sad person, because she always wore a scarf covering her mouth. But I sometimes heard her shrill laugh. She loved life. She loved her daughters. She loved to sit outdoors under a tree in the patio, telling stories and gossiping until late at night.

My grandmother had four sons – the only one I remember was Margarito, who made cinder blocks at his home across the street, next to the school – and four daughters: Maria, Chelita, Luz Alba (my mother), and Rosita. (Of all her daughters she loved the youngest, Rosita, the most – so much that right before she died, she wanted to tie herself to Rosita and never be left alone.) Tia Maria and Tio Roberto owned a store three blocks away from my grandmother's house, and they provided the family with daily meat and fruit. Chelita often did the laundry and handled all family business matters. Luz Alba, the prettiest, brought beautiful fabrics from the

United States every summer. Rosita, the best dressmaker of them all, made dresses without using a pattern, just by taking a person's measurements.

In the early morning, my cousins and I would sit in the patio and wait for my grandmother to feed the chickens. The chickens especially liked the old kitchen in the patio, a thatch-roofed and plaster-walled little building virtually abandoned when my grandmother got appliances for the house. The chickens lived all over the land surrounding her new cinder-block house and even ventured out into the road. Yet when they heard her rustle the bag of feed, they ran toward her. "Abuelita, throw some corn over here," we would shout with excitement. The chickens would rush at us and peck up the kernels of corn, even peck at our shoelaces. We laughed loudly.

One day, I saw her go to the pecking chickens and grab one by the neck. In one quick motion she twisted its neck as she walked toward the kitchen. She slapped the dead chicken on the table and began to pluck its feathers with both hands. The chicken was soon cut up into parts and put into a pot of boiling water. I never forgot that chicken – or that chicken soup.

I have few specific memories from those summers with my grandmother, but I remember her voice in the air. She liked to talk and talk – about the neighbors, about this and that, about memories from her youth. I remember her hands always warm from cooking or ironing or cleaning. I remember her laughter. She was a woman with a heart full of love for her family, her home, her country, and all the animals she fed and killed.

Abuelita Concepción's Chicken Soup

This is the chicken soup that I often watched my grandmother make. Since she cooked without measuring her ingredients, you, too, are welcome to vary the proportions according to your desires.

We usually sat down for lunch in her small kitchen by one o'clock. After squeezing a wedge of fresh-picked lime into the soup, we would eat with blue metal spoons that were speckled with white. Always there was Coca-Cola, and La Joya sodas in bright orange, red, yellow, or brown. After lunch we were ready to take a siesta, but first we had to mop the floor. The large heavy mop made pretty designs on the floor, like long hair flowing in the wind, before the concrete dried to a dull gray. Then we went to our Abuelita to have her bless us and make the sign of the Cross on our foreheads with her warm hands. We slipped under the beds onto the cool concrete floor and tried to imagine a cool breeze coming from the open door before we fell asleep.

1 cup dried garbanzo beans
1 whole chicken, cut into
    8 to 10 pieces
2 garlic cloves
1 small onion, chopped
Salt
½ cup uncooked white rice
1 tomato, cut into wedges
¼ cup cilantro, chopped
2 corn or flour tortillas per
    person (corn tortillas are
    best with chicken)
1 lime

Peel the garbanzo beans, if you like, by removing the light-colored skin that encases them.

Place the chicken pieces, garlic cloves, and chopped onion into a soup pot and cover with water. Simmer for 1 hour, seasoning with salt to taste. Then, add the rice, garbanzo beans, and tomato. Cook for 30 minutes longer, or until the garbanzo beans are tender, adding water as necessary. Stir the chopped cilantro into the soup just before serving.

Serve the soup with tortillas and fresh lime wedges. The lime "whitens" and clouds the soup and produces a delicious, light flavor. This soup, or *caldo,* will feed 4 adults — or one grandmother and many grandchildren.

My Next-Door Neighbor

Nancy DeNicola Cicerone
1905–1992

BY DEBORAH LOMANNO DOENGES

When I was very little, I was taught in Sunday school that we should love our neighbors. The teacher asked whether we knew our neighbors. "Of course I know my neighbor," I exclaimed. "I love my neighbor. She is my grandmother!" We didn't need neighbors; we had Nona.

Being the oldest granddaughter and living next door had its privileges. Nona loved to take me shopping with her. And I loved to go, because I would inevitably come home with something new and because we would always stop for something to eat, usually a grilled cheese sandwich at Woolworth's. I felt wonderful just to be with her. She made sure I was acting like a lady and gave me advice on everything from not swinging my pocketbook when I walked to washing my hands every time I entered the house. She had a funny laugh; it always made me laugh. And a funny sneeze, very loud. We would tease her and yell "God bless you" from our house.

She used to tell me she would probably die before I was married. She must have been feeling her mortality, since my grandfather died when I was nine. I cried to think that she might not be around when I was older. Luckily, she walked down the aisle at my wedding and attended the christenings of all four of my children. They, too, remember her with great fondness.

After my grandfather died, my older brothers and I took turns sleeping over at her house; she didn't want to be alone at night. I was sometimes afraid, sleeping in the same room where my grandfather died, but because I knew she needed me I never said anything.

When I was an adult, Nona began to need me in different ways. Now I took her shopping. She loved the supermarket and would take forever browsing. She liked spending the time there with me, a sweet echo of our earliest expeditions.

Loving Nona, my neighbor, was one of the easiest and most important experiences of my life. I take with me her loving and caring examples of how to treat people, how to open the heart and the home. My mother, her daughter, is very much like her, and many times when I look at my mother I can see my grandmother in her. Living so close and being there for one another was a blessing to us all. We learned firsthand how to love our neighbors, wherever they may live.

Nona's Easter Bread

An immigrant at the age of one, Nona became a mother of five and a grandmother of twenty. Her house was always full of people, with something wonderful always cooking on the stove. This, I learned, was the normal Italian house.

Nona made her famous Easter bread only for Easter Sunday. The recipe is not elaborate or fancy. Still, I remember the love she put into the well of flour, and her determination in kneading it just right, so it is very special to me. Sharing this recipe is like sharing a piece of Nona.

Now that Nona is gone, I make Easter bread for my family, privileged to be the one to carry on this simple but wonderful tradition. As we sit around our large table at Easter and count our blessings, we pass this bread and remember Nona with love.

7 cups flour

2 eggs

2¼ cups warm water

1 tablespoon sugar

1 tablespoon salt

2 tablespoons pepper (optional)

⅓ cup vegetable oil

1½ envelopes (1½ tablespoons) active dry yeast, dissolved in ¼ cup warm (not hot) water with 2 teaspoons sugar

Place the flour in a large bowl and make a well in the center.

In a separate bowl, drop the eggs into the warm water (if the water is hot, the eggs will curdle). Add the sugar, salt, pepper, and vegetable oil. Mix well. Pour this into the middle of the flour, then mix a little flour into the liquid. Add the yeast water to the well of flour. Gradually mix until you can no longer handle the dough with a fork.

Knead the dough well, but not too hard. Cover it with a towel and let it rise until doubled.

Punch down the dough, divide it into two loaf pans, and let it rise again. Meanwhile, preheat the oven to 375 degrees.

Bake the bread for 40 minutes. For the last few minutes, take the loaves out of the pans and place them directly on the oven rack to brown. Tap the bottom of the bread; if it is done, it will make a hollow sound.

Makes two 9½ x 5½-inch loaves.

Taking Measure

Hilda Amsler McElhattan
1906–1996

BY NANCY PRICE GRAFF

Even as my maternal grandmother lay dying, I had trouble conjuring up a picture of her in my mind's eye. In part this was because we lived far from one another, and my children – two of her eight great-grandchildren – compromised my mobility while her declining health compromised hers. But it was in large part, too, because of a phenomenon that dates back years, decades, perhaps to the very start of my life.

When I was a young child, I thought of my grandmother as a large woman, unusually tall and solid. Although she was by nature gentle, she had a physical presence, as if her broad bones were filled with sand. At least a head taller than my paternal grandmother, she rose before me as a skyscraper soars in the imagination.

In her prime, she probably scratched the underside of five foot nine, a strapping height for a woman born at the turn of the century. She was reared on a small farm amid the crossroad villages and rolling fields of western Pennsylvania. Valedictorian of her high school graduating class, she married a man who never finished high school, and, except for brief stints in Chicago and New York – where my grandfather's work took them for a while – she never left the small towns of her childhood.

I remember how much she loved words. Whenever we visited we played Scrabble, and she played to win, conjuring up words on the board that I am sure she never used conversationally in all her life. Once she beat me by laying "booze" across triple word points, and I looked at her astonished that a woman who neither drank nor used slang would even have such a word in her vocabulary. For my high school graduation, she gave me a Webster's dictionary, inscribed, which I still cherish. The last time I visited her, not long before her death, she challenged me to a game of Scrabble, and we played, her frail hand trembling like a hummingbird over the board while my young daughter squirmed on my lap.

Time and events have now complicated my memories of her physical presence. I do remember that when I was nine years old, my grandfather died. Despite my youth, I could see that my grandmother was diminished by her loss, that the wear of his long illness and her grief had shrunk her physically, compressing her skeleton and dissolving some substance of her being.

Meanwhile, I kept growing. By the time I was sixteen, I had passed her and made my own mark on the doorway at five foot nine. Then she broke her hip, and although she healed and regained the use of her leg, she rarely walked without a cane. Except in her apartment or my parents' home, she now walked bowed over to clutch the cane's rubber-knobbed handle. When I kissed her, I was forced to lean down, to reach past the silver hair spun fine as spider webs to the warm cheek below.

Only when I had been married a number of years did my grandmother start to grow again. Without physically regaining any of the height she had lost, she nevertheless began to grow before me, to take on mythical proportions. For the first time, I began looking at her as my grandfather's wife, a woman who gave thirty-six years of her life to a marriage. I also gained an intimate appreciation of her tenacity and faith as I began to experience myself the insidious depression that had whittled away at her spirit for so many decades. As the years of her widowhood stretched on past thirty, fully a third of her life, the depths of her loves and losses grew even more poignant and heroic in my thoughts.

My grandmother died of breast cancer at eighty-nine. During the last decade of her life, every time I saw her she was smaller than the time before. Her bones drained of sand and she grew bird-like in her apparent weightlessness and vulnerability. Yet there was still something indomitable about her presence that overrode her frail corporeal being, something monumental that cemented her place as matriarch over four generations of women.

Grandma McElhattan's Chicken and Noodles

Each of my cousins remembers a different favorite dish from the days when our grandmother cooked. We cannot recall one another's choices; it's as if she treated us as distinct, unrelated units and not like the sprawling brood of her own family. More likely, we are simply showing our tastes.

I had an affinity for the noodle dishes that were part of her German heritage. This chicken and noodle dish is a modest recipe from a woman who lived a modest life, but there is something filling and appropriate about it that makes it deeply satisfying. I remember it being served whenever the family gathered.

4 cups chicken broth
(my grandmother always
used homemade)
3 cups water
2 whole chicken breasts, split,
skinned, and boned
1 egg, beaten
Flour for dredging the chicken
2 to 3 tablespoons butter
½ medium onion, chopped
1 (16-ounce) bag
extra-wide egg noodles

Bring the broth and water to a boil in a large kettle. Simmer the chicken over low heat until it is tender. Turn off the heat, remove the chicken from the broth, and set the broth aside.

Cut the chicken breasts in half. Pat them dry, then dip them in the egg and dredge them in flour.

Melt the butter in a skillet. Add the onions and sauté them until soft. (Do not brown them.) Remove the onions and set them aside. Add more butter to the skillet, if necessary, then brown the chicken.

While the chicken is browning, bring the broth to a boil again. Add the noodles and cook them until soft. Do not drain them. When the noodles are done and the chicken pieces are brown, add the chicken and onions to the soupy noodle mixture and serve. Makes 4 servings.

The Wildness in Her Hair

Margaret Doty Duffield
1907–1979

BY SUZANNE DUFFIELD KINGSBURY

By the time my grandmother died, she was so frail she could have been my age, not yet ten. Cancer lined her pancreas. Her lovely face, once beautiful in brown and white photos, had been aged to a rubber-softness by gin. She died from drink, from boredom, from selling her intelligence to crossword puzzles.

I know my early grandmother from a journal she kept between 1934 and 1940, the story of a twenty-something couple living in New York City. She wrote of FDR, of the buys at Bloomingdale's, of black nursemaids, walks down Fifth Avenue, cocktail parties, houses on Long Island Sound, and a circle of friends who drank champagne and played charades, went to the theater and published articles, became editors, playwrights, actors, and directors. In her writing I see my contemporary of sixty years ago, and I know we would have been friends.

In our ancient home movies, she looks elegant: dark eyelashes, a petite frame dressed in lace, and the kind of walk that said "lady." She left behind a treasure chest of costumes for me to dress up in: sequined flapper dresses, beaded shawls, feather boas, and Spanish taffeta skirts down to the ankles.

My grandmother understood magic. My cousin Jill had a magic hat; when she put it on, strange things happened – she communicated without talking, she dreamed in different languages. Grandma would nod her head, "Yes, yes, that can happen. I, too, had a magic hat when I was young."

As a youngster at Grandma's I was never told to clean up or to eat all of my dinner. I was allowed to watch late movies on TV and stay up all night long, then eat as many pancakes as I wanted for breakfast. This was not because my grandmother liked to spoil me, but because there were no rules. A true eccentric, she didn't understand them and never cared about them.

Her wildness, unapparent in her quiet disposition, could be noted from her hair. Once a week she would go to the Guilford Beauty Shop to tame it, but within the next seven days it would spiral out of control into a frenzy of loose ringlets that traveled upward, downward, and sideways, framing her face like a lion's mane. The unkempt frivolity was especially noticeable at a time when women were ironing their hair, plastering it to their heads in shiny curls that looked painted on. My mother once found crumpled pictures of my grandmother in an old wastebasket. The photos showed her sitting demurely on the beach, stylish bathing suit, legs crossed, a slight smile across her lips — and hair spiraling around her like an unkempt animal's. Grandma had thrown these pictures away, as if ashamed that it would dare to creep out, her wildness, into broad daylight.

She made us extravagant meals from recipes she had written on wrinkled pieces of paper and stuck into old cookbooks. (She reminded me of a frustrated songwriter scribbling music on napkins.) Saying she wasn't hungry, she often sat down with a giant chocolate chip cookie as her only course for dinner. I dreamed of the day when I might be adult enough to eat dessert as my main meal.

Back then, cooking was a woman's trademark. If you could cook, you could be. But my grandmother rebelled: she drank gin while she cooked. My grandfather drank, too, keeping his drink in a hole in the floor of the front closet. He in the front of the house, she in the back, drinking their entertainment, drinking the New York social scene back into their marriage.

The family has many excuses for my grandmother's drinking: "because her husband did," or "because suburban life didn't suit her," or "because she was bored." In his journals my grandfather wrote of the humor in her drunkenness, sidestepping her illness to grope for entertainment in its foulness.

What did I learn from her? To die early? To hide my writing? She wrote in secret while her husband's work was widely published in the *Herald-Tribune* and in books on world politics. I have devoured her journals. Her vitality has given me permission to let my own wildness creep out. From this woman I have learned to be unashamed of the wildness, whether it shows in the fiction I write, the places I explore, the drums I beat, or the men I choose as lovers. I will let it flourish in deference to her memory. Only nine when she died and not understanding her wisdom at the time, I have brought it with me into womanhood.

Grandma's Vermouth and Chicken

Along with her costumes and journals, I still have those scribbled recipes she stuck into cook-books. They speak of her memory, of good taste, of pizazz, and of a little sorrow. Below is one of her recipes. From her comments you can see her laissez-faire attitude creeping around the corners of the page.

2 chicken breasts, halved
2 tablespoons butter
¼ cup dry vermouth
    or dry white wine
Juice from ¼ lemon
Salt and pepper
2 (10-ounce) packages of
    artichokes
½ onion, diced (optional)
2 garlic cloves, diced (optional)
1 cup heavy cream (optional)

"This chicken-do involves as many half chicken breasts as there are bodies to feed. Brown the chicken in butter – partially cook – finish cooking in vermouth, lemon juice, salt, and pepper. Meanwhile, cook frozen artichokes (2 packages for 4 to 6 people), put artichokes in ovenproof pan with chicken and arrange on bottom, shake around a bit, cover, and leave until dinnertime. Just before serving, heat in a 350-degree oven but do not broil. You can do all of the above any way you wish as it always seems to come out."

Note: To make this dish even more flavorful, sauté the onion and garlic in the butter, then add the chicken. Once the chicken is nearly cooked, remove it and set it aside. (No need to cook the chicken in the oven.)

Add the vermouth to the pan and allow the leftover butter to dissolve. Then add the lemon juice and cream. Simmer for 3 to 5 minutes, stirring occasionally. Place the chicken and the artichokes into the cream sauce, allow them to heat through, then serve over pasta. This recipe serves 4 people.

Grandma's Ham and Wild Rice *(Jambon Lauré)*

Here is another of her delicacies, made even more delicious to me by her own words.

1 cup uncooked wild rice

4 cups water

1 tablespoon salt

4 tablespoons butter

½ pound button mushrooms,
    stems discarded

4 (¼- to ½-inch thick) slices
    baked ham

½ cup dry white wine

1 cup sour cream

"Wash the rice as thoroughly as possible. I find it best to put the rice in a deep bowl and cover it with cold water. Swish it around a bit and then carefully pour off the dirty water. Next, put the rice in a sieve and wash again under the cold water tap. Oh, be sure to skim off any bits of stick or whatever that float to the top in the bowl. Eventually, put it to boil in the 4 cups of water and, when it is done, wash it again in a sieve if necessary but in any case drain it very dry.

"Melt the butter, add the peeled mushroom caps, and cook gently for about 8 minutes. [Peeling the mushrooms wasn't so much a rule with Grandma, she just believed in the clean, white, untouched beauty of the peeled caps. It's sufficient, though, simply to wipe the mushrooms with a damp cloth.] Put the ham in a casserole (cut in bite-size pieces if for buffet) and add the mushrooms. Put the well-drained rice into the pan in which the mushrooms were cooked, and add the wine and then the sour cream. Warm and mix well. Pour this mixture over the mushrooms and ham and bake about 20 minutes." Serves 6.

One True Red Rose

Dortha Juanita Gans Thomas
1907–1988

BY TANYA THOMAS RYBARCZYK

Like my grandmother, I love roses. And, like her, I'm proud, and stubborn, and a bit of a loner. We were never close; we lived on opposite coasts, and she died before I became a woman and could understand her as such. I know her now from a few scattered childhood memories, and from a video my father created before she died from her second bout with lymphoma. Dot was one of eight children and, according to my great-grandmother, the only one not borne in pain. She spent her childhood on a farm in the state of Washington; her parents were homesteaders from North Dakota. She loved to go barefoot, to pick flowers as she gathered the cows, and to spend the early mornings on a swing that her father had built just for her between the house and the barn.

Only once did I spend any extended time with my grandmother. It was early spring, in the weeks following my parents' divorce. I was seven, living in New York. The day after the news was announced, I was pulled from school, told to study my times tables, and sent off to travel by car with my grandparents to their home in California. I had been warned that my grandfather thought me an unruly child, so I was on my best behavior. Grandma would sneak me treats and smiles when my grandfather wasn't looking, and I would take them quietly and smile back at her.

Each night, when the three of us stopped at a motel, I quietly curled up in my sleeping bag on the floor. Before turning out the lights, my grandmother came near, whispered to me for a while, and kissed me good night. At one motel, there was an extra bed in the room for me, and Grandma and I celebrated. She clapped her hands together, and her eyes got all wide. "Now isn't this wonderful?" she exclaimed, and we laughed and laughed as I jumped on the bed, until my grandfather glanced over and said I'd better not get used to the luxury.

The car we were traveling in was small, and I was packed in the back seat between the luggage and the door. Occasionally Grandma convinced Grandpa to rearrange the luggage so she could sit next to me. There she helped me with my times tables and taught me to play Dots – a game she was good at, she said, because it sounded like her name.

"We were never close; we lived on opposite coasts, and she died before I became a woman and could understand her as such. I know her now from a few scattered childhood memories, and from a video my father created before she died."

A picture of me and my grandmother at Four Corners shows us standing with each of our legs in a different state, my grandmother's hands resting on my head. I remember the cold wind blowing up under our jackets, whipping our hair across our faces. My grandmother's hair was short and white; mine was long and brown. Her hands were keeping my ears warm and holding my hair back for the picture. I still remember my grandmother's hands, how it felt to hold them, how they felt resting tentatively on my head. Her skin was soft and loose. I liked the feel of her hands, though I never would have told her that; I was trying so hard to be good, and I see now that she was too.

Inside my grandparents' house, everything was neat and orderly. It smelled, to me, like old people. In the living room where my grandfather would sit and read, a clock on the mantel went tick, tick, tick. But outside was my grandmother's rose garden, full of hybrid teas six feet high: reds, yellows, whites, pinks, peaches. The sweet smell intoxicated me as branches swayed above my head and bees buzzed about my ears. The blooms were so large I could not cup them in my hand. I don't remember seeing roses before then.

My grandmother accomplished many things before her death: She earned a master's degree in Christian education (rare for a woman of her time), taught, raised a family, kept her faith, and lived to celebrate her fiftieth wedding anniversary. And yet it is said that she spent the whole of her life searching for a true red rose.

Dot's Beer Bread

More than food, my grandmother craved the conversation and sense of connection that came with company. She had little patience for cooking, and little confidence in her abilities in the kitchen. The easier a dish was to cook, the better: it was more likely to turn out well, and she was able to move more quickly into the living room where the others were sitting and talking.

Dot's beer bread is healthful and easy, a favorite recipe by all accounts. And a favorite family story tells how Dot – a Church of the Brethren teetotaler – endured embarrassment each time she purchased the necessary beer.

The recipe is printed just as it appears on the blue recipe card my grandmother gave to my aunt.

½ cup raw sunflower seeds, cooked rye grain, or cooked oatmeal (optional)

2½ cups all-purpose flour

2½ teaspoons baking powder

½ teaspoon baking soda

½ teaspoon salt

½ cup whole wheat flour

½ cup soy flour

¼ cup sugar

¼ cup molasses

1 (12-ounce) can beer

"To dry ingredients, you may add ½ cup raw sunflower seeds, or ½ cup cooked rye grain, or ½ cup cooked oatmeal, or anything else that won't absorb much liquid.

"Mix all ingredients well (I usually mix the dry ones first). Put into greased loaf pan. Bake about an hour at 400. Test for doneness with wooden toothpick – it often looks done when it isn't.

"You can play with this recipe, so long as you keep the 2½ cups of flour (and the baking powder and soda) and the beer constant. If you want it less sweet, cut down on the sugar. The smaller portions of flour may be varied as you wish: 1 cup soy, no whole wheat, all whole wheat, or rye can be put in instead.

"Standard loaf pan is OK. If you can find a smaller one, you'll get a little better shaped loaf, but the quality of the bread is the same. If you want to wait, I'll bring you an extra loaf pan at Thanksgiving."

Grandma's Corn Custard

I will always smile over one of my grandmother's favorite sayings, spoken often at the dinner table. With only a bit of corn custard left in the serving dish, she would look around and ask sweetly, "Now, does anyone want this more than I do?"

She used to call this "Mrs. Minnick's Corn Custard" to honor her friend and its creator. But to me it will always be "Grandma's."

2 eggs
1 cup milk
2 tablespoons sugar
2 tablespoons cornstarch
½ teaspoon salt (optional)
1 (15-ounce) can cream-style
    sweet corn

Preheat your oven to 350 degrees.

Beat the eggs together in a medium-sized mixing bowl. Add the milk, sugar, cornstarch, and salt. Stir until blended. Add the corn and stir well.

Pour the custard into a greased 1-quart casserole dish. Bake uncovered for 1 hour and 15 minutes, or until the top has browned a bit. To test for doneness, shake the dish gently; it should be somewhat firm. Serves 4 to 6 people.

Mildred Blanche Sincraugh Houses
1908–1992

ℬlackberry Summers

BY JANIS HASHE

My grandmother was a born storyteller.

"What kind of a story do you want?" she'd ask, as we settled into bed, warm and pj'd. "A regular story or one made up out of my head?"

"Out of your head," the three of us would chorus.

So my grandmother would tell us stories "out of her head" – wonderful stories with many chapters and no real endings, because we never wanted them to end even if they had to stop for a while. Stories about the Little Shmoo Boy, whose personality and physical description changed to match the tone of the tale, and many, many stories about all kinds of animals, including her faithful dog Sheppy. She would probably have been hurt if we had ever picked a store-bought story over hers, but we never did, so everyone had fun.

My grandmother Mildred grew up dirt-poor in Arizona, the daughter of Effie Scott Sincraugh, a woman used to shooting rattlesnakes with a shotgun. Mildred married the love of her life, Clark, at seventeen, and stayed married to him until her death sixty-seven years later. She was not quite five feet tall, and she was plump. You sort of *sank* into her when you hugged her. As we got older we grew taller than Grandma, but she remained huggable.

She smelled of talc and Calgon Bouquet and she loved to dress up – always with a cardigan sweater draped jauntily across her shoulders and held in place with rhinestone sweater guards. But being, as she put it, "Scotch" (she was actually Scots-Irish-Dutch-German), she was proud of having paid a dime for the peach-colored bag that was a perfect match for her peach-colored pumps. The pumps had probably cost a nickel at the local Goodwill. Her early poverty had taught her that money wasn't important. Work, family, laughter, treating others with respect – these were the things she valued. Only as an adult have I realized how lucky I was to have her, and how much I learned from her.

Her storytelling instinct sometimes caused her to "embroider" real stories. She'd tell a family anecdote, and my grandfather – a tall, quiet man who worked with his hands all his life – would look at her, shake his head in amusement, and say, "Mildred, you and I have been living separate lives for the last sixty years." *His* version of the story was much less colorful.

Mildred loved to read, though she never finished high school, and her reading took her around the world – in her imagination. Had things been different, she might well have been a writer, putting down on paper the tales she spun so easily for her audience of three. As it was, she worked twelve-hour days alongside my grandfather as a rancher's wife. Later, when life got a little easier, she was still canning, darning, and saving for another Depression. She was proud of my mother for finishing college and becoming a teacher.

Toward the end of her life, I wrote to her that she had been my inspiration for becoming a writer. When I next saw her, I knew by the look on her face that I had given her something precious. Not nearly as precious, though, as what she had given me.

She still comes to me in dreams, urging me to "get on with it." (She was never one to beat around the bush.) Now that my novel is finished, it will be dedicated to her – in memory of those stories that were always better than any we found in books.

Mildred's Wild Blackberry Tarts

Mom taught school throughout our childhood, so we often spent afternoons with Grandma. In the California beach community where we grew up, there were fields of wild blackberries. "If you kids go out and pick enough blackberries, we'll make a pie," she'd say. She probably just wanted to get us out of the house for a few moments of peace. When we came back, we always wanted our own "pie," so we'd end up making wild blackberry tarts.

Don't be afraid to get messy making these. (Mildred never minded when we did.) You can use store-bought blackberries, but you might want to wait until you can pick wild ones — or until some little kids can do it for you.

The Filling

4 heaping tablespoons honey
Cinnamon
4 cups blackberries, washed
    and well drained

The Crust

2 cups unbleached flour
Salt
⅓ cup vegetable oil
⅔ cup boiling water

To prepare the filling: add the honey and cinnamon to the blackberries. Toss the berries until they are coated, then set them aside.

For the crust: combine the flour and a pinch of salt. In a separate bowl, whisk the oil into the boiling water. Add the flour mixture and stir until a dough is formed. Cover and refrigerate for at least 20 minutes.

Preheat your oven to 400 degrees.

Remove the pie dough from the refrigerator. Divide it into 8 pieces. On a floured board, roll out each piece with a lightly-floured rolling pin. The dough should be rolled to a thickness of about ¼ inch.

Line 4 individual tart pans with rolled-out dough. Trim the edges, leaving an overhang of ¼ to ½ inch. Scoop the berries into the center of each pan.

Lay a top crust over the filling. Using your fingers, pinch together the edges of the top and bottom crusts. With a fork, prick the top of each tart in several places.

Place the tarts in the oven and bake them until the tops are golden brown, about 45 minutes. (Watch the crusts carefully. Do not let them burn — adjust the heat accordingly.) Makes 4 tarts.

Note: Tarts can be served either hot or cold. Mildred served them hot (we couldn't wait) with cold condensed milk. Heavy cream or vanilla ice cream are good, too.

A Bright Orange House

Angela Hernandez Lugo
1910–1993

BY CAROLINA GUERRA KILBOURN

When I turned nine, my grandparents moved from the country to the city, two blocks from where I lived in Saginaw, Michigan. Grandma quickly turned her plain house into the brightest house in the neighborhood. It was pumpkin orange, with the rocks bordering her flower gardens painted every imaginable color. My face would flush when I heard people commenting about this house. We pleaded with her to try a quieter green, or a brown, but the house stayed orange. After many years, the house did change – to yellow! It was still the most beautiful house on the block, and I was secretly proud of it.

Having my grandparents so close meant that I always had a place to escape to. When I didn't like the rules at my house, I'd jump on my blue Huffy and ride to Grandma's. She never took sides, just made small remarks like "aye" or "hmmm" or "too bad." She always had enough food for me – tortillas, beans, rice. In fact, she could have fed anyone who walked through the door. She was an expert at feeding a large crew; she had raised twelve children (and given birth to fifteen).

Everyone called her "Angelita," for "little Angela." She was born in Weslaco, Texas, to a migrant woman who raised two children on her own. (A single parent in those days! What a scandal!) As a child, a teenager, even as a pregnant mother, Angela worked in the fields. They lived wherever the crops were plentiful, traveling in their car to wherever there was work. They never had enough money for doctors, and she delivered one of her babies under a tree with the help of the other migrant women who were working in the fields. When that baby died soon afterward, she blamed only herself.

The life of a migrant farmer is harder than anyone can imagine. But she endured this and more, burying three grown children and her husband before she died. She had diabetes from the age of fifty, and her weak heart and lungs were a further source of suffering (she smoked cigarettes from the age of ten).

In spite of all the pain and hardship, she had a life filled with joy and music. Whenever I hear certain songs, I picture her sitting at her kitchen table crocheting and listening to the Mexican radio station. She was a regular at the fiestas on Friday and Saturday nights in Saginaw's large Mexican-American community. After she became ill, she continued to attend the fiestas in her wheelchair. While the music didn't mean much to me at my young age, it was everything to her. She thought Mexican music was the best music – maybe the only music – to dance to. She drew sustenance from the music, and from the food, the color, and the people around her.

"It was pumpkin orange, with the rocks bordering her flower gardens painted every imaginable color. My face would flush when I heard people commenting about this house. We pleaded with her to try a quieter green, or a brown."

I have much more than color, food, and music from Angela Hernandez Lugo. From my grandma I learned strength and determination. She always made a positive experience out of a negative one. Even in her worst pain she would say, "Oh God, please give me the strength to live."

She had endured so much in her life, and until the very end she was always ready to endure more. There were times when she showed more courage than any one person should be expected to have.

Throughout my house are vibrant objects that once belonged to her. Pictures and pottery. Pillows and rugs. These things have inspired me to keep alive the color, food, and music that meant so much to my grandmother. Her music is now my music, and her food is now the food that I prepare for my family and friends. But more importantly, her spirit is alive in me, and the example of her strength will always be with me.

Angelita's Flour Tortillas

Tortillas have been on our table for as long as I can remember. Everyone in our family takes pride in making them. Grandma had her own recipe, and her five daughters had their own. Grandma never wrote down her recipes, of course, and never used measuring cups or spoons. We all learned by watching.

2 cups flour
1 to 2 teaspoons salt
1 teaspoon baking powder
⅔ cup warm water
¼ cup vegetable oil or
   shortening

Mix together the flour, salt, and baking powder. Add enough warm water to make a stiff dough. If the dough is too sticky, add more flour.

Form the dough into 12 to 14 balls. Roll each ball out to a thickness of about ⅛ inch.

Heat a heavy frying pan or iron skillet on medium-high, then add the vegetable oil. Fry the tortillas for 30 to 60 seconds on each side, or until they start to brown. Place the finished tortillas in a cloth to keep them warm until you're ready to eat. Makes 12 to 14 tortillas.

Note: Tortillas are good with butter and salt, or they can be filled with meat, stir-fried vegetables, refried beans, and rice.

Angelita's Refried Beans *(Frijoles)*

I often watched my grandma make refried beans, as she probably watched her own grand-mother make them. Frijoles *were a staple in her house, as they are now in mine.*

I have always enjoyed sharing my Mexican culture with friends and neighbors. I do so especially on Cinco de Mayo (May 5th). This is the Mexican holiday celebrating the Mexican victory over the French. It is a day symbolic of Mexican resistance to all outside forces. On this day I make frijoles *to share with others, and to remember.*

1 pound dried pinto beans
2 to 3 tablespoons salt
1 to 2 tablespoons vegetable oil

Rinse the beans and soak them in cold water for 2 hours. Drain and transfer them to a pot of fresh water, then bring the water to a boil. Reduce the heat, add salt, and continue to boil the beans for 1½ to 2 hours, or until they are soft and pink.

Once the beans are fully cooked, mash them in a hot, well-oiled skillet over medium heat for 10 to 15 minutes. Add water if necessary.

Serve hot, perhaps inside a warm tortilla, or use as a dip with nacho chips and salsa. This recipe serves 10 to 12 people.

Note: The neat thing about refried beans is their simplicity and economy. Angelita fed many mouths on little money with this dish. But to make the beans even more flavorful, consider mixing in cumin, Mexican oregano, onion powder, and garlic powder; garnish with cilantro.

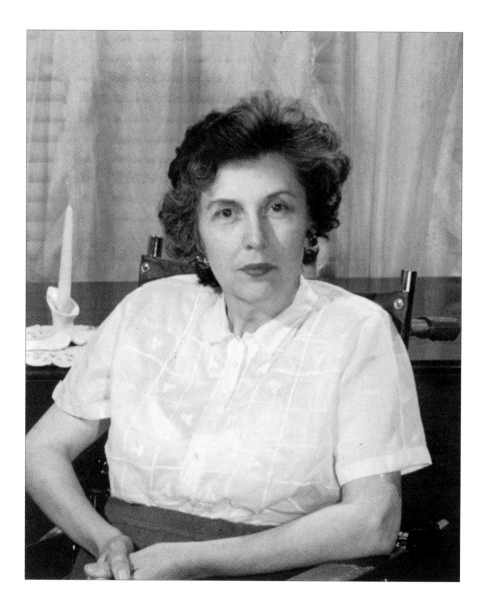

Triumph of the Spirit

Erma Williams Hipple
1911–

BY KATHY HIPPLE

On her thirtieth birthday, my grandmother wrote her first check to Mayo Clinic. Thus began her search for the cause of her mysterious symptoms – temporary blindness and sporadic loss of motor control. The search would conclude with a diagnosis of multiple sclerosis, for which there is still no cure. Armed with little more than pithy advice from the doctors – "Never work to the point of exhaustion, and stay away from people with colds to the point of rudeness" – Erma returned to Utica, a tiny town in rural Illinois, to begin her life as a disabled wife and mother.

For a lesser woman, this would have marked the end of a vibrant, active life. For Erma, it did not. No doubt she was devastated. The more she learned about the disease, from its crippling effects to its fifteen-year life expectancy, the more frightened she must have become. But she had a five-year-old boy (my father) to raise and a household to run. She made mental and physical adjustments. Ramps were installed, a wheelchair purchased. And as she declined physically, her spirit seemed to swell.

By the time I was born, my grandmother had become a vital force in Utica. She helped found the town library, hosted Bible study groups at her home, taught nearly every kid in town to play the piano (at fifty cents a lesson), and almost always had a visitor sitting at her kitchen table or on her screened porch. Despite her college education and formidable intelligence, she had many friends among the less educated factory workers and farmers who lived in town. Her next-door neighbor, a Mexican-American man, visited daily. When she failed in her efforts to teach him to read English, she had him teach her Spanish instead. After my father left home for college and my grandfather died, my grandmother's friends rallied around her, doing her shopping, bringing in her mail, running her errands, planting her flower boxes, trimming her hedges. These daily acts of kindness – along with part-time home healthcare – allowed my grandmother to live alone at home, despite advancing MS, well into her eighties.

Her house was always filled with neighborhood kids. My grandmother, it seems, was as irresistible to them as she was to my brother, my sister, and me. She found children amusing and fascinating. The minutiae of our lives commanded her deepest attention. But when we needed to run from her queries, to explore the abandoned darkroom upstairs, or to play outside, she smiled and sent us on our busy way. She understood children.

When I was eight, we three kids spent a glorious summer at her house while our parents attended college nearby. In the mornings we went to a Baptist summer camp. Each day at camp, if we had memorized a Bible verse, we could reach thumb and forefinger into a penny-filled jar and extract as many pennies as we could lift through the jar's opening. Most children were content to grab only a few pennies. Not my brother. Despite his near-eidetic memory, he took great pride in locating the shortest Bible verses. Then, he would grab as many pennies as possible, carefully organizing them into something resembling a penny roll without the wrapper, and ease them out of the jar. It was a precarious mission, often yielding only one or two pennies. But if he succeeded – Hallelujah! – nearly forty cents. We then raced off to spend our pennies on candy or ice cream. Then to my grandmother's. She was in her wheelchair on the porch, waiting to hear the results of our daily penny caper and other adventures, waiting to laugh at our exuberance.

We were her biological grandchildren, but her heart overflowed with love for her "Utica grandkids" as well. She watched us all grow up, through the stubbed toes of our childhood to the square dances of our teens and the ghost stories at night on the porch.

As an adult, I've spent many happy days watching my children visit my grandmother and explore her house and town. The house is exactly as I remember it. The town, I realize with the jaded eye of a New Yorker, is more rust belt than small-town paradise. But not to my children. They marvel that they can walk by themselves along the sidewalk to Main Street, where they can buy candy or ice cream. As I drive along behind them, I'm not really in the car but skipping alongside them, eight years old again. My grandmother is not really in a nursing home in a neighboring town, where she moved last year, but sitting in her wheel-chair on her porch, waiting to hear of our adventures downtown.

Grandma Hipple's Cherry Torte

Grandma Hipple came from an English family that arrived in America in the 1700s. Raised on a farm, she had little time or strength for the complicated foods of her heritage. Her husband, Bruce Hipple, from a German-American family, had been a butcher and an Oscar Mayer salesman for many years, and most meals included the best cut of meat he could bring home each day. As a child, I found the desserts more exciting than the meals. Grandma Hipple's desserts were usually simple to prepare, even when they had to be baked. No meal was complete without a healthy portion of cake, pie, crumple, or torte.

The Torte

1¼ cups sugar
1 cup flour
1 teaspoon baking soda
1 teaspoon cinnamon
¼ teaspoon salt
1 (14-ounce) can pitted
  sour cherries
1 egg, beaten
1 tablespoon butter, softened
1 cup chopped nuts

The Topping

Juice from the can of cherries
½ cup sugar
1 tablespoon cornstarch
1 tablespoon butter

To make the torte: preheat your oven to 350 degrees.

Sift together the sugar, flour, baking soda, cinnamon, and salt.

Drain the sour cherries and set the juice aside.

In a medium-sized bowl, combine the cherries, the egg, the butter, and the nuts. Add the dry ingredients and mix well.

Spread the batter in a greased 9 x 13-inch pan and bake for 45 minutes.

Meanwhile, prepare the topping: in a saucepan, combine the cherry juice, sugar, cornstarch, and butter. Bring the ingredients to a boil, then immediately remove the mixture from the heat and let it cool.

When the torte has cooled, drizzle the topping over it and serve. Makes 10 to 12 servings.

Elsie Bernice Hodge
1912–1988

Among the Leprechauns

BY RHODA JANE BARRETT

Magic and a sense of otherworldliness are what I associate with my grand-mother, Bernice Hodge. She took a life of hardship – living in the backwoods and small towns of Kentucky, West Virginia, and Ohio, raising twelve children through decades of poverty, uncertainty, and turmoil – and wove a magical web of love and imagination to inspire her children, grandchildren, and generations to come.

When I was three years old, my family lived with my grandmother for a year while my father was off in Vietnam. That time with her opened a world of magic and wonder that I still visit today. Spellbinding entertainment was her forte. We'd have tea parties with real china (and, on special days, with her grown-up friends as my guests). We'd take long walks to collect flowers, then press the blossoms between wax paper for fancy placemats. She would tell me stories about her real-life adventures: how she had lived above the restaurant that she ran with my grandfather, serving as cook and dishwasher and simultaneously caring for six children; how they moved to a makeshift cabin in the mountains with no one around for miles; how she and her family later subsisted off farm-land and, through hard work, managed to meet almost all their needs (except for her cherished coffee). Grandma could recite poetry and sing folk songs, and she never tired of teaching me to follow along. Her ultimate gesture was the penny in the birthday-girl's slice of cake. Did she bake the penny in the batter, or did she slip it in, unnoticed, as she served the cake? (With all such family folk-lore, we are just as happy not knowing the truth; we only need to tell the story over and over again.)

Many women of Grandma's generation lived on farms and in small towns, surviving the Depression and two world wars partly because they knew how to make something out of nothing; these were the ways of rural America. But Grandma took American ingenuity to a higher level, perfecting the art of making the ordinary seem magical.

> **"My mother had been too beautiful, too rare, to live among the weeds and ordinary flowers. The leprechauns had been sad to see her go, but they promised to keep tending the other flowers, and some day there would be more like her that God could take home."**

Grandma was a blend of Scots-Irish blood for stubbornness, German for strength, and Cherokee Indian for high cheekbones and a bit of fury. She was a truly American mix, an auburn-turned-white-haired beauty with hazel eyes. Her looks defied the hardships of her past – having given birth to and raised twelve children with a hard-working yet alcoholic and manic-depressive husband. Perhaps she knew that if she didn't look around her and find beauty, color, and magic in her world, she'd see a grim and depressing grayness. Whatever the impetus, Grandma did so much more than "get by." I was lucky to visit her often while growing up, and to attend college near her home in her last years. I saw up close the indomitable ways of this woman whose blood I am proud to carry in me.

A testament to Grandma's determination are her children – all of them successful by society's standards. Her sons fought in our country's armed forces, some rising to the rank of colonel; her daughters made their mark as businesswomen and writers. All of her children became leaders in their communities and raised large families of their own.

My mother is one of Grandma's two children no longer living, but even her death, which occurred before Grandma's, was portrayed as part of the magic and wonder of the cycle of life. My mother would be even closer to me now, said Grandma, living in my heart and at the same time looking down at me from heaven, always there to talk to me and guide me no matter where I went in life. We'd never be separated, my mother and I, for she was now in my soul and I would always have her there.

Such thoughts consoled my tender thirteen-year-old heart, but even more comforting was Grandma's rendition of why my mother went to heaven. The story she told had undoubtedly been passed down from her ancestors in Ireland. The world was a beautiful garden, she said. This garden was tended by magical little leprechauns and was visited daily by God. On the day my mother died, God was taking his stroll in the garden and looked down to see the most beautiful flower he'd ever seen. He decided to transplant that flower to his own garden, where only the most rare and beautiful blooming flowers thrived. My mother was that beautiful flower, and God took her home to be with him. My mother had been too beautiful, too rare, to live among the weeds and ordinary flowers. The leprechauns had been sad to see her go, but they promised to keep tending the other flowers, and some day there would be more like her that God could take home.

Ten years after my mother passed, my Grandma joined her dear daughter in heavenly bliss. I knew that she was presented by the leprechauns, just as I know that I live among the leprechauns and that they watch out for me. Some day, when they show God my beauty and rarity, he'll take me home, too. In the meantime, I am able to think of the magic and wonder of life, as my Grandma did, and I feel close to her still.

Grandma's Leprechaun Salad

Married at age sixteen and thrust into a life that rivals any frontier woman's, my grand-mother always knew how to "make something out of nothing," or, as I like to think of it, how to make something wonderful *out of almost* nothing. *This salad of hers is made from ingredients that might be found in the average kitchen. She liked to say that the salad was made by the leprechauns. It always did seem magical.*

1 (12-ounce) package spinach
    fettuccine
Juice of 1 lemon
2 (6-ounce) jars marinated
    artichokes, drained
    (reserve the oil)
2 tablespoons capers (optional)
½ cup chopped green onions
1 head broccoli florets, steamed
    crisp but tender
2 large tomatoes, cut into
    eighths, or 10 cherry
    tomatoes, halved
1 (6-ounce) can ripe black
    olives, halved
1 (6-ounce) can water-packed
    tuna
3 tablespoons Italian salad
    dressing, or ⅛ cup oil mixed
    with 1 tablespoon vinegar
Freshly grated Parmesan

Cook the fettuccine according to the directions on the package. Drain off the water, then squeeze the lemon juice over the pasta.

Mix together the artichokes, capers, green onions, broccoli, tomatoes, black olives, tuna, Italian dressing, and 1 to 2 tablespoons of the artichoke oil. Add this mixture to the noodles.

Chill the salad in the refrigerator. Before serving, sprinkle Parmesan cheese on top. Think of the leprechauns as you eat. Serves 8 people.

 Resting Place

Pauline Wilson Burg
1912–1992

BY ANDREA KATHLEEN ORRILL

Through all our days together, Grandma's house was the safest place I knew. The seven-hour drive – cramped in the VW with my parents and sister – was worth it, because in the end I'd be sitting on a stool in Grandma's kitchen, a fluffy "sugar cake" cookie in my hand and Grandma asking me about school, friends, boys. Even after I'd finished college, visiting Grandma made me feel secure and protected, as though nothing else mattered except our being together.

There were many Pauline Wilson Burgs. Most of them I knew only from the stories that she and my mother told. There was Polly the A-student, who went to college at a time when few women did. There was Pauline, the May Queen with the beautiful legs, who posed with her court for the university yearbook and fell in love with John Palmer Burg, a handsome dental student from her hometown. There was Mother the homemaker, who treated her job of managing home and children as seriously as any business.

To me, though, she was just "Grandma." The woman who made my Halloween costumes, hemmed my skirts, knitted my sweaters. The woman who served milk in pitchers and made wheat toast for her grandchildren with chunks of butter and pink sugar on top. The woman who searched the Pennsylvania countryside from Papaw's Cadillac for a glimpse of her favorite white horse. Who sat beside me in the back seat as we wound along the roads. Who patted my leg, called me "My Andrea," and passed out peppermints when the hills made me queasy. With Grandma, I felt special and safe.

It was Saint Bernard of Clairvaux who said, "We find rest in those we love, and we provide a resting place in ourselves for those who love us." No one has made me understand the truth of these words more than Grandma. Since her death, my safe place is no longer a house in Red Lion, Pennsylvania. It's wherever Grandma is, and to me that's everywhere. On autumn walks, on Christmas Eve, on Easter Sunday, I feel her with me. Through four grueling semesters of graduate school I felt her support, and I worked to make her proud. She was there when I went into the hospital for surgery, her presence comforting me in my fear. She was there when I married, her joy mingling with my own. She's part of all things special and everyday – the wind, the sun, the scent of lilac. She's wherever her grandchildren remember. Mostly, she's resting in my heart.

Polly Burg's Corn Fritters

Each summer, soon after we arrived for our annual visit, Grandma would give us a report on the quality of the season's corn. Her appraisals were lengthy and descriptive and a source of humor for my sister, Jeannie, and me. Thoughtless children, we were amused by so much concern for a mere vegetable. Fortunately, Grandma forgave our laughter and prepared for us some of the best corn dishes I've ever tasted. Here's my favorite.

2 cups raw corn, grated
   straight from the cob
2 eggs, well-beaten
1 tablespoon sugar
½ to 1 teaspoon salt
Pinch of baking powder
1 to 2 tablespoons flour
Vegetable oil for deep-frying

Combine the corn and the beaten eggs.

In a separate bowl, mix the sugar, salt, baking powder, and flour. Add this to the corn mixture.

In a saucepan or kettle, heat the vegetable oil to 365 degrees. Reduce the heat if the oil begins to smoke. Drop the corn mixture by spoonfuls into the hot oil and allow the fritters to brown until cooked all the way through.

Serve hot. (You may wish to blot the fritters with a paper towel to absorb the oil.) Makes enough fritters to feed 4 to 6 people.

Polly Burg's Chicken and Dumplings

When it came to comfort food, Polly Burg was a step ahead of the chicken soup contingent. Her steaming chicken and dumplings, packed with hearty noodles and sweet potatoes, soothed the spirit and restored calm on the most hectic of days. A bowlful always makes me feel better, even when I'm feeling good to begin with!

The Dumplings

2 cups flour

⅛ teaspoon salt

½ teaspoon baking powder

1 tablespoon butter

1 egg

1 to 2 tablespoons water or
    milk, if needed

The Chicken

1 whole chicken, cut into pieces

1 medium sweet potato,
    thickly sliced

1 teaspoon chopped parsley

Stew the chicken in a large pot of water for 45 minutes to 1 hour, then remove it from the broth. Keep the chicken warm in a casserole dish until ready to serve.

While the chicken is stewing, prepare the dumplings. Mix together the flour, salt, and baking powder. Using two knives (or your fingers), cut in the butter, then add the egg. If the dough is too dry, add a little water or milk.

Roll out the dough on a floured board and cut it into 1 x 2-inch strips. Leftover dough can be stored in the refrigerator for two weeks.

After you have removed the chicken from the broth, add the sweet potato. Increase the temperature until the broth begins to boil. Drop in the dumplings one at a time so the broth continues to boil. Cook the dumplings for 20 to 25 minutes. The dumplings will thicken slightly as they absorb the broth. Once the dumplings are cooked through, add the parsley. Ladle the sweet potatoes, dumplings, and broth over the chicken. Makes 4 to 6 servings.

$\mathcal{K}$nowing about Your Days

Teresa Margaret Hoebel Bielmann
1919–1996

BY KIM BIELMANN

The summer after she died, my grandmother visited me in the form of the huge white gladiolas (her favorite flower) that I had planted in her memory. I went out and talked to her every day, as I do with all the plants in my garden. Grandma always wanted to know about my days.

Five years before she died, I had driven eleven hours from Norfolk, Virginia, to her home in Buffalo, New York. My family had tried to prepare me for the changes I would see in her, telling me she had aged quite a bit. This did not prepare me. My first-generation German-American grandmother had always been gruff and opinionated, sharp and outspoken. Now she seemed to be living somewhere far behind her blue eyes. She appeared at first not to hear me.

Searching for something to anchor me, I went to her kitchen and took inventory of the old metal bread box, then of the white metal cabinets that held cookie tins and colored plastic cups. How absurd, I thought. She is there in the next room and I am here in the kitchen searching for her.

But always when I go back in my memory, this is where I find the spirit of my grandmother: in the kitchen. And indeed, a life filled with kitchen-generated warmth began at her birth. Born prematurely, she had to be surrounded with oven-warmed bricks to bring her temperature up to normal.

During her life she had jobs outside the home (working at a soda fountain, testing machine gun clips during World War II, clerking in one of Buffalo's finest confectionaries), but her life was defined by her work – and especially her nurturing – as a homemaker.

Every summer our family would drive up to Buffalo to visit her. Upon arriving, my younger brother and I would throw open the refrigerator to find every kind of pop imaginable. We would brave the dark basement to find the metal tins full of cookies. The week would be filled with food: all the treats that my parents couldn't afford, and all the rich foods that Grandma (who had been diagnosed with diabetes at forty-five) couldn't eat. She surrounded herself with temptations, all for us. And even as we ate her fried eggs and kuchen for breakfast, she was on her hands and knees cleaning the floor. (She prided herself on floors so clean you could eat off them. But we never did.)

Grandma's sense of purpose — caring for her family — was disrupted when my grandfather died of a heart attack while using a snowblower. She was fifty-five, her son and daughter had their own families, and the only man she would ever love was gone. That's when Grandma began to visit us. With us she had a family to cook for every night, and she busied herself by constantly cleaning after my brother and I "schlopped" everything up. It was in these years that Grandma taught me to play rummy at the kitchen table. She also taught me to bake, starting with the old-fashioned Toll House cookie. (It remains one of my most popular recipes.) She tended to boss me more than I liked, but I always anticipated her arrival with excitement. Between visits, we kept in touch with letters. At least once a week she would write to tell me the details of her days. And I would write to tell her about my days: school, friends, family.

One snowy Buffalo day in January 1996, I went to the hospice where my grandmother lay dying. In the absence of noisy machines and intrusive hospital staff, I was able to sit at her bedside, to take in the familiar smell of her skin, to tell her about work and school, friends and family. I stroked her soft white hair and told her that I loved her, that I knew she was tired, and that I was okay if she needed to go. She was not conscious. Nothing much happened in that quiet room. Except that she died, peacefully. This was the first "close" death I had experienced, and I will be forever grateful for such a gentle introduction to this event, grateful that in some way she "heard" me.

And to my grandmother herself, I am grateful for the profound lessons I learned from her. Because of her, I know the importance of having someone who always wants to know about your days.

Grandma's Pork and Knadels

Today, I live in a tiny apartment on the water, where I manage to cook using a toaster oven, microwave, and portable burner. I love to cook and bake slowly, as a meditative and creative process. It reminds me of our times in Buffalo.

In those days, the best meal of the week was Grandma's pork and knadels. This is no health food by today's standards, but I try to resist labeling foods "good" or "bad." Instead, I try to eat the things I know to be more nutritious, and then occasionally allow myself to enjoy without guilt the grandmotherly foods I find so comforting. My grandmother's food was about indulgence. I indulge myself, as she indulged me, with love and with this food.

For the Pork

1 (3- to 4-pound) pork roast
Salt and pepper
2 medium yellow onions, chopped
½ cup water
2 tablespoons cornstarch mixed with 1½ tablespoons water

For the Knadels

1 loaf stale white bread
2 small potatoes, peeled and grated
2 eggs
¼ teaspoon salt
1 heaping tablespoon flour

Preheat the oven to 350 degrees.

To prepare the pork: rub salt and pepper on the roast. Place the pork in a roasting pan with the onions and water. Roast the pork for 30 minutes per pound.

When the roast is done, transfer the drippings to a frying pan. Bring the drippings to a boil, then slowly add the cornstarch water. Stir and cook the gravy until it thickens. Add salt and pepper to taste.

To make the knadels: remove the crust from the bread and cut the bread into cubes.

Wet your hands with cold water, then use your hands to mush together the bread cubes, grated potatoes, eggs, salt, and flour.

Form the dough into 8 balls and drop them into boiling water. The knadels are done when they rise to the top.

Serve the pork and knadels while they are hot, with hot gravy ladled on top. Makes 5 servings.

About the Contributors

Teresa R. Amuso, born in Pittsfield, Massachusetts, raised five children in Lenox, mostly as a single parent. Not able to start college until the age of thirty-seven, she graduated valedictorian from Berkshire Community College and was encouraged to fulfill her dream of academia. After earning her Ph.D. from the University of Massachusetts at Amherst, she taught for many years and was particularly active in the New England Modern Language Association, presenting papers or chairing sections every year. Recently retired from her position as associate professor of English and philosophy at the University of Maine at Machias, she is now writing literary criticism, a philosophy book, and her memoirs – special to her heart – written with love for her family.

T. J. Banks has written fiction, poetry, book reviews, and essays for a variety of journals. A graduate of Trinity College in Hartford, Connecticut, with a B.A. and M.A. in English literature, she has won numerous honors from the Cat Writers' Association and has written two books, *Houdini,* a cat novel for young adults, and *Souleiado,* a time-travel novel. Her essay "Letter to Tim," about the untimely death of her husband, won *The Writing Self's* Spring 1996 contest "Sorrow Was the Source: Writing as Catharsis." She and her young daughter Marissa live in Avon, Connecticut.

Rhoda Jane Barrett received an A.B. in public policy studies and psychology from Duke University, then did graduate work in management and administration at George Washington University and the University of Baltimore. In the late 1980s, she did grant writing for child welfare programs at the Anne Arundel County Department of Social Services, State of Maryland. She then worked for four years as account manager, editor/writer, and vice president of a public relations firm before shifting gears again to become a consultant to the Carlisle Collection designer fashion company and a stay-at-home mom in Vienna, Virginia, raising two daughters, Michelle and Laura, with her husband, Ron. She serves as president of the advisory board of American University's chapter of Chi Omega Fraternity and is active in her community.

Ellen Perry Berkeley was a senior editor at the *Architectural Forum* and *Architecture Plus,* moving from New York City to Shaftsbury, Vermont, upon the demise of these professional journals in the 1970s. She then wrote the award-winning *Maverick Cats: Encounters with Feral Cats* (Walker, 1982; New England Press, 1987), the only comprehensive book on the domestic cat gone wild, and was volume editor of *Architecture: A Place for Women* (Smithsonian Institution Press, 1989). She taught writing and criticism in leading architecture schools in the 1970s, and was one of seven founders of the innovative Women's School of Planning and Architecture in 1975. She has a B.A. from Smith College, spent several years studying architecture at the Harvard Graduate School of Design, and for her provocative writing received a mid-career Loeb Fellowship in Advanced Environmental Studies at the Harvard GSD. Her articles, essays, and reviews appear in national and regional publications. She lives in a house of her own design with her historian/writer husband, Roy, and their formerly feral pussycats April, Leona, and Roscoe.

Simi Berman, who lives in Chesterfield, New Hampshire, is an artist widely known for her ceramic sculpture, a form of three-dimensional illustration, which she has exhibited and sold throughout the country for many years. Her work appears in several important private collections of American folk art. She is a self-taught artist, having a degree in linguistics from City College of New York. In the past few years she has taken to pen and brush. This is the work she now most enjoys. Her pen drawings have appeared in the *New York Times* and her watercolors have most recently been exhibited at the Tea Tray Gallery in Cambridge, Massachusetts. She is currently working on the illustrations for a children's book. Her husband is architect Leopold Berman. They have a son and grandson nearby.

Kim Bielmann lives in Norfolk, Virginia, where she graduated from Old Dominion University with a B.S. in interdisciplinary studies (a minor in women's studies) and an M.S. in education. She teaches in the gifted program of the Norfolk public schools, raising student awareness of racism and sexism and helping female students cope with the challenges of adolescence. Kim also glazes and sells ceramic tiles. Her favorite author is May Sarton, who illustrates that it is possible to live a quiet life that is both intellectually and creatively fulfilling. Sarton, says Kim, also shows the reader that beauty and comfort can be found in domesticity.

Mary Hard Bort is a native Vermonter educated in nursing at the University of Vermont; she has worked in Vermont and California as a pediatric nurse. As an army wife she lived in Alaska, California, North Carolina, Maryland, Virginia, and Germany. Since her return to Vermont in 1975, her "golden years" have been enriched by her immersion in local history and by a second career as a librarian and writer. She is curator of the Manchester Historical Society, writes a continuing column for the *Manchester Journal* on matters of local history, and does freelance writing for Vermont periodicals.

Adriana Millenaar Brown was born of a German mother and a Dutch father. At the age of nine, she began living in her third country and learning her fourth language. Since her marriage in 1967 she has lived in Williamstown, Massachusetts, where, for the last ten years, she has been sorting out her first ten years through writing. Adriana has a B.A. in English literature from Williams College. She has taught French at a local private school and Dutch at Williams College, and she currently teaches English as a second language at Massachusetts College of Liberal Arts. Her stories have been published in English and German.

Frances Ferguson Buttenheim is a freelance writer for such publications as *Country Living,* the *Berkshire Eagle,* and the *Cleveland Plain Dealer.* Previous endeavors have included a paid position as executive director of the Williamstown Community Chest in Massachusetts, and an unpaid – and far more demanding – position as trustee of the Williamstown Public Library. She has an A.B. in European and Russian history from Wellesley College and an M.A.L.S. (master of arts in liberal studies) with a focus on art and theater from Wesleyan University. Her granddaughters, Francesca Dmitrievna Eremeeva, born in 1997, and Claire Marriner Saint-Amour, born in 1999, spend summers in Williamstown with Frances and her husband, Peter, just as Frances spent summers with her maternal grandmother in North Carolina when she was a child.

Adele Chatfield-Taylor, since December 1988, has been president of the American Academy in Rome, a center for independent study and advanced research in the fine arts and humanities. She has lived and worked in New York and Washington since 1967 as a professional historic preservationist. She was on the staff of the New York City Landmarks Preservation Commission from 1973 to 1980, at which time she established and became executive director of the New York Landmarks Preservation Foundation. From 1984 to 1988, she was director of the Design Arts Program for the National Endowment for the Arts. Her M.S. is from

Columbia University's Graduate School of Architecture, Planning, and Historic Preservation. In 1996 she was elected a Fellow of the American Academy of Arts and Sciences. She is married to playwright John Guare.

Elizabeth Linder DaGue, born and reared in the deep South, holds an undergraduate degree in English from Auburn University and an M.A. from Southern Illinois University. She has done additional graduate work at various other universities. After teaching composition at Auburn University and Indiana University, she taught essay and research writing at the high-school level to college-bound seniors. Also for high-school students, she has developed curricula and taught honors courses in computer-based composition and research writing. Now a freelance writer living in rural Illinois, she has published articles on subjects as disparate as teaching English and buying real estate in Scotland. She is seeking a publisher for her first novel, which is set in Scotland.

Alba De León is an artist and educator. She lives in San Antonio, Texas, and teaches at Palo Alto College, one of four colleges of the Alamo Community College District. She works at Studio 106B of the Blue Star Arts Complex in the following media: photography; handmade paper; and acrylic paint on canvas, screen, and cloth. During the summer, she creates paper works at Trout Paper, a handmade-paper studio in upstate New York.

Sheila deShields has used her experiences as a reporter, teacher, editor, software systems engineer, and mother in her writing. She received a Rotary International Fellowship to Wales, where she completed her master's degree in British literature. Her poetry, articles, and stories have appeared in *West Wind Review,* the *Halifax Herald, Scriblerus,* and Mortar Board's *Forum.* Living now in San Jose, California, she is writing a historical fantasy on finding our grandmothers.

Deborah Lomanno Doenges comes from a family of seven children whose parents always found an occasion to bring good food to the table. She married David Doenges in 1978 and they have four children: Michael, Andrea, Daniel, and Dominic. She earned a medical secretarial A.S. from Aquinas College in Milton, Massachusetts, but has chosen to stay at home and raise her children rather than pursue a career. An administrative assistant to the principal of the Sherburne Elementary School in Killington, Vermont, she loves to play tennis, read, walk, watch her children grow, and cook, bake, and eat.

Stella Ehrich received her B.F.A. in painting from the Memphis Academy of Art. After graduation she moved from Tennessee to Italy with her husband, sculptor Fred X. Brownstein, and they lived and worked for sixteen years in northern Tuscany. During that time Stella commuted to Florence for seven years to study painting and figure drawing in the atelier of Professor Nerina Simi. With their children Eric and Vanessa, they now have their home and studios in North Bennington, Vermont, where Stella received an M.F.A. in painting at Bennington College. Her work has been exhibited in England, Italy, and the United States and is in many public and private collections in all three countries.

Lydia L. English grew up in Chicago. There she began a twenty-year career in banking, becoming the first African American and first woman to hold a banking position as vice president of the Independence Bank of Chicago. She subsequently managed several branches of Citibank in the Virgin Islands. Making a major career change, she matriculated at Brown University in 1981, earning an A.B. magna cum laude in 1985 and then, at Yale, a Ph.D. in anthropology in 1991. Her dissertation was on the relationships of females and males in the newly liberated Commonwealth of Dominica, West Indies. She spent some years back at Brown, as an associate dean of the college and an adjunct assistant professor; she is now with the Andrew W. Mellon Foundation as program officer in higher education.

Hilda McDonnell Farrell, born in Everett, Massachusetts, survived the Depression, the hurricane of 1938, and World War II to become a secretary and marry a young veteran. When he died prematurely, she raised their seven children alone; within one year of his death, all were teenagers at the same time! Resuming college as the children grew, she earned her A.B. cum laude from Framingham State College at the age of sixty. She has been writing all her life – essays, articles, columns, memoirs, and letters, many of them published. Her grandmotherly credentials: twenty-one grandchildren.

Ruth Ferber, born in Ripley, Mississippi, briefly attended West Tennessee State Teachers College, then became a registered nurse. She graduated summa cum laude in 1936 from Norwalk General Hospital in Connecticut (which was affiliated with Yale University School of Nursing). Specially trained in contagious diseases, she worked in hospitals in Memphis, Detroit, and Ann Arbor. Ruth is married to Leon Ferber, M.D., and they have three children. She has written two novels, three short stories, and a low-cholesterol cookbook.

Sally S. Finn, raised in New Jersey and New York, graduated magna cum laude with a B.S. from New York University. She then worked briefly as a researcher for the Federal Reserve Bank of New York and the American Bankers Association. For the last thirty-four years she has lived in Vermont, where her five children thrived on recipes handed down from their grandmothers and great-grandmothers. For seventeen years she was assistant to the principal of Waterbury Elementary School. She is founder of the former Mid-State Writers Guild, and writes reminiscences and other essays as a contributor/correspondent to several publications.

CB Follett's poems have appeared in many magazines and anthologies around the world. She has received numerous awards and grants — among them, five nominations for the Pushcart Prize in Poetry in 1993; runner-up for both the Robert Winner Prize and the George Bogin Award and finalist for the Alice Fay De Castagnola Award (all from the Poetry Society of America); and a grant for poetry from the Marin Arts Council in 1995. She has three collections of poetry, *The Latitudes of Their Going* (Hot Pepper Press, 1993), *Gathering the Mountains* (Hot Pepper Press, 1995), and *Visible Bones* (Plain View Press, 1998). Her latest anthology is *GRRRRR: A Collection of Poems about Bears* (Arctos Press, 1999). A graduate of Smith College, she lives in Sausalito, California, perched between the coastal range and San Francisco Bay.

Nancy Price Graff is a writer and editor. She has a B.A. in American studies from Middlebury College and an M.A. in American cultural history from the University of Vermont. She grew up outside New York City but has lived in Vermont since 1971. From 1983 to 1985 she served as editor of *Vermont Life*. A freelance writer and historian, she has written extensively about Vermont history and is the author of four children's books: *The Strength of the Hills* (Little, Brown and Company, 1989), *The Call of the Running Tide* (Little, Brown and Company, 1992), *Where the River Runs* (Little, Brown and Company, 1993), and *In the Hush of the Evening* (HarperCollins, 1998). Her husband is a journalist with the Associated Press, and they have one son and one daughter.

Barbara Marie Gravinese grew up in the Bronx and Manhattan, attended the High School of Music and Art, and received a B.S. in studio art and art history at the City University of New York. She has taught art in her studio and has given workshops on book illustration. The creator of New York City's water conservation program, she spent five years there as director in the mid-1980s. During this time she wrote a water conservation gardening book that was distributed nation-wide. She then went to New York University Medical Center to study medical ultrasound and was a perinatal sonographer for the next eight years. She is a new resident of Vermont.

Nora Richter Greer is a freelance writer specializing in architecture and urban affairs. Previously an editor with *Architecture* (the journal of the American Institute of Architects) and an editor for the National Trust for Historic Preservation's *Forum*, she is the author of four books: *Architecture Transformed: New Life for Old Buildings* (Rockport Publishers, 1998), *Architecture as Response* (Rockport Publishers, 1998), *The Search for Shelter* (AIA Press, 1986), and *The Creation of Shelter* (AIA Press, 1988). A graduate of Connecticut College, she has an M.S. in journalism from Northwestern University, and this past year she received an M.A. in creative writing from Johns Hopkins University. She lives in the nation's capital with her husband and two cats and is currently finishing a novel.

Marilyn Gustin is a craniosacral therapist practicing in Tucson, Arizona. Over the years she has managed a halfway house for recovering mental patients, founded and directed a hospitality center for German merchant sailors, provided administrative assistance and retreat leadership at Picture Rocks Retreat House in Arizona, and taught Bible and spirituality in undergraduate and master's level curricula. She has over twenty published books and booklets, plus dozens of published articles. She received her doctorate, with honors, in cross-cultural spirituality studies from the Graduate Theological Union, Berkeley, California, in 1987.

Hannelore Hahn founded the International Women's Writing Guild (IWWG) in 1976, and has guided it as a diverse network for the personal and professional empowerment of women through writing. She represented the IWWG in Beijing at the Fourth World Conference on Women and, as a survivor of the Holocaust, gave two-hour video testimony that was documented by the Survivors of the Shoah Visual History Foundation (Steven Spielberg, founder and chairman). She served as a translator of the *Scientific Correspondence of Albert Einstein* and is the author of the award-winner memoir, *On the Way to Feed the Swans* (Tenth House Enterprises, 1982). Her essays have appeared in the *New York Times* and other publications.

Janis Hashe is a professional journalist, national columns editor for United Parenting Publications, and a produced playwright. She is president of the board of directors of the small avant-garde Theatre of NOTE in Hollywood, which produces new work and new writers. She has a B.A. summa cum laude from San Francisco State University and an M.A. from San Jose State. Partly because of her beloved grandma, she loves to cook; also partly because of her, she has just finished her first novel.

Kathy Hipple lives with her husband, Brad Steitz, and their three children, Samantha, Jeffrey, and Max, in New York City. After earning her bachelor's degree at Tulane University, she worked briefly as a writer in Manhattan, then became a vice president on Wall Street selling bonds to Japanese institutions. She left Wall Street to raise her children and is now studying part-time at Columbia University for a degree in social work.

Jeannetta P. Holliman is a writer, performance artist, teacher, and workshop facilitator. Her writing, which is personal and spiritual, weds poetic prose with the collage form. One such piece, *Myth, Madness, Magic,* a collaborative work, was produced off-Broadway in New York City in 1996. A former textbook and freelance editor, Ms. Holliman currently teaches creative writing to public school students in Columbus, Ohio, where she lives with her husband, George, their two sons, Darrin and Chonce, and their feline, Sam.

Mary Ann Horenstein is a writer and a retired educator who directed CIPED, a high-school experiential learning program in New Jersey that took students into the community for part of their education. She wrote *Twelve Schools That Succeed* (Phi Delta Kappa, 1993), a book on innovative education, and is the lead author of *Reel Life/Real Life: A Video Guide for Personal Discovery* (Fourth Write Press, 1995). She has a bachelor's degree from Smith College and a doctorate from Rutgers University. With her husband, Donald, she lives in Burlington, Vermont.

Noel Candice Horn was a medical technologist in her first life, working in rheumatology research at a university center. After marriage, she raised three children and earned a business degree. She also volunteered at her community's schools, at its hospital, and at her church, presiding over organizations and holding elected public office. Now in her second life, with children grown, she follows her passion for all forms of writing, particularly that of the (almost) lost art of letter writing. Noel is an avid reader, an incurable book collector, and an inveterate traveler. Her essays, articles, and memoir pieces have appeared in numerous publications. She lives in Grand Rapids, Michigan.

Jane Jacobs is the author of such seminal works as *The Death and Life of Great American Cities* (Random House, 1961), *The Economy of Cities* (Random House, 1969), *Cities and the Wealth of Nations* (Random House, 1984), and *Systems of Survival* (Random House, 1993) – all still in print. Her recent book, *A Schoolteacher in Old Alaska* (Random House, 1995), is a memoir by her grandmother's sister, with added commentary by Jane. Her newest book is *The Nature of Economies* (Modern Library, 2000). Born in 1916 in Scranton, Pennsylvania, Jane attended business school to learn shorthand, and later worked without pay for a year as a newspaper reporter. In her twenties she took two years off from secretarial jobs and freelance writing for further education at Columbia University. She was an editor and writer for the Office of War Information during World War II, and for the State Department's information agency afterward. She joined the professional journal *Architectural Forum* as an associate editor in 1952; her article for *Fortune* on the mistakes of city planning led to the Rockefeller Foundation grant that enabled her to write her first book. Since 1968, Jane has lived in Canada. Her beloved husband, architect Robert H. Jacobs, died in 1996.

Katherine Quimby Johnson is a native Vermonter. She graduated magna cum laude from Colby College, received her M.A. from the University of Vermont, and studied in Vienna, Austria, courtesy of the Fulbright Commission. She now writes a weekly newspaper column, as well as children's books and middle-grade novels, and is the administrative assistant for the Center for Holocaust Studies at the University of Vermont. In her spare time she reads, gardens, and knits (a skill she learned from her grandmother). She lives with her husband and their daughter in a former train depot in Cambridge, Vermont, a home they share with a rabbit and a parakeet.

Paula E. Kautz-LaPorte lives a modest Vermont life with her husband, daughter, and son on a small piece of fertile land in the friendly town of Shaftsbury. She is a professional seat weaver and operates their family business, the Bennington Bus Station. She is an active member of the Vermont Girl Scout Council and the Bennington County Choral Society. Paula is a sports enthusiast, a vegetable gardener, and a creative writer. She has an A.S. in business from Southern Vermont College.

Carolina Guerra Kilbourn has lived in Michigan and Colorado, and now lives in Burlington, Vermont, with her husband and family. While raising three children, Carolina has worked with elementary school children to improve their reading skills. She enjoys sharing her Mexican cooking and culture with friends and neighbors. Like her grandmother, she enjoys working outdoors and tending her gardens.

Suzanne Duffield Kingsbury works as regional associate for the Africa programs at the School for International Training in Brattleboro, Vermont. She is also a drummer, dancer, writer, mixed-media artist, and world traveler. A graduate of the University of New Hampshire in 1991, she received a Fulbright grant to Sri Lanka in 1993, where she began writing in Buddhist monasteries and drumming and dancing in small Sinhalese villages. She is currently at work on her first novel and, having studied at the Harkness Dance Center in New York City, is certified to teach dance to young children and teens.

Florence Ladd, author, psychologist, and social critic, was born and reared in Washington, D.C. With a B.S. from Howard University and a Ph.D from the University of Rochester, she has taught at Simmons College, Robert College in Istanbul, the Harvard Graduate School of Education, and the Harvard Graduate School of Design. In the 1980s she was dean of students at Wellesley College, and from 1989 to 1997 she was director of the Bunting Institute of Radcliffe College. She is currently Writer-in-Residence at the Radcliffe Institute for Advanced Study. Her novel, *Sarah's Psalm* (Scribner, 1996) received the 1997 best fiction award from the American Library Association's Black Caucus. Ladd's short stories have appeared in *The Golden Horn* and *WRagtime*. She is the mother of poet and performance artist Mike Ladd, and she lives in Cambridge, Massachusetts, and Putney, Vermont.

Kathleen LaPlante was born and raised in Winsted, Connecticut, until the family moved to upstate New York. She has taken many courses in local colleges but has no claim to any degrees. Her interests include photography, rubber stamping, singing, writing, and caring for the many cats and dogs that have joined her on her journey through life. Married to Bernard LaPlante, she is the mother of a son and daughter, and has one grandson and one granddaughter. She and Barney were in the restaurant business for fifteen years. They live in Old Chatham, New York, on the farm that once belonged to Barney's great-grandparents.

M. Katherine Layton grew up in Princeton, New Jersey, but has lived in Vermont for thirty years. She earned her B.A. from Lake Erie College for Women, where she studied art. She is a professional watercolorist, works as the assistant to the director of women's studies at the University of Vermont, loves gardening, and takes lots of art and writing classes. Passionate about children's literature, she is doing research for a book about a female artist from Vermont. Remembering the gifts that Grandma Layton passed on to her, she has recently become Grandma to her granddaughter, Grace.

Joan Lederman lives in Woods Hole, Massachusetts, where her studio sits 150 feet from the ocean, near ferry travelers and world-class science institutes. She uses ocean moods and a vibrant intellectual climate as sources for her work as a ceramic artist and "imagineer" (in the latter role, imagining how intuitions and visions can be implemented or engineered into the seen world). Since 1996, she has been a pioneer in her field, using deep-sea sediments (harvested for scientific research) as glazes on her stoneware clays. The B.F.A. degree she earned from Boston University in 1968 only minimally prepared her for the imaginative and collaborative work that unfolds with every day.

Dianne S. Lodge-Peters goes by three names: "Nana-Skip" to two grandsons, "Fraudoktorprofessor" to former students, and "Intrepid" to writing colleagues. After earning her Ph.D. from the University of Michigan, she held professorships in the study of higher education at major state universities throughout the United States, doing research and teaching graduate courses in various subjects related to the social psychology of higher education. Now retired from research, she writes travel stories and memoirs, and gives workshops to women's groups about rites of passage in family life.

Jane Berry Marcellus has worked as a newspaper reporter, tenured community college professor, and freelance writer. A native of Oklahoma, she has also lived in New England, the desert Southwest, and the Pacific Northwest. With degrees from Wesleyan University, Northwestern University, and the University of Arizona, she is currently working on her Ph.D. at the University of Oregon, focusing on gender issues in the press. She continues to write essays and memoirs. In 1991 she legally changed her last name to Marcellus, her maternal grandmother's birthname, because she wanted a permanent matrilineal name.

Maureen Teresa McCarthy lives in the Finger Lakes area of upstate New York, where she writes, walks, gardens, and bakes bread. She attended San Francisco State for her B.A., lived in Europe and Mexico for two years, then studied at San Diego State and Syracuse University for her M.A. in American literature. She is the mother of two teenage boys, a teacher at a community college, and a freelance writer. In her spare time, she is renovating the 200-year-old house she lives in. She has published work on various writers (most recently May Sarton) and on the Finger Lakes. She is currently writing a novel set in the Vietnam era.

Donna Lee Bowen McDaniel is a freelance journalist living in Southborough, Massachusetts. She appreciates the opportunities in her life that were not open to her nana's generation: among them, going to college (Donna graduated from Tufts University with a B.A. and Boston University with an M.Ed.), living in Asia and Europe, and following her passions – from reporting on a daily newspaper and serving as the first selectwoman in her town, to traveling with a chorus to Siberia, China, South Africa, and points in between. Now a nana herself, she is sad that her five grandchildren are growing up far away in Colorado.

D.H. Melhem, poet, novelist, playwright, independent scholar, and author of over fifty published essays, is a former member of the faculties of Long Island University and the New School for Social Research. Her work has been praised by many distinguished writers and has won many awards. *Gwendolyn Brooks* (University Press of Kentucky, 1987), the first comprehensive study of the poet, earned her a nomination for a Woodrow Wilson Fellowship in women's studies. *Heroism in the New Black Poetry* (University Press of Kentucky, 1990) won her an American Book Award. *Blight,* her first novel, was published by Riverrun Press in 1995, the same year that *Rest in Love,* her acclaimed elegy for her mother, was reissued by Confrontation Press. Her fourth book of poems, *Country* (Cross-Cultural Communications), came out in 1998; a chapbook, *Poems for You* (P&Q Press, 2000), is forthcoming. She is coeditor with Leila Diab of *A Different Path* (Ridgeway Press, 2000), the first anthology from RAWI (Radius of Arab American Writers, Inc.). She graduated cum laude with a B.A. from New York University, then went on to earn an M.A. in English from City College of New York and a Ph.D. in English from City University of New York. She is vice president of the International Women's Writing Guild.

Colleen J. Miller received her B.S. in nursing from the University of Vermont. Over the past two decades, she has been employed as a nurse at schools, hospitals, a medical center, a convalescent center, and a nursing home. Since 1993 she has run her own antiques business in Burlington, Vermont. She has three children – Jeffrey, Peter, and Amy – and reports that they are creative, artistic, and funny. She loves to read, hook rugs, hunt for antiques, and dowse. She is a member of the American Society of Dowsers.

Ruth Ann Myers was innkeeper of the Munro-Hawkins House Bed and Breakfast Inn in Shaftsbury, Vermont, for five years in the 1980s. Before, during, and after that period she was a psychotherapist in private practice in Bennington, Vermont. Her B.S. degree is from Bucknell University; her M.S.S. is from Bryn Mawr. She has worked in mental health agencies and hospitals in Pennsylvania, Rhode Island, and Vermont.

Lea Bertani Vozar Newman, professor emerita of the Massachusetts College of Liberal Arts and a former Fulbright scholar to Italy, has an M.A. from Wayne State University and a Ph.D. from the University of Massachusetts at Amherst. She has written books on Hawthorne and Melville and is currently working on two new projects: a memoir about growing up in Chicago's "Little Italy," and *Robert Frost's New England Poetry: The Places, People, and Stories Behind the Poems* (New England Press, 2000). From her home in Bennington, Vermont, she tries to keep up with five children, two step-children, and a growing number of grandchildren and great-grandchildren all over the country.

Takayo Noda was born in Tokyo, Japan, and moved to New York City with her then-husband in 1961. After raising her son, who is now an accomplished pianist, she went back to school to pursue her interrupted career in art, working with Michael Ponce de León, Seong Moy, and Leo Manso at the Art Students League of New York. Her work has received numerous awards and is in many private and public collections. Her many exhibitions include a recent solo show in the Tiffany windows in New York City, as well as group exhibitions at the National Academy of Design in New York City; the Portland Art Museum in Portland, Oregon; and the Roopankar Museum of Fine Arts in Bhopal, India. In 1998, one of her works was selected by the Metropolitan Transportation Authority for display as a poster throughout the New York City subway system.

Dorri Olds did wheelies on motorcycles with drunken school chums at age thirteen; at fifteen she dropped out of high school and ran away to Greenwich Village; at sixteen she went to college, then transferred four times and took a two-year leave of absence to become a rock star; at twenty-six she sold her first painting. Now thirty-six, she has sold fifty-one paintings and has had seventeen gallery exhibits. She owns a busy graphic design company and has just illustrated a newly published children's book, *Irving Goes to Town,* written by Kenneth F. Williams. She lives in New York City.

Erika Kreis Olmsted spent her childhood and early youth in Germany, living close to her grandparents. In 1948 she returned to the United States. and attended Vassar College, graduating with a B.A. in art history. A job at the Metropolitan Museum of Art was followed by a twenty-year marriage, during which she lived in Mexico, Japan, and suburban Connecticut. After a divorce, and after her four children had left home, she chose to live in Vermont, still pursuing the arts and crafts and greatly enjoying hikes in the Green Mountains.

Andrea Kathleen Orrill has written fiction, essays, and poetry for books and journals, as well as articles for national and international publications. A graduate of the State University of New York at Albany with a bachelor's degree in English and a master's in social work, she now works as a psychotherapist in Saratoga Springs, New York. She and her husband, Paul, devote much of their time and energy to raising their children, Liam and Madison.

Huguette Vitu Peck was born in France, in the town of Besançon in the Jura Mountains. World War II prevented her from finishing her engineering degree, but the University of Grenoble told her she had earned the equivalent of a B.S. She recently wrote about her experiences during and after the war in *France, 1939, Part I: Lost and Found* (Academy Books, 1994) and *France, 1939, Part II: The Dark Years and the Light at the End of the Tunnel* (Academy Books, 1997). She moved to the United States with her American husband in 1954, teaching French and science in a private school until 1971 when the Pecks moved to Vermont and bought a weekly newspaper. She and her husband (formerly with the *Herald-Tribune* in Paris and New York) worked together at the *Vermont News Guide* until 1986, then retired to active community work. She has two sons and five grandchildren in France, and two sons, a daughter, and five grandchildren in the United States.

Karen Phelps, an award-winning author and photographer, has written extensively in fields as diverse as shamanism and dog breeding. She is currently working on a memoir about her experiences showing dogs over the past three decades. A native of Westchester County, New York, she lives in a little house in the woods with three collies and a cat. She has a B.S. in behavioral science and an M.S. in organizational leadership, both from Mercy College.

Keri Pickett has won a Bush Foundation fellowship, a Jerome Foundation grant, a National Endowment for the Arts fellowship, and other prestigious awards for her photographs. She is a regular contributor to *People* magazine and other national publications. Her photographs are in the permanent collection of the Minneapolis Institute of Art and the Houston Museum of Fine Arts. In addition to *Love in the 90s: B.B. and Jo. The Story of a Lifelong Love* (Warner Books, 1995), she is also the author of *Faeries: Visions, Voices and Pretty Dresses* (Aperture, 2000). A graduate of Moorhead State University, Keri lives in Minneapolis.

H.H. Price is a native Vermonter who has lived and worked in Maine for thirty years. She is the author of *Blackberry Season: A Time to Mourn, a Time to Heal* (Lura Media, 1993), which is a series of stories set in Vermont about growing up without her mother. She is currently collaborating on two books about hidden Maine history: one on African Americans and the other on the Underground Railroad. She is a graduate of Northwestern University and was later a student of Heinz Westman, a pioneer in the theory and practice of psychotherapy. She and her husband have two grown children and one grandchild.

Gail Moses Rice grew up in Bennington, Vermont, spending her summers baking with her Granny Stuart in Pepperell, Massachusetts. After graduating from Castleton State College she taught fourth, fifth, and sixth grades in Manchester and Bennington, then every grade (simultaneously!) as the only teacher in a two-room schoolhouse in Mt. Tabor, Vermont. Among other educational work, she has supervised student teachers for the state Department of Education. Gail works as librarian of the Mark Skinner Library in Manchester, Vermont. Her children are now adults, and she and her husband live in Sunderland, Vermont.

Christine May Roblee is a single mother living in the San Francisco Bay Area, where she supports herself, her daughter, and her writing habit by working as a software systems engineer with a major insurance company. Since moving to the suburbs, she finds the pace slower, more relaxing, and much more conducive to writing – her lifelong passion and favorite hobby. Her writing these days centers around stories and plays, as well as the development of Internet web sites for Bay Area nonprofit groups.

Susan W. Rushmore is a New Yorker who finds herself living in Bennington, Vermont. She is a writer, musician, and artist who attended New York University, Oberlin Conservatory, and the University of Vienna. In recent years she has written for *Many Voices, AccessAbility,* the *Women's Times,* and *Healing Options.* For most of her life she has struggled with anorexia, agoraphobia, and a dissociative disorder. Her art, music, and writing reflect the intensity of her struggle.

Cynthia Sterling Russell has been writing since the age of five. One of her essays, "Coming Home," was reprinted in seven languages; her second book, *Double Duties,* was chosen by the Woman Today Book Club and was selected Book of the Year by the New Haven Public Library. She teaches psychosynthesis (a system of personal and professional growth that uses a foundation of journal writing), she has a private practice of psychotherapy and supervision, and she is on the clinical faculty of the Department of Psychiatry (Psychology) of Yale University School of Medicine. She graduated magna cum laude from Radcliffe College and received an M.S.W. from Columbia University and a Ph.D. from Union Institute.

Tanya Thomas Rybarczyk is a writer, educator, and yoga instructor. She earned her M.A. in English literature in 1991 from the State University of New York at Binghamton, and followed this with postgraduate work in creative writing at Old Dominion University in Norfolk, Virginia. She has recently published several stories and articles and finished her first children's book. An avid hiker and kite flyer, Tanya has traveled extensively in the United States and abroad. She, her husband, Greg, and their greyhound, Luna, currently reside in West Hartford, Connecticut, where Tanya serves as the director of middle-school ministries at Asylum Hill Congregational Church.

Sharon Lloyd Spence is the author of eight travel guides and over 300 magazine articles on adventure, culture, sports, and food. Her *1998 Adventure Guide to Southeast Florida* (Hunter Publishing) won top honors from the western chapter of the Society of American Travel Writers. A graduate of Northwestern University with a B.S.S. in speech, she teaches travel writing at Taos Institute of Arts and at writing conferences nationwide. She lives in Los Alamos, New Mexico, with her husband, photographer Warren Lieb, and her beloved cat, Roscoe.

Claire L. Steiger, a resident of Greenwich, Connecticut, is a retired mother. She graduated from Vassar College, earned an M.S.W. from the University of Denver, and has worked in psychiatric settings, in a domestic abuse program, and as financial manager for her husband's practice in psychiatry. Widowed, she has four daughters and five grandchildren. She was elected a member of the National League of American Pen Women after her local branch awarded a first prize to one of her poems, and she was on the list of finalists in a contest judged by Rita Dove, U.S. Poet Laureate 1993–1995. She travels yearly with family and friends to her home in County Cork, Ireland.

Em Turner was born Em Turner Chitty and raised in Sewanee, Tennessee, a college town on the Cumberland Plateau. She has a bachelor's degree in comparative literature from the University of the South (located in Sewanee) and a master's in English from Virginia Polytechnic Institute. Fluent in Italian and French, she teaches English as a second language at Pellissippi State Technical Community College in Knoxville, Tennessee. She has lived in New York City; Florence, Italy; and Washington, D.C. She now lives in Knoxville with her writer husband and their young son and daughter. Em enjoys playing fiddle in a traditional and contemporary folk-music band.

Dianalee Velie has had poetry, short stories, and nonfiction articles published in literary journals and anthologies nationwide and in Canada. She has received numerous awards; most recently, her poem "Notes to a Would-Be Lover" won second place in a contest sponsored by the National League of American Pen Women. She is a graduate of Sarah Lawrence College and has an M.A.W. from Manhattanville College, where she now teaches the craft of writing. She also teaches workshops in poetry, memoir, and short story writing at Norwalk Community-Technical College, and poetry at the State University of New York at Purchase. Her play, *Mama Says,* was performed off-Broadway in 1998.

Lilla M. Waltch is a fiction writer who has published mysteries for both children and adults. Her novels include *Miss Starr's Secret* (Sterling Publishing, 1959), *Cave of the Incas* (Parents' Magazine Press, 1968), *The Third Victim* (Dodd, Mead and Company, 1987), and *Fearful Symmetry* (Dodd, Mead and Company, 1988). A graduate of Radcliffe College, she earned a Ph.D. from Brandeis University and has taught literature and writing at the college level and also at the Cambridge Center for Adult Education. She is a recipient of a Massachusetts Fiction Fellowship and is now at work on a suspense novel that includes a devoted grandmother in its cast of characters.

Katherine Komninos Wilder (better known to her readers as K.K. Wilder) is a columnist, writer, writing coach, and editor who has lived all over New England. She has taught college English and writing in Vermont and Maine, and now makes her home in Burlington, Vermont, overlooking Lake Champlain and New York's Adirondack Mountains. She has edited two cookbooks: *Our Cook Book II: Timeless Recipes 1808–1994* (Unitarian-Universalist Society, 1994), and *Sinfully Good: Food for the Goddess* (4 Friends Press, 1996). Her columns and articles appear in national and regional publications. She is coproducer and cohost of the cable access TV show *Wild Spirit: The Writing Life.*

Joanne Chow Winship is an architect, an arts administrator, and the mother of Wesley. She practiced architecture in New England before taking a lead in arts development as executive director of the Vermont Council on the Arts and as director of cultural affairs for the City and County of San Francisco. Joanne earned her Bachelor of Architecture degree from the University of California at Berkeley, and her M.S. from the Arthur D. Little School of Management. When she is not contributing her skills to strengthening organizations like those concerned with the Presidio of San Francisco (a new national park), she follows her eye in photographing the patterns and interactions of people and nature around the world.

Micaela Nechkin Woodbridge lives in Granby, Connecticut. After earning an M.A. in English from the University of Hartford, she taught college English before pursuing a career in corporate advertising and public relations. Believing, like Cato (and Babi), that one is never too old to learn, she retired in her early fifties to acquire a second M.A. – this time in ancient Mesopotamian art history – from the University of Pennsylvania. Micaela enjoys playing and singing bluegrass and traditional old-time music with her husband, Tim, and has recently taken up the fiddle.

Nancy Means Wright holds an A.B. from Vassar College and an M.A. from Middlebury College. She is the author of eight books – the latest, *Poison Apples* (St. Martin's Press, 2000) is a sequel to *Harvest of Bones* (St. Martin's Press, 1998) and *Mad Season* (St. Martin's Press, 1996); all three are set in rural Vermont. She lives, writes, and teaches in Vermont and in New York's Mid-Hudson Valley. Her seven small grandchildren have been brought up vegetarian, so she, her husband, and one "carnivore" son are the only beneficiaries of Jemima's delectable recipes.

Index

Monterey Jack, in enchiladas, 212
mozzarella, in frittata, 117
Parmesan, in frittata, 117
pecorino Romano, in frittata, 141
pecorino Romano, in baked haddock, 142
Swiss, in scalloped potatoes *(gratin dauphinois),* 92
Cherry torte, 263
Chicken
    curry, 38
    and dumplings, 271
    and noodles, 242
    soup, 227, 236
    and vermouth, 245
Chocolate mousse, 84
Cinnamon
    buns, 224
    dough strips, 158
Cognac, in chocolate mousse, 84
Cookies
    almond half-moon, 126
    applesauce molasses, 95
    biscotti, 21
    honey-nut squares *(teiglach),* 200
    ladyfingers, 43
    mincemeat, 114
    mon (poppy seed), 60
    potato chip, 204
    "pussy feet," 125
Corn
    custard, 251
    fritters, 270
    see also "Indian pudding"
Crêpes
    Finnish pancakes, 126
    French pancakes, 155
Cucumbers
    in bread salad *(gaspache),* 193
    in Thousand Island pickles, 29

Currant(s)
    in holiday pudding, 88
    jelly, in red cabbage, 121
    in "rock cakes," 13
    teacakes, 64
Curry, chicken, 38
Custard
    with caramel sauce, 53
    corn, 251

D
Dough, leftover
    cinnamon dough strips, 158
    "rag-a-muffins," 146
Doughnuts, 30
Dumplings
    and chicken, 271
    and pork, 275

E
Easter bread, 238
Eggs
    frittata with parsley and cheese, 141
    spinach frittata, 117
Enchiladas, with shredded beef, 212

F
Fettuccini, in "leprechaun salad," 267
Finnish pancakes, 126
Fish
    baked haddock with tomato, 142
    tuna, in "leprechaun salad," 267
French pancakes, *see* Crêpes
Fresca fasolia me lathe (green beans, Halki style), 177
Frijoles (refried beans), 259
Frittata
    spinach, 117

parsley and cheese, 141
Fritters, corn, 270
Fruitcake, 34

G
Garbanzo beans, in chicken soup, 236
Gaspache (bread salad), 193
Green beans Halki style *(Fresca fasolia me lathe),* 177
Green peppers
    in bread salad *(gaspache),* 193
    in enchiladas, 212
"Groom's cake," *see* Fruitcake

H
Haddock, baked, with tomato, 142
Ham
    and bean soup, 209
    in "Wednesday casserole," 110
    and wild rice *(jambon lauré),* 246
Hardtack loaves, in bread salad *(gaspache),* 193
Hoecakes, 221
Holiday pudding, 87
Honey-nut cookie squares *(teiglach),* 200

I
Icings and dessert sauces
    bourbon hard sauce, for "yellow cat," 79
    burnt caramel, for blackberry spice cake, 47
    caramel sauce, for custard, 53
    cherry glaze, for cherry torte, 263
    foaming sauce, for holiday pudding, 87
    sugar icing, for "pussy feet," 125
Indian chicken curry, 38
"Indian pudding," 107

J

Jambon lauré (ham and wild rice), 246

Jam
    raspberry, 103
    violet, 216

K

Keftedes sto fournou (baked meatballs), 179
Kern (currant) teacakes, 64
Kidney and steak pie, 9
Knadels and pork, 275

L

Ladyfingers, 43
Lamb-pockets, deep-fried *(tcheburiki),* 134
Leek soup, 91
Lentil-spinach-macaroni soup *(adas b'hamod),* 75
"Leprechaun salad," 267
Lime, in chicken soup, 236

M

Macaroni-lentil-spinach soup *(adas b'hamod),* 75
Maple syrup
    in cinnamon buns, 224
    in "rag-a-muffins," 146
Meatballs, baked *(keftedes sto fournou),* 179
Mincemeat cookies, 114
Molasses
    applesauce molasses drops, 95
    in beer bread, 250
    in fruitcake, 34
    in holiday pudding, 88
    in "Indian pudding," 107
Monterey Jack, in enchiladas, 212

Mon (poppy seed) cookies, 60
Mousse, chocolate, 84
Mozzarella, in frittata, 117
Mushroom(s)
    and barley soup, 56
    in chicken curry, 38
    in ham and wild rice *(jambon lauré),* 246

N

Navy beans, in soup, 137, 209
Noodles
    and chicken, 242
    see also Dumplings
Nuts
    in cherry torte, 263
    in potato chip cookies, 204
    in Swedish apple pie, 233
    see also Peanuts, Walnuts

O

Oatcakes, 8

P

Pancakes
    Finnish, 126
    French (crêpes), 155
Parmesan
    in spinach frittata, 117
    in "leprechaun salad," 267
Parsnips, in potato cakes, 25
Peanuts, in chicken curry, 38
Pecan(s)
    pie, 69
    in honey-nut cookie squares *(teiglach),* 200
Pecorino Romano
    in frittata with parsley and cheese, 141
    in baked haddock with tomato, 142

Pectin, for violet jam, 216
Persimmon pudding, 98
Pickles, Thousand Island, 29
Pie
    blackberry tarts, 254
    pecan, 69
    steak and kidney, 9
    Swedish apple, 233
Pilaffe tou fournou (baked rice, Greek style), 178
Pineapple upside-down cake, 183
Pinto beans, in refried beans *(frijoles),* 259
Popover with bourbon hard sauce, 79
Poppy seed *(mon)* cookies, 60
Pork
    and knadels, 275
    tenderloin, with ginger and soy sauce, 130
Potato chip cookies, 204
Potato(es)
    cakes, 25
    French fried, 170
    and leek soup, 91
    mashed, in cinnamon buns, 224
    in pork and knadels, 275
    scalloped *(gratin dauphinois),* 92
    in "Wednesday casserole" 110
Puddings
    holiday (steamed), with foaming sauce, 88
    "Indian," 107
    persimmon, 98
    rice, 197
    see also Chocolate mousse
"Pussy feet," 125

R

"Rag-a-muffins," 146

Raisins
 in babkas (Polish bread), 174
 in chicken curry, 38
 in fruitcake, 34
 in holiday pudding, 88
 in "Indian pudding," 107
 in persimmon pudding, 98
 in rice pudding, 197
Raspberry jam, 103
Refried beans *(frijoles)*, 259
Rice
 in bean soup, 137
 baked, Greek style *(pilaffe tou fournou)*, 178
 in chicken soup, 236
 pudding, 197
 in stuffed cabbage, 162
 see also Wild rice
"Rock cakes," 13
Rolls, 166
Rutabagas, in potato cakes, 25

S
Sake, in pork tenderloin with ginger and soy sauce, 130
Salad
 bread *(gaspache)*, 193
 "leprechaun," with spinach noodles, artichokes, and tuna, 267
Scalloped potatoes *(gratin dauphinois)*, 92
Scones, *see* "Rock cakes"
Soup
 bean, 137, 209
 borscht, 52
 chicken, 227, 236
 leek and potato, 91
 lentil-spinach-macaroni *(adas b'hamod)*, 75
 mushroom and barley, 56
 "Thursday night soup," 187
Spaghetti sauce, 230
Spinach
 fettuccini, in "leprechaun salad," 267
 frittata, 117
 -lentil-macaroni soup *(adas b'hamod)*, 75
Steak and kidney pie, 9
Strudel, 150
Swedish apple pie, 233
Sweet potatoes, in chicken and dumplings, 271
Swiss cheese, in scalloped potatoes *(gratin dauphinois)*, 92

T
Tarts, wild blackberry, 254
Tcheburiki (deep-fried lamb pockets), 134
Teiglach (honey-nut cookie squares), 200
Thousand Island pickles, 29
"Thursday night soup," 187
Tofu, in stuffed cabbage, 162
Tomato(es)
 in baked rice, Greek style, 178
 in bean soup, 137
 in bread salad *(gaspache)*, 193
 in chicken soup, 236
 in enchiladas, 212
 fried, with gravy, 4
 in green beans, Halki style *(fresca fasolia me lathe)*, 177
 in baked haddock, 142
 in "leprechaun salad," 267
 in mushroom and barley soup, 56
 in spaghetti sauce, 230
 in sweet and sour stuffed cabbage, 162
Torte, cherry, 263
Tortillas,
 with chicken soup, 236
 in enchiladas, 212
 flour, 258
Tuna, in "leprechaun salad," 267
Turnips
 in chicken soup, 227
 in potato cakes, 25

V
Vermouth and chicken, 245
Violet jam, 216

W
Walnuts
 in applesauce molasses drops, 95
 in apple strudel, 150
 in biscotti, 21
 in cinnamon buns, 224
 in fruitcake, 34
 in "pussy feet," 125
Wild rice and ham casserole *(jambon lauré)*, 246

Y
"Yellow cat," *see* Popover